The Hollywood Greats

Barry Norman
The Hollywood Greats

HODDER AND STOUGHTON
BRITISH BROADCASTING CORPORATION

Illustration Acknowledgments

The Kobal Collection: *pp 116 and 119*
Melbourne Spurr Portraiture: *p 167*
By courtesy of Metro-Goldwyn-Mayer: *pp 15, 17, 18, 19, 67, 141, 142, 143, 144, 189, 191, 192, 193, 217, 218, 219, 220, 221, 222 and 247*
Metro-Goldwyn-Mayer/Kobal Collection: *pp 69, 190 and 194*
Popperfoto: *pp 42, 43, 44, 65, 95, 147, 223 and 224*
Radio Times Hulton Picture Library: *pp 66 and 117*
By courtesy of RKO Pictures: *p 248*
By courtesy of Twentieth Century-Fox: *p 68*
By courtesy of Warner Bros., Inc.: *p 170*
Warner Bros./Kobal Collection: *p 115 and Bogart portrait on jacket*
Warner Bros./© United Artists Corporation Ltd. All rights reserved: *p 94*

420471650

British Library Cataloguing in Publication Data
Norman, Barry
    The Hollywood Greats
  1. Moving-picture actors and actresses
 — United States
 I. Title
791.43′028′0922   PN1998.A2

ISBN 0-340-23332 X (H & S)
ISBN 0-563-17751 9 (BBC)

This book is dedicated to my wife, Diana,
whose help, suggestions (and not least typing)
were invaluable. And also to
Barry Brown
Margaret Sharp
Judy Lindsay
Sally Stockford
Sue Mallinson and
Jill Talbot.
Without them, their research and their organisation,
none of this would have been possible.

Preface

The Golden Age of Hollywood lasted for about thirty years, from 1920 to 1950 (the dates are approximate), at which time the Fairy Godmother waved her wand, turned the whole town into a pumpkin and invested heavily in television.

But during that brief period, Hollywood was a place such as the world had never seen before and will certainly never see again — a place that could take truck drivers and waitresses and turn them into gods and goddesses or at least creatures who, when seen from the back of a darkened cinema, could reasonably pass for gods and goddesses.

It was the place where every day the American Dream came true for somebody. All that was necessary for instant success was good looks, a modicum of talent (and sometimes not even that) and the ability to photograph well. Given these modest attributes, and an introduction to the right people, an ambitious young man or woman could be transformed virtually overnight into a minor Deity on whom was lavished fame and fortune and the uncritical adoration of the stalls and the back circle.

Hollywood was a unique combination of factory town and fairyland. The stars were the product, the movies were the wrapping and just so long as the package made a profit the favoured ones continued to live in their mock-Spanish castles in Bel Air and Beverley Hills, earned enormous sums of money and were so well-protected by their studios that for anything much short of rape, murder or armed robbery they were practically immune from prosecution. In the Golden Age of Hollywood anything could be bought for a price, even the law.

This book is about that time — not about the place but about some of the people, the gods and goddesses, who dwelt there, although neither the book nor the television series on which it is based was originally intended to be so. When towards the end of 1976 Bryan Cowgill, then the Controller of BBC 1, approached Barry Brown, the producer of what was then *Film '76* and was

to grow in the fullness of time into *Film '77*, *'78*, and *'79*, and
offered five fifty-minute documentary slots during the next
summer, Barry Brown's first instinct — and, come to that, mine
too — was to present him with five profiles of contemporary film
stars. But in this we were faced by an unforeseen difficulty: the
stars we wanted, at the time we wanted to interview them, would
either be busy or scattered about the world or both. Given an
elastic schedule and a vast budget this would not have proved
insurmountable but because of other commitments (chief among
them the necessity of producing *Film '77* every fortnight) we
had only five weeks in which to film all the interviews. And
because the BBC is rather careful with the public's money, no
matter what certain inveterate cynics may believe, we only had
a modest budget — adequate, but far from enough to finance
some ambitious globe-trotting enterprise.

So we thought again, Barry Brown, the rest of the production
team and I, and we hit upon the idea of the "late Greats". Quite
apart from the fact that all the people we wished to talk to would
be in Hollywood or New York when we wanted them — which
was highly convenient — we couldn't really imagine why we
hadn't thought of this before.

The modern Hollywood Greats, after all, represent a new kind
of film industry, one which is, admittedly, capable of producing
films as good as (and in some cases better than) anything turned
out in the Golden Age; but it's a fragmented industry dominated
by accountants, package deals, percentages, front money and
elaborate bargaining on the lines of "You get Brando and we'll
invest five million." The late Greats, on the other hand, epitomised an era when films were the biggest and, more important,
most glamorous entertainment industry anyone had ever seen.
Money talked even then, of course, but romance and excitement
talked just as loudly and the people who ran the film factories
were showmen who responded as much to gut-reaction as to the
message of the accountant's calculator (or, in those early days
perhaps, abacus).

And so we set off in the spring of 1977 to look into the life
stories of Gable and Flynn, Tracy, Cooper and Bogart — names
which must figure fairly prominently on almost everybody's list
of Hollywood Greats. And we discovered that, quite by chance,
we had hit upon a formula that would provide us with better
and more interesting programmes than our original conception
could have done. Profiles of living movie stars invariably tend to

be eulogies; nobody ever tells the truth, or at least not the whole truth. Friends of the subject are there to tell the world what great, indeed they might almost say what all-time great, human beings the subjects are. And the subjects themselves, modestly concurring with the view that they are great, if not all-time great, human beings are anxious to put forward only the very best view of themselves.

But when the star is not only great but also late, a much closer approximation to the truth emerges. Friends and relatives are inclined to talk fondly but more frankly than they would have done if the subject of the profile were still alive. So on to the portrait it is possible to paint both the beauty spots and the warts. This, as I said, we discovered by accident. The stories, for example, of Errol Flynn's drug habits or Spencer Tracy's violent alcoholism or Joan Crawford's harsh treatment of her adopted children emerged without prompting. But such tales were not told maliciously; mostly, indeed, they were told affectionately and with sympathy because they could no longer embarrass or diminish the stature of the people concerned and because they helped to complete the picture.

Now you may wonder whether it is strictly necessary to include such details in a profile of a film star. There is a theory much put about by professional movie buffs — those whose entire lives are devoted to the cinema and whose work consists solely and, in my view, parasitically, of criticising films and writing about film-makers — that to know what an actor is like it is necessary only to look at his work. This, however, is manifest nonsense.

Some quite dreadful people have enjoyed successful careers in movies by presenting themselves as shining heroes made of stainless steel; a number of homosexuals of both sexes have been foisted on an innocent and admiring public as heterosexual fantasy symbols. To look only at the work of such actors and actresses is not to know them at all.

Anyone making a documentary — or writing a biography — about a politician or a soldier or even an author or artist would be failing in his job if he didn't point out the weaknesses of his subject as well as the strengths. Why should the rules be any different if the subject happens to be a movie star?

Yet a double standard seems to exist.

After the programme on Joan Crawford I came in for a certain amount of hysterical criticism for presenting her not mistily and dreamily and, as it were, photographed through gauze, but as the kind of woman I believe her to have been: ruthlessly ambitious and self-centred; admirable in a way but not, I should imagine, very likeable. It was as if even journalists, a dispassionate breed as a whole, preferred the myth to the reality. (Incidentally, when I said a double standard existed I think I meant a triple standard: the group of newspapers that squealed most loudly and with greatest outrage was printing much harsher, even indeed scurrilous, stuff about Joan Crawford barely a month after my programme was shown.)

Particularly in the 1930s and 40s, the decades when the people in this book were at their peak, film stars had a quite enormous influence not just in their own countries but internationally. They were the arbiters of fashion in dress, in looks and in speech; they were the very centres of millions of people's dreams; they were the leaders of a mass culture that affected pretty well the entire world. I believe it is as valid and as natural to wonder what they were like when they stepped away from the camera and wiped off the make-up — exposing among other things the hang-ups and neuroses which were so constant a feature of their careers — as it is to wonder about the private lives of statesmen and generals.

So the object of our TV portraits — well, sketches really, for a fifty-minute documentary is not a portrait in oils but a pen and ink sketch — was neither deliberately to enhance nor to belittle the actors (and, as we moved into the second series in 1978, the actresses) concerned. No eulogies, but no iconoclasm either. We tried only to put together a candid and honest picture of our chosen subjects. And in the following chapters these pictures are reproduced, or rather, expanded and enlarged; they're still not portraits in oil, perhaps, but at least they've been upgraded from pen and ink sketches to, let us say, studies in water-colour.

One word of warning, though: those who are looking for film biographies — details of which pictures the stars made and when — should look elsewhere. This is a collection of brief biographies wherein many of the films are mentioned only as landmarks. The work of the stars is there to speak for itself; I'm far more interested in the people who created the work. Thus it seems to me that the exact role Spencer Tracy played in, for instance, *Woman of the Year* is less important in trying to provide an insight into the man than the fact that it was on that film that he met Katherine Hepburn, who was to have a huge influence upon his life and even his personality.

In the ten chapters that follow many of the interviewees (whose accounts I extensively recorded and whom I now formally thank) will crop up again and again, playing a major role in one life perhaps and a walk-on part in another. The chief reason for this is quite simple: in its best days Hollywood was less a town than a village, the richest village probably in the world, and those inhabitants who settled and survived there came to know everyone else and, at one time or another, to work with everyone else.

Today Hollywood is still rich but it's no longer a village, merely part of the general urban sprawl of Los Angeles. Some, though not all, of the old Hollywood remains but what is left is dowdier and tattier than it was. The corner of Hollywood and Vine, once one of the most glamorous spots in the world, is now the hangout for teenage prostitutes of every imaginable sex and drug addicts of every possible kind. Graumann's Chinese Theatre is simply Mann's Chinese Theatre. The famous Romanoff's has become a Chinese restaurant and is not even called Romanoff's any more. Sunset Strip has at least one hooker to every fifty yards of sidewalk.

Furthermore, while the stars in this book lived nearly all their lives in Hollywood, because it was the centre of their world, the modern stars — the Newmans, Redfords, Eastwoods and Brandos — live elsewhere and visit Hollywood only when necessity demands.

The place used to be a fairyland, a fairyland run by ogres — men like Louis B. Mayer of MGM and Harry Cohn of Columbia of whom it was said, "You had to stand in line to hate him." And these ogres, who could create a star on a whim, could just as easily destroy him on another whim.

They, not the celluloid gods and goddesses, had the real power. It was the ogres who built Hollywood and made it flourish by selling dreams cheaply. But the trouble with any cut-price business is that it's always in danger of being itself undercut. So when the old ogres died, their successors, the ogres-elect, looked for a way of selling even cheaper dreams and found it in television. Technically anyway, Hollywood is still the film capital of the world but films are no longer all-important there. Universal Studios, for example, now make a large part of their annual income by running conducted tours of the lot, including such points of interest as Andy Hardy's house, the mock-up of the giant shark in *Jaws* and the tank where de Mille parted the Red Sea for his *Ten Commandments*. Many of the other studios have either closed or contracted or turned themselves over to the making of television pictures and the luxurious suburbs which were once the exclusive habitat of the movie set have been invaded by upstarts from the newer and bigger multi-million dollar industries of pop culture.

Somebody once said, "Strip the phoney tinsel off Hollywood and you'll find the real tinsel underneath." With hindsight, of course, we can all see that any place that was constructed by weaving patterns of phoney tinsel on a foundation of real tinsel was bound to fall sooner or later but even so I regret its passing. For that reason, as for many others, I'm glad now that for the TV series and for this book I happened upon the Hollywood Greats, the late Greats who lived and worked in tinsel town in its finest days. Bryan Cowgill presented us with the opportunity to look into the lives of the first five; Bill Cotton, Cowgill's successor, gave the go-ahead for the series on the second five — Crawford and Colman, Harlow, Garland and Laughton. To say they don't make 'em like that any more is simply to state the obvious. These were giants at a time when there were giants, men and women who bestrode Hollywood during the Golden Age when, just for a little while, all that tinsel did look most remarkably pretty. The tinsel is still there but it's television tinsel now and, whatever you may feel about television, fairyland it ain't.

Contents

1. Clark Gable   15
2. Errol Flynn   41
3. Spencer Tracy   65
4. Gary Cooper   91
5. Humphrey Bogart   115
6. Joan Crawford   141
7. Ronald Colman   167
8. Jean Harlow   189
9. Judy Garland   217
10. Charles Laughton   245
    Index   271

Clark Gable

*The youthful Gable with
new teeth and, at this angle,
the sugar-bowl ears
slightly disguised.*

above : Gable with Gilbert Roland, Constance Bennett and, on his right, his second wife, Ria Langham.

opposite : At their ranch — now a housing estate — with wife No. 3, Carole Lombard.

*above : Gable's fifth and final wife, Kay Williams, bore him a son a
few months after her husband's death. Between them his wives
enjoyed (if that's the word) 17 husbands.*

*opposite : Sylvia Ashley, Gable's fourth wife, gallantly
accompanying him on a hunting trip.*

One day when Clark Gable was at an age when death was something that afflicted others and would never have the effrontery to come seeking him, he was asked to suggest an epitaph for himself. The one he resolved upon was both modest and accurate: "He was lucky and he knew it."

Clark Gable was lucky and he did know it. And because neither the luck nor his awareness of it ever deserted him — except on one dreadful night when a plane crashed in flames in the mountains near Las Vegas — he became and remained for the best part of thirty years the biggest male star Hollywood had ever known. Such a statement, of course, has to be treated with some reservations, for Hollywood, after all, is a town that deals only in superlatives. The story of the forthright hireling who, after a private screening of a new film, told its producer with a regretful shake of the head that in his opinion the movie was only great is not much of an exaggeration.

Nevertheless, and scaling everything down accordingly, Gable was the biggest, although at this distance, nearly two decades after his death, it's not easy to see why. But then nothing about Gable is easy. With him, more perhaps than with any other Hollywood star, it's difficult, if not indeed well-nigh impossible, to sort the man from the myth. Hollywood has always followed the dictum of one of its finest directors, the late John Ford, who said: "If the legend is more interesting than the truth, print the legend," and with Gable that is precisely what it has done.

He stood, for instance, 6 feet 1 inch tall, a respectable height in the 1930s when people generally tended to be shorter than they are now. But there are still men about, his contemporaries, taller than he, who speak of him with awe as though he were a veritable giant, a Colossus under whose huge legs petty men walked. There are people, too, who tell of the ease and charm with which he could devastate the most sophisticated of women. Well he had his share of those as every leading man must have done (it is, after all, one of the perks of the job) but the indications are that he was more at home chatting up waitresses and messenger girls and the friendly hookers from the house of Madame Frances.

The actress Virginia Gray, who loved him and indeed loves him still despite his rather cavalier behaviour towards her, says: "He had a brain that didn't quit — it was always going." But against that Joseph L. Mankiewicz, a director and scriptwriter of exceptional ability and one of the shrewdest observers of the Hollywood scene, sums him up somewhat differently: "Not very bright. Pleasant and undemanding."

In the end, perhaps, Gable was all those things. He was whatever appeared in the eye of the beholder. Seven years after he died, Joan Crawford, with whom he had once enjoyed a brief but ardent affair, wrote without fear of contradiction: "Clark Gable was the King of an empire called Hollywood. The empire is not what it once was — but the King has not been dethroned, even after death." Indeed not. In fact what happened was that the King died and they dissolved the monarchy, an act of which, to do him justice, Gable himself might well have approved.

"The King business," he said once, with a rich but less than regal turn of phrase, "is all bullshit. I was in the right place at the right time and I had a lot of smart guys helping me — that's all."

Bullshit or not — and oddly enough there was less bullshit involved than one is wont to find in Hollywood — Gable was the King. He was accorded the crown in 1938, at a time when Hollywood and possibly even America itself felt the need of a king of some kind and as the result of a competition in Ed Sullivan's syndicated newspaper column. "Who do you think," the readers of this column were asked, "are the King and Queen of Hollywood?" Twenty million people responded — or so it's alleged and maybe the real bullshit attaches to that figure — and Gable was overwhelmingly elected. Myrna Loy was named the Queen, a fact which, forty years later, is probably known only to the most devoted movie buff.

On Gable, though, the title sat quite easily. In those days, even before the release of *Gone With The Wind*, he was Hollywood's leading leading man. He was larger than lifesize because the cinema audience wanted him so. Already, partly through his own qualities and partly through the efforts of the publicity machine, he had become an almost mythical creature, a dream figure desired by every woman and admired by every man. And if this public Gable bore only a passing resemblance to the good-looking and competent actor of the same name who worried about whether his fame and good fortune could possibly last and who fished his false teeth out of a glass every morning, it really didn't matter.

Once again Hollywood had successfully printed the legend.

In this case the legend began in Cadiz, Ohio, on February 1st, 1901, when a son, William Clark, was born to William H. Gable, a sometime farmer and sometime itinerant oil-driller, and his wife Adeline.

Adeline Gable, a frail and epileptic woman, endured a difficult pregnancy, having already endured a brief and largely unhappy marriage and died eight months after her son was born. For a while young Clark, known in those days as Billy, was looked after by his maternal relatives, although they, being Roman Catholic, hardly won the approval of his Protestant father. But when the boy was two William Gable was married again, to Jennie Dunlap, a milliner, of whom Clark later said: "She was a wonderful woman, although I didn't realise it then. She must have loved me very much because I was certainly not what you would call well-behaved. I was rather spoiled."

Clark Gable's scholastic achievements, first at Hopedale Grade School and later at Edinburgh High School, were distinctly less than spectacular. He was a useful baseball player but his grades were indifferent and he hardly seems to have been the answer to an adolescent maiden's prayer. A girl who dated him in his high school days said later, with more brevity than charity: "He wasn't particularly good-looking. His ears were too large." This latter criticism, of course, was to be levelled at him regularly for the rest of his life.

When Clark was sixteen, the family moved from Hopedale to a farm sixty miles away at Ravenna, Ohio. The lad didn't take very kindly to farm life nor, in fact, did he and his father take very kindly to each other. Their relationship at that time and for a long time afterwards was decidedly cool but in the frequent quarrels between father and son, Jennie, the stepmother, sided invariably with the boy and thanks to her intervention he left school at sixteen and went to Akron, Ohio, to work as a labourer in a tyre factory.

It was soon after he arrived there that he visited the music hall and developed such an interest in the theatre that he took on an unpaid, part-time job as call boy with the local stock company. Within a year, however, Jennie became seriously ill and Clark returned home from Akron to be with her when she died. The funeral over, he left home again, this time for New York where he found work on Broadway as a call boy for a play called *The Jest* starring John and Lionel Barrymore.

Neither the play nor the job lasted and Clark rejoined his father, who was now oil-drilling in Oklahoma, and became an oil-field apprentice, labouring for twelve hours a day at a dollar an hour. He hated this rather more, if anything, than he had hated farming.

So, when at twenty-one, he inherited three hundred dollars

from his grandfather he decided to try the stage again, to the total horror of his father who, having only the slightest acquaintance with the theatre, was well aware that it was inhabited entirely by perverts and was adamant that acting was no job for anyone with the remotest claim to being a man. After a series of frightful rows father and son parted, not to speak to each other again for ten years.

Clark, whose interest in the arts — such as it was — had been imparted solely by his stepmother, joined a touring company in Kansas City and, when that folded, worked in a lumberyard and then sold ties in a department store. In the summer of 1922 he signed on with another insignificant theatre company in Oregon and there, largely because there was virtually nobody else available, he began to play supporting roles of respectable size, although by all accounts he was an extraordinarily unimpressive actor. "If he had any experience," said the wife of one of his producers at that time, "it must have been restricted to putting up and taking down the tent. He could get on and off the stage but didn't even always manage that successfully." He must, come to think of it, have been a quite remarkable sight — a big, clumsy, country boy with jug ears, a mouthful of bad teeth which, though his own in those days, looked as though they'd been designed for somebody else and huge hands for which, on stage, he could never find an adequate use.

He was always conscious of his hands. Years later, in 1933, when he made two films (*The White Sister* and *Night Flight*) with Helen Hayes he told her that it was on account of his hands that he could never have become a successful stage actor since he had no idea what to do with them. "What he thought was wonderful about films," said Miss Hayes, "was that when his hands, or his bananas as he called them — his bunches of bananas — got out of control the director could always cut to a close-up and therefore he was safe on the screen. But in the theatre nobody could help."

However, back in Oregon in the early 1920s, young Gable met the second of the three older women who were to figure so importantly in his life: Josephine Dillon, a former New York stage actress turned drama coach, who was fourteen years older than he. His stepmother, Jennie Dunlap, had taught him that there was more to life than scratching around on a farm and now Josephine Dillon began to turn him into something which, on casual inspection, could be taken for an actor. She persuaded him to drop the name Billy and use the more distinguished-sounding

Clark; she taught him how to act and how to move and how to lower his rather high-pitched voice to a deeper, sexier and more impressively butch level. When, in 1924, Miss Dillon disbanded her theatre troupe and went to Hollywood, Gable followed her and in December of that year they were married.

The marriage itself does not appear to have been much of a success, the relationship being more on the lines of pupil and teacher, or even perhaps mother and son, than of husband and wife. And Gable's first attempt to establish himself in Hollywood was even less successful. Mrs Gable did manage to find her youthful husband a few jobs as an extra in silent pictures but, outside the marital home, nobody cared; nobody even noticed. The likes of John Gilbert and Gilbert Roland were the men the public fancied at the moment and alongside their elegance and sophistication the large, ham-fisted Gable must have looked like the neighbourhood thug. Trading on his brief acquaintance with Lionel Barrymore he got himself a small part in a stage revival of *The Copperhead*, in which Barrymore starred, but when the run came to an end he left Hollywood. With both his career and his marriage virtually drifting hand-in-hand towards oblivion, the town seemed to have little more to offer him. So he accepted a contract with a stock company in Houston, Texas, and there met Ria Langham.

Throughout their married life Josephine Dillon had been acutely afraid that she would lose her husband to a younger girl. As it happened she had been worrying needlessly: she actually lost him to an even older woman. Ria Langham, a wealthy, thrice-married socialite and divorcée was, in fact, seventeen years older than Gable. Clearly he had considerable impact on her for when he left Houston she followed him to New York where she accorded him her patronage and, no doubt, other things as well. If Josephine Dillon had turned the theatrical tyro into an actor, Ria Langham converted the gauche country boy into a man of the world, teaching him dress-sense and the kind of manners demanded in the café society in which she moved.

At this stage, I suppose, Gable's chief success had been, to put it cruelly, as a sort of gigolo, the plaything of a pair of older women. But now in New York in 1928 he enjoyed a small triumph on the stage in a play called *Machinal* and partly as a result of that and partly as a result of Mrs Langham's sponsorship he landed the leading role in the touring version of *The Last Mile*. This was a play about a convict which had already provided Spencer Tracy with a short-cut to a film contract and now, when he played it in Hollywood, was to do the same for Gable.

Mervyn Leroy, who was later to direct him in *The Homecoming*, was among those who witnessed Gable's performance and he described the experience to me thus: "I was sitting in about the second row and I saw this man with his arms on the bars, you know, because it was a jail scene and I couldn't take my eyes off of him because he had such power. Doing nothing he had such power. And I knew he was a star, absolutely knew. There was no argument about it." This latter statement, of course, may owe a great deal to hindsight, but nevertheless Mr Leroy was sufficiently impressed to arrange a screen test for Gable at Warner Brothers Studio. Mr Leroy says he thought the result was great which, allowing for Hollywood hyperbole, means that it must have been at least adequate but unfortunately Jack Warner, the head of the studio, and Darryl F. Zanuck, his acolyte, were less moved. They thought Gable's ears were too big and for that reason turned him down.

Later on, as Mr Leroy tartly remarked, Warners would have been delighted to have him just to photograph his ears but by then it was too late because Metro-Goldwyn-Mayer had got him. Before that happened, however, he had played his first speaking role in a western called *The Painted Desert* in which he was shot by Hopalong Cassidy, a fate which, to judge from his performance, was no worse than he deserved and then, ironically, he went back to Warners to appear with Barbara Stanwyck in *Night Nurse*. This film was to do a great deal for Gable but, because its release was held up, he was already under contract to MGM by the time Warners realised what kind of a prospect they had allowed to escape them.

The original MGM contract came about as a result of a screen test arranged by Lionel Barrymore and was offered without much enthusiasm. One of the casting directors said that with those ears he looked "like a giant sugar bowl" and Louis B. Mayer, the studio's omnipotent little dictator, dismissed him as a passing fad — "a gigolo with brass knuckles". Nevertheless his impact on the public was immediate and by the time *Night Nurse* came out as the seventh of eight Gable pictures released in 1931, his name, despite the comparative smallness of his role, was almost as important a selling-point as that of Barbara Stanwyck.

It was in *Night Nurse* that Gable, playing the chauffeur, portrayed for the first time "the gigolo with brass knuckles". To a

public which in the early years of the Depression had grown tired
of, or at least needed a change from, silky Latin lovers like
Valentino and Ramon Navarro, Gable was something new and
different. He brought to the screen an all-American ruggedness
and just a touch of the blue-collar worker. Unlike, say, the remote
and gorgeous Valentino, he was the kind of man that men thought
they might become and women thought they might acquire and
his mildly brutish treatment of women somehow pandered to both
male and female wish-fulfilment.

What he had drawn in that role in *Night Nurse* was the outline
of the screen image that was to make him the King. As the director
Howard Hawks, Gable's cousin-by-marriage and frequent hunting
companion, put it: "What you should realise about Gable is that
in all his pictures that were any good he played a heavy. He played
it with a grin and people liked him and he was the first to do
that."

By the end of 1931 Gable's career was securely established and
he had also managed to straighten out the somewhat tangled mess
of his private life. Josephine Dillon divorced him in March that
year and as soon as the divorce was final he married Ria Langham.
Why he was so attracted to these far more mature women — at the
time of their marriage, after all, Gable was only thirty but Ria
Langham was forty-seven, old enough indeed to be his mother —
is not quite clear. The easy and glib answer, I suppose, is that a
mother-figure was precisely what he was seeking, but perhaps
that's too easy and too glib. Gable himself was never forthcoming
on the subject, but there is little doubt that without the help of
these two women he would not have succeeded as an actor;
certainly he would not have succeeded so quickly and it's difficult
to escape the conclusion that, even assuming he had been fond of
or in love with both of them at one time or another, he was also
consciously using them. Josephine Dillon seems to have been in
no doubt about that. "Clark told me frankly," she said, "that he
wished to marry Ria Langham because she could do more for him
financially. He is hard to live with because his career and ambition
always come first." One has to bear in mind, of course, that there
spoke a woman scorned, a woman who was openly bitter about his
desertion of her and what she regarded as his subsequent financial
meanness towards her. Even so, it is a fact that he abandoned both
her and Ria as soon as something more attractive and possibly
more beneficial came along.

It's also a fact that neither of those first two marriages was distinguished by any great fidelity on his part. In that eventful year of 1931 he made two films (*Dance, Fools, Dance* and *Laughing Sinners*) with Joan Crawford and by the time they appeared together again in *Possessed* in 1932 their relationship was a good deal more than professional and a long way removed from platonic. They were both married at the time — she to Douglas Fairbanks, Junior — although it has often been said in their defence that these marriages were already unsuccessful and heading for divorce. This, however, sounds like a typical Hollywood whitewash job, certainly in Gable's case for he had been married only a year and even during the Crawford entanglement he was also at least dallying with Loretta Young.

The Crawford romance was a clandestine affair. They would both arrive early at the studios and leave late, presumably snatching odd moments in their dressing-rooms for the serious business of the day. But, clandestine or not, it was no great secret. Also, although it was clearly based on a fierce physical attraction, it's doubtful whether it had much to do with love. Joe Mankiewicz dismissed the very suggestion by saying, a shade cynically: "No one ever had a big love affair with Joan Crawford." And the writer Adela Rogers St Johns, who was a friend to both of them, and more than a friend to Gable, said: "It was just a volcanic explosion, nothing to do with a love affair at all. It scared everybody out of their wits because Joany was married to young Doug and Gable was married to Ria, and Irving Thalberg (the production supervisor at MGM) took the matter in hand and sent everybody off in different directions."

This was all part of the paternalism of the studio system. The big Hollywood studios would cosset their money-making stars and even protect them from prosecution if the need arose. But in return they positively forbade any action — adultery or general immorality — that could reflect on the studio image or damage the box-office take. An extra-marital relationship between Gable and Crawford could have had both those undesirable effects and thus Thalberg was swift to move in and order the affair to end.

Adela Rogers St Johns knew Gable from his earliest days in Hollywood and in fact Thalberg asked her to look him over to see if he was suitable for the role he eventually played in one of his first films, *A Free Soul* (in which, incidentally, he did his tough image no harm at all by slapping Norma Shearer around). She remained deeply fond of him until the day he died and probably knew him as well as almost any other woman, and better, in fact, than some of the five he married. She wasn't, she says, in love with him herself although "we had an affair because it was more convenient". But the closeness of their relationship can perhaps be gauged by the following anecdote: "He always remembered my birthday and my fiftieth was coming up and he said, 'I want to give you a party.' And I said, 'Well, that's very darling of you.' He said, 'All right, let's say eight o'clock on the evening of your birthday.' So he sent a car for me and I got to his home and there wasn't a soul anywhere in sight and I said, 'Where's the party?' And he said, 'Well, look, you don't think I'm going to waste your fiftieth birthday with a lot of strange people running around here? You can always say for the rest of your life, to your grandchildren and everybody, you can always say you spent your fiftieth birthday in bed with Clark Gable."

With such credentials to support her views, she has perhaps a point worth considering when she dismisses Gable's first two marriages thus: "I've always put it down to the same reason that one of my sons gave when he married. He said to me, 'You know, Ma, if I could afford a good Filipino I would not have had to marry.' You've simply got to have somebody around to pick up after you and send your cleaning out and keep a pad with your engagements on it."

Whether he had married her for such ignoble reasons or the equally ignoble reason that she could help him in other, more material ways, Gable remained married to Ria Langham until 1939 in which period he established himself unquestionably as the biggest male star in the world: "Valentino in Jack Dempsey's body" as the publicity men put it with their usual understatement. By the end of 1932 — thanks largely to *Red Dust* in which he pursued the ladylike Mary Astor while he himself was pursued by the adoring but shop-soiled prostitute, played by Jean Harlow — he was in the list of the top ten box-office stars and he remained there until the war. Meanwhile, his image was being gradually refurbished. He had all his teeth taken out, some say at the behest of Louis Mayer who, according to Joe Mankiewicz, went through a bizarre medical phase during which, at his instigation, a dentist moved on to the MGM lot and started taking everybody's teeth out. Mankiewicz's personal opinion is that Gable's teeth were removed at the behest of the teeth, which were ugly and bad. Gable was not too pleased about losing them — as Mankiewicz said: "It wasn't very pleasant being the world's greatest lover on screen knowing your dentures were likely to start clacking any moment," — but in private he could make jokes about them. On hunting trips, for instance, he would poke his head out of his tent in the mornings with his false teeth in his hand and, bestowing upon his companions a wide and gummy grin, would say: "Well, fellers, here's America's sweetheart."

The hunting itself was also part of his new image. He enjoyed it anyway, but the public view of Gable the muscular hunter was heavily promoted by the MGM publicity department and he went along with it because he was essentially the company man, biddable, undemanding and, despite his success, strangely insecure. When Helen Hayes made her two pictures with him in 1933 she found him "running scared".

"He was afraid," she said, "of his future, even of tomorrow. They were all afraid. I remember the first impression I had when I first went out there. I thought I was going to see a whole lot of actors so completely rich and secure and happy and romantic and I saw people terrified. Someone explained it to me by saying: 'Well, you're only as good as your last picture.' Clark was frightened all the time. And he was having a great battle with Metro because they were pushing him into pictures he didn't want to do. Not that he had any artistic ambitions or desire; he just didn't like the films he was being put into. And they didn't care what he liked or didn't like; he was under contract. I remember Clark playing with such ease and carelessness in a scene and being so gay and funny and then, as soon as the director called 'Cut' he would look at the camera in terror as if there were someone with a gun behind it. You know? As if he expected to be fired right on the spot."

That insecurity and the memory of his poverty during the pre-Hollywood (or, more accurately, the pre-Ria Langham) years also influenced his attitude towards money and helped to account for his reputation for meanness. The latter probably owes most to the complaints of Josephine Dillon who, for years after their divorce, maintained that he had treated her with appalling stinginess. But it was widely accepted among his friends and acquaintances that Gable had a clear idea of the value of a dollar. Where money was concerned he was cautious. Wayne Griffin, his friend and hunting companion and, at one time or another, his agent, producer and business adviser, said: "I never felt that he was tight but he had been very poor for a long time before he became successful and he didn't want to have that experience again. So he kept a lot of his wherewithal in cash funds in the bank and the safety deposit box.

I tried to counsel him to get more investments but he was a little careful about that."

Jean Garceau, who became Gable's secretary when he married Carole Lombard and stayed with him until his last marriage, said: "I had an awful time getting him to invest his money — just terrible. He would run around town with maybe three thousand dollars in his pocket. He liked to have his hands on his money always. He didn't ever want to put anything into real estate because he couldn't get it out fast enough." Gable himself is alleged to have said that he never gave tips because he didn't want to buy anybody's friendship, which, if true, must have left a lot of disgruntled waiters in his wake and which would, not surprisingly, have given a strong impression of meanness. But against that all his friends have ample stories of his generosity towards them and of his willingness to pick up the bill in restaurants.

However, no matter what the cause or the symptoms of his insecurity, the insecurity itself was clearly unnecessary because, throughout the thirties, his reputation simply increased. In 1934, albeit to his own indignation, he was loaned by MGM to Columbia to make *It Happened One Night*, with Claudette Colbert. MGM did this largely to punish him because he had turned down a gigolo-type role opposite his erstwhile lover, Joan Crawford, and he was also demanding more money. Frank Capra, who directed the film, said that Louis Mayer agreed to lend Gable out because that was his way of sending people to Siberia, and added: " The first day Gable came down to the set he was dead drunk and he made it very apparent that he didn't want to be sent to Siberia."

Nevertheless, *It Happened One Night*, a simple tale of a run-away heiress and a tough newspaper reporter, won Gable his only Academy Award and, incidentally, almost ruined the American underwear industry at a stroke when it was revealed that the great man wore no under shirt. That film also marked the beginning of the most fruitful period of his career when he made pictures like *Mutiny on the Bounty*, *San Francisco* and *Test Pilot* and eventually *Gone With The Wind*.

At one time Errol Flynn was being considered for the role of Rhett Butler but it came to Gable virtually by public acclaim, this being the year when he was voted "the King" in the Ed Sullivan competition. It has been said that Gable didn't want the part but the truth is that he was afraid of it, rather than unenthusiastic, and anyway thought it better suited to Ronald Colman. When David

Selznick, the producer, first approached him Gable said he "didn't want the part for money, marbles or chalk". But Selznick had made a deal with MGM and Gable, now separated from Ria, heavily involved with Carole Lombard and obliged to support two homes, could not afford to be suspended by the studio. Louis Mayer, knowing this, persuaded Mrs Gable's lawyer to keep up the financial pressure and then, offering both the carrot and the stick to his recalcitrant star, undertook to pay a 286,000 dollar divorce settlement to Ria so that Gable and Lombard could marry.

Gable finally gave in but not without the gravest reservations. He told Jean Garceau that he was going in to the film with ten million critics and he had serious doubts about his ability to satisfy any of them. Nor, when the filming began were his fears at all allayed. Gable had never before worked with the director, George Cukor, and the two men were hardly compatible. Gable felt that Cukor was neglecting him and devoting too much time to coaching Vivien Leigh, so for five days he stayed away from the set. Selznick, faced with the choice of losing his director or his star, supported the star. Cukor was removed from the picture and Gable, given the privilege of naming the new director, chose Victor Fleming, a hunting and motor-cycling companion of his and a man whose aggressively "macho" personality and offhand attitude towards women Gable much admired. Fleming, who was in the middle of making *The Wizard of Oz* at the time, was initially no more receptive to *GWTW* than Gable had been. But eventually he was persuaded to change his mind and so Gable made the film which, if all his other pictures were destroyed, would alone guarantee him a permanent place in any Hollywood hall of fame.

Meanwhile, he had once again settled his marital status. He and Ria were divorced in March 1939, and later the same month he married Carole Lombard, the former wife of William Powell. She was actually seven years younger than Gable, which made a nice change, a delicious and high-spirited blonde comedienne with great style and, when occasion demanded, a vocabulary that could make a stoker blush. Her affair with Gable had been common knowledge for some while and though it was generally regarded with affectionate approval, it had aroused the terrible wrath of such relentlessly respectable groups as the Daughters of the American Revolution. To some extent, no doubt, it was to appease this kind of pressure group, which carried a fair bit of clout in the 1930s, that Mayer had agreed to make the divorce settlement to

Ria, so enabling Lombard and Gable to marry and win a tight-lipped nod of approval from the revolutionary daughters and, just as importantly, ensuring that MGM's box-office receipts from Gable movies — not least *Gone With The Wind* — did not suffer from the fact that the star was an unashamed adulterer.

The newly-wed Gable and Lombard bought themselves a twenty acre ranch in the San Fernando Valley, called each other "ma" and "pa" and somewhat unpredictably, bearing in mind their previous track records, settled down to a life of happy domesticity. It seems, by all accounts, to have been a perfectly idyllic marriage. She was more than a wife: she was a hunting companion and, being an inventive girl, introduced softer diversions during the lulls in this bloodthirsty sport. On one occasion, recalled by Howard Hawks, they were duck shooting but, as it was a foggy morning, no ducks were about. Gable said, rather sulkily, that there was nothing they could do till the fog cleared and Carole said: "Well I know something we can do," and she took him off to a nearby hide and proceeded to do it. Even Gable had to admit that this was a lot more fun than duck-shooting.

Adela Rogers St Johns said of the marriage: "The only woman, as far as I know, that he ever was in love with was Carole. It was the finest kind of romance, man-woman thing, you ever saw in your life. They were devoted to each other." Among her many other attributes Lombard apparently had the gift of making Gable laugh (a thing most of the women who pursued him never thought to attempt) and of deflating his ego when, at times, he began to believe his own publicity.

But idyllic though it seems to have been, the marriage was also tragically brief. In January 1942, America having by now entered the war, Carole Lombard undertook a Government-sponsored tour to sell war bonds. She was supposed to travel back to Los Angeles from Indiana by train but, impatient to be home, she decided to fly instead. The plane ran into a storm and crashed in the mountains near Las Vegas, bursting immediately into flames. All the passengers, including Lombard and her mother, were killed.

When Gable learned of the accident he rushed to Las Vegas and was barely restrained from climbing the mountain himself to look for the bodies. Later, when it was certain that Carole was dead, he locked himself in a hotel room and refused to eat or talk to anybody for twenty-four hours. Then when his friends had coaxed him into returning to his home, Jean Garceau handed him a note from Carole. She had left him a series of *billets-doux*, one for every day she was away and this was the last of them. Jean Garceau said: "That was just too much. He'd borne up very well up to that point but when he read that last note he simply went to pieces and broke down and cried and that's pretty hard to see in a big man like that."

Howard Hawks, who was Carole Lombard's cousin, believed — as did most of his friends — that Gable never really recovered from his wife's death. Hawks felt it significant that Gable's fifth and last wife was "quite a lot on the same order as Carole, not as beautiful but quite a bit like her".

In August 1942, Gable joined the American army air force. He enlisted as a private but graduated an honourable 700th in a class of 2,600 from Officers' Candidate School in Florida. He sought, and was apparently given, no special privileges. Indeed, having trained as a gunner and been promoted to captain, he joined the 351st Bomber Group in England, flying several missions over Germany as an aerial photographer and winning the Distinguished Flying Cross and the Air Medal. The Germans even put a price on his head — a reward of 5,000 dollars, instant promotion and leave for anyone who captured him alive.

Why he joined up and volunteered for combat duties when he had no need to do so is not entirely clear. He was after all forty-one when he enlisted and he could, quite reasonably, have stayed in Hollywood, as many younger actors did, making patriotic films and doing his bit for the war effort while remaining safely on the home front. Shortly before she died Carole Lombard had urged him to "get into this man's army" and he may have done so partly in deference to her wishes as well as from a sense of patriotism. Whatever his reasons his war record was distinguished by any standards and coincidentally it played an important part in strengthening and perpetuating the Gable legend.

Throughout his career he always had the good fortune to catch the mood of the age. In the Depression and post-Depression years of the thirties he epitomised a peculiarly American glamour. He was rough and tough and yet, when occasion demanded, gentle. In a matriarchal society he was one man who, on film at least, dominated his women, firmly, sometimes physically but also with charm and even courtesy. John Wayne also treated women firmly, but the difference was that he seemed to regard them as recalcitrant mustangs whose spirit had to be broken before they could be ridden with any degree of comfort. Gable, on the other hand, appeared quite happy to tolerate or even admire a high-spirited woman so long as she was finally able to accept that in a partnership of equals he was a little more equal than she was.

In the forties the image changed and was refined as Gable became a classically romantic figure; a grieving widower and a returned war hero. And in the fifties as America settled down to a period of avuncular conservatism under Eisenhower, a president whose most notable achievement in office was to lower his golf handicap, Gable was the archetypal middle-aged Establishment man. Perhaps that is why he was never deposed as King: he always gave his subjects what they wanted of him.

But the Gable who came back from the war was a greatly altered figure — a restless, disillusioned man of forty-four, bereaved, deeply affected by the action he had seen over enemy lines and out of patience with the make-believe of Hollywood. His first post-war film was a forgettable romance called *Adventure*, in which he co-starred with Greer Garson. "Gable's back and Garson's got him!" said the film publicity, to Gable's great disgust because he didn't like Greer Garson very much. Nor did the idea of appearing opposite the young actresses who had emerged during his absence appeal to him greatly. Playing love scenes with them he felt like an ageing lecher. So the first few years after his return to civilian life were unhappy ones. Much of his spare time was devoted to serious drinking and the earnest pursuit of women.

The drinking could have landed him in serious trouble in 1945 were it not for the power of MGM. Driving home drunk one night he crashed into a tree, cut himself rather badly and knocked himself out. Fortunately the man with whose tree he had collided was also in the film industry and knew the ground rules. The MGM trouble shooters were informed before either the police or a doctor. Indeed, the police were kept out of it entirely and so, quite as importantly, were the Press. It was just part of the paternalistic service provided by the major studios for a property as valuable as Gable.

The women at this time posed fewer problems. He became a valued customer of Madame Frances, his friendly neighbourhood brothel-keeper, who provided him with a handy take-away service: a girl delivered to his door at night and tidily whisked away the next morning. Gable, of course, had no need to pay for his diversions: he was pursued ardently and constantly by some of the most beautiful women in Hollywood but Gable, the hunter, had no taste for being hunted himself and besides, such women made him uneasy. As Joe Mankiewicz said, they weren't really looking for Gable the man, they were looking for Rhett Butler, for Gable the King of Hollywood, Gable the great performer — in every sense, no doubt — and he felt, as any man might, that he could not rise to such expectations. To these women he would merely have been a conquest, one more notch on their suspender belts and he was more at ease with humbler and less voracious companions. "More than anything," Mankiewicz said, "Gable believed in the one-night stand, or the easy conquest, the messenger girl or the publicity girl. He was never, remotely, the great lover."

There was, however, in these post-war years one girl who neither pursued him nor fell into the category of easy acquisition or one-night stand and that was Virginia Gray, who had appeared with him in a minor role in *Idiot's Delight*. They met again at the home of a mutual friend soon after he returned from the war and started going out together. "He was very, very guarded," she said. "Didn't want to get involved and said so. Spelled it out. And I thought, 'Well, who in hell do you think you are?' The women were throwing themselves at him and this he hated. The more they did it, the more he would run and he figured all women were alike. If, in a relaxed moment, he showed any emotion he'd scare himself to death and disappear for a month."

He had many fears, she said, about himself and about his career. He was not even sure whether he wanted to continue acting and the films in which he appeared — *The Hucksters*, a story about the advertising business with Deborah Kerr, *Homecoming*, in which, co-starring with Lana Turner, he played a wartime surgeon, and *Command Decision*, another war story with Walter Pigeon — were unsatisfying. From time to time he would raise the question of marriage with Virginia Gray but immediately, petrified at the thought of any such commitment to anybody, he would turn and run.

Nevertheless, in 1949 to everyone's astonishment, not least perhaps his own, he took a fourth wife, Sylvia Ashley, a former London chorus girl, who had already been married to Douglas Fairbanks senior and a couple of titled Englishmen. They took the decision to marry after a party in December that year and both regretted it almost immediately. She, the famous society woman still clinging fiercely to the title of Lady Ashley to which she no longer had any right, and he, the hard-drinking outdoor man, quickly proved to be, as they had appeared, quite incompatible, although of the two it was she who tried harder to make the marriage work. She even went hunting with him, a noble effort on her part if not exactly rewarding for either of them. But Gable rapidly lost interest in the union and, after a lengthy separation, they were finally divorced in 1951. It was just before then that he returned, for the last time, to Virginia Gray.

"One day I was out in the backyard fooling around with something," she said, "and I came in through the patio and there he was, sitting in the living room, just as though nothing had happened. I thought, of all the nerve! You rip a person apart then you come in and sit with that silly grin on your face as if it all happened yesterday and let's pick up where we left off. Well, then again, the serious discussions went on and he ran again. He was going to Reno to get a divorce but by that time I knew there was just no way for us and it hurt too much. I cared too much. And I knew, as long as I'd be around it would be this way and so, as rough as it was, I made the decision to end it. I thought, either it's going to be one way or the other. I'm not asking for marriage but I can't take this, and of course the rest is history."

And so, single again, Gable moved into the last phase of his career. Since the war he had made ten films, none of them comparable with the best of his 1930s pictures, but in 1953 he had a genuine success with *Mogambo*, a remake (directed by John Ford) of *Red Dust*, with the Mary Astor and Jean Harlow roles played respectively by Grace Kelly and Ava Gardner. It was his penultimate film for MGM because the now failing studio could no longer afford to pay him his 520,000 dollars a year salary and decided to drop his contract. When the *Mogambo* box-office returns started to come in the studio had a change of heart and made an attempt at reconciliation but by then Gable had made up his mind to go. He had long been resentful of the fact that MGM had never offered him a percentage of the huge profits from *Gone With The Wind* and had also refused him a percentage of his subsequent films. Thus, after making *Betrayal*, another war drama, with Lana Turner, he left the studios in 1954 to become a freelance.

Ahead of him lay eight more films and one more wife, Kay Spreckles, née Williams, a former actress whom he had known for several years and whom he finally married in 1955. He was then fifty-four and somewhat surprised to find himself still in demand for romantic leads in films like *The Tall Men*, a western and *Teacher's Pet*, a comedy with Doris Day. The pictures he made in these last years of his life did nice business and Gable was, at last, on a percentage, though the really big money never did come his way until his last film, *The Misfits* in 1960.

Like *Gone With The Wind* this was a picture Gable did not want to make. It was a strenuous role for a man of his age and the part he was asked to play, that of a latterday cowboy rounding up wild horses for slaughter, went strongly against the Gable image. But both Arthur Miller, the writer, and John Huston, the director, were keen to sign him and the fee he was offered, 750,000 dollars, was a great deal higher than had ever come his way before. Unable to make up his mind he finally decided to raise his asking price to a million in the belief that he would be turned down.

Gable was at breakfast with Al Menasco, a wealthy business-man and his closest friend, when the producers arrived to find out whether he would play the part or not. As he went out to spring on them what he thought would be his unacceptable demand for the extra 250,000 dollars, he said to Menasco: "This won't take long. Keep my coffee warm." He was away for more than half an hour and returned, according to Menasco, with a bemused expression on his face. All he said was: "They took it."

His co-star in *The Misfits* was Marilyn Monroe and for many reasons, not least Miss Monroe's psychological problems and notorious inability to be anywhere on time, the filming was a lengthy, laborious and frustrating business. Gable did many of the roping and horse-handling scenes himself and Menasco, who was present for much of the shooting, believed that this arduous work in desert heat, combined with the on- and off-set tension caused by Monroe's disintegrating relationship with her husband, Arthur Miller, simply wore him out. "At that time Clark was nearly sixty years of age and beginning to show it and his breath was short and when he came off camera and sat down in the shade he was a pretty exhausted man."

Whether the effort of making *The Misfits* contributed to his failing health or not, Gable was dead before the film was released. John Huston has said: "Like a gentleman he made his last shot and then died a day later," but that, too, is simply part of the Gable myth. In fact he died in November 1960, a few weeks after shooting finished and as the result of a heart attack. He was three months short of his sixtieth birthday. John Gable, his only child, was born a few months later.

Gable's reviews for *The Misfits* were undoubtedly the best he had ever received, as only befitted what was perhaps the best performance he had ever given. And that, too, helped to sustain him posthumously in his pre-eminent position among Hollywood's male stars; the King had died, as the King should, at his peak.

The Hollywood that Gable knew no longer exists. Television and the record industry are more important there now than the movies. MGM which once boasted more stars than there are in heaven, has sold off most of its land and is simply a small cluster of buildings in which independent pictures are made. Gable's old ranch is an expensive middle-class housing estate and his former home, the one he bought for Carole Lombard, is occupied by two interior designers.

But if the kingdom is sleazy and run down, the King himself remains undiminished.

Gable was never a great actor; he was always Gable in another hat. But he was a serious professional, a contract star who, for most of his life, was content to follow the company line and never make waves and that gave him durability. Nobody, in a competitive business like the movies, could ever become king unless he had staying power but, equally, he could never become king if he only had staying power. And Gable added to that a number of other qualities, none of them perhaps individually outstanding but rarely found in combination.

He knew his limitations and was careful not to step beyond them. He had an innate sense of dignity that kept his fans slightly in awe of him. Other stars, especially in the thirties, were mobbed and had their clothes ripped from their backs but it never happened to Gable. He was an actor who not only played a hero but behaved like a hero when the time came. He was a figure of glamour and a figure of tragedy. He was a sex symbol whom men could identify with: women chased him, he didn't chase them. He was, men felt, a man's man at heart, a guy who liked to take a drink and go hunting with his friends, who treated women with casual gallantry and was not above slapping them down if they got out of hand. As the *New York Times* said in its obituary of him, he was "as certain as the sunrise. He was consistently and stubbornly all man."

"The camera liked him," said Howard Hawks. "He couldn't

do any wrong. When he grinned the whole audience felt better."
And, of course, as he moved with as much serenity as anyone
could expect in a place as fickle and mercurial as Hollywood
through a thirty-year career that embraced sixty-seven films and
five wives (who between them got through seventeen husbands)
he had one other vital, incalculable, irreplaceable quality going
for him: he was lucky and he knew it.

Errol Flynn

The youthful Flynn — Michael Curtiz's "beautiful puppet".

*above : Flynn met his second wife, Norah Eddington, while he was
on trial for statutory rape.*

*opposite : Flynn with first wife Lily Damita, whose alimony — he
insisted — always kept him broke.*

*above : Flynn, face ravaged by time, drink and drugs, in his last film
"Cuban Rebel Girls", with Beverley Aadland, his 17-year-old
companion at the end of his life.*

*opposite : Flynn married his third wife, Patrice Wymore, in France
— and promptly faced another charge of rape.*

Errol Flynn died in Vancouver on October 14th, 1959. It was a heart attack which killed him, though such technicalities hardly matter really, since it must have been a photofinish between his heart, his liver and his kidneys as to which would put the finishing touches to him. Flynn was only fifty when he died but he could hardly be said to have been cut off in his prime because, by then, he was a quite awe-inspiring wreck, his body utterly ruined by a surfeit of drugs, a surfeit of booze, a surfeit in fact of practically everything which, taken to excess, might reasonably be expected to kill a man. At the inquest the coroner remarked that he had had the body of a tired old man, to which Flynn, had he been around to hear it, might very probably have said "Amen" and felt himself vaguely complimented. He had often said, had he not, that anyone who died with more than ten thousand dollars in his pocket must have been a failure, since he clearly had no idea how to spend his money to its best advantage. By the same token, therefore, he may well have felt that anyone who died with more than a vestige of good health left in his body could not have lived his life to the full. Flynn, dying diseased and quite likely broke—though this is not entirely certain as his financial affairs were in such a magnificent mess that they have not been sorted out to this day—was not guilty on both counts.

As evidence of the fullness with which he had led his life one has only to look at the reasons for his dying in such an improbable place as Vancouver. He had not gone there, as might have been supposed, to set up a new film. Nor had he gone there for a holiday or for the good of his health — too late for that in any event. He had gone there, quite simply, to escape the law. Back in California the sheriff, with or without posse, was waiting to pounce and charge him either with statutory rape (for the third time in his life) or, at the very least, with contributing to the delinquency of a minor.

The fact that the minor, a seventeen-year-old actress named Beverley Aadland, had fled with him to Vancouver and did not in any way feel herself to have been rendered delinquent by their relationship was neither here nor there. Today a liaison between a fifty-year-old man and a seventeen-year-old girl might still occasion the odd "Tut" of disapproval, but nobody goes to prison for it. In 1959, however, morality, even in Hollywood, was made of sterner stuff and Flynn, as usual, was its whipping boy. Despite all the scandal that attaches to his name, his greatest fault was this: he was born out of his time.

46

Of course, it's hard to say what would have been the right time for Flynn to be born: much earlier, probably, rather than later. Had he been born later his drinking and his sexual peccadilloes would have attracted little attention, though his drug addiction would have got him into trouble. Had he been born earlier, in the eighteenth century for example, the adventurer and buccaneer that he played best on screen and that he tried to be, as far as the twentieth century would allow, in his private life, might have been actively encouraged. Flynn's most attractive quality was that he lived exactly as he wished to live, without a thought for convention and, by extension perhaps, without a thought for anybody else. It's easy to say, as his admirers do, that he hurt nobody except himself but it's impossible for anyone to pursue the ruthlessly self-centred path that Flynn pursued without leaving a number of walking wounded in his wake.

That being so, the story of Flynn's life, viewed from the point of view of a strict puritan or even from the point of view of ordinary, respectable, God-fearing people, reads like a most satisfactory cautionary tale. He had astonishing good looks, a small but highly saleable talent, a magnificent physique and such sex appeal that he seemed to walk through life on a carpet of prostrate and willing females. (He once estimated that he had spent between 12,000 and 14,000 nights making love. Since that would have meant every night for the best part of forty years it's difficult to believe, but he certainly had his share.)

Yet with all those priceless advantages he managed to finish up wrecked and virtually alone, on the skids and a fugitive from justice, a textbook example of one who, against all the odds, had managed to wrest defeat from the jaws of victory.

The saga of Flynn's journey up to the top of the hill and straight down the other side began in Hobart, Tasmania, on June 20th, 1909. Errol Leslie Thomson Flynn was the son of Professor Theodore Flynn, a marine biologist and zoologist and his wife, Marelle. To the father, the wild and rather spectacular boy he had begotten was a constant source of wonder. I met Professor Flynn on two occasions in England some years after Errol's death. He was a tall, spare, gentle and scholarly man who still talked of his son with deep but bemused affection. The relationship between them had clearly been one of love and mutual admiration, although just as clearly the elder Flynn had long abandoned any attempt to understand the ways and motives of the younger.

But the relationship between Errol Flynn and his mother was very different, being based on a mutual suspicion, dislike and at times even hatred. Flynn himself made that plain enough in his autobiography, *My Wicked, Wicked Ways*, published while his mother was still alive, although he offered no real explanation for the distaste she seems to have felt for him from birth. He was her first child and she didn't have her second, a daughter, till ten years later, so perhaps his arrival was unplanned and therefore unwelcome. Perhaps, there being nothing in the rules which says a mother is obliged to love her children, she simply resented him as an interference with her way of life.

Whatever the cause of her antipathy, the amateur psychiatrist might well feel it unnecessary to look any further for an explanation of Flynn's irresponsible and self-destructive passage through life. Certainly it seems probable that his dislike for his mother, of which he never made any secret, had a profound effect on his relationship with all other women.

The young Flynn grew up and was educated, to a point, in Hobart, London and Sydney where, at the age of sixteen he was left to fend for himself when his parents and younger sister moved to Europe. After a few shiftless months in Sidney he set off for the goldfields of New Guinea, joined the Government service as a clerk and was fired when caught in *flagrante delicto* with an official's wife. Thereafter he worked on a copra plantation, acquired part-ownership of a yacht which he hired out for documentary filming and, except for a brief spell when he returned to Sydney to be cured of gonorrhoea, made New Guinea his base for the next few years. During that time he made his acting debut as Fletcher Christian in a low-budget picture called *In the Wake of the Bounty*. It was a totally inauspicious beginning although, with hindsight, one can detect a note of prophecy in one of the lines he was called upon to deliver: "The future holds the most awful adventure of all."

The chief affect of this production was that it inspired in him an ambition to earn his living as an actor and, to this end, he went to England in 1933, advertised himself mendaciously as the star of various non-existent films, did a brief stint with the Northampton Repertory Company, appeared forgettably in two equally forgettable West End plays and made a picture at Twickenham Studios called *Murder at Monte Carlo*, the result of which was a summons to Hollywood and a successful screen test with Warner Brothers.

By then Flynn was twenty-six and, professionally, he got off to what one can only call a quiet start, playing a corpse in a film called *The Case of the Curious Bride*. Privately, his beginnings in Hollywood were much more dramatic. Within months of his arrival in 1935, he had met and married the first of his three wives, Lily Damita, a volatile French actress eight years older than himself. The marriage only lasted seven years, but he was still paying for it when he died. In fact, it lasted for seven years in name only, having been considerably less than successful from the start.

When it ended in divorce in 1942, Lily, her case strengthened by the fact that she had borne him a son, Sean, extracted lavish alimony from her husband and, since she refrained from marrying again, continued to draw it until his death; not that the payments were always as regular or complete as they should have been. Flynn blamed that alimony settlement for the fact that, from the time of his divorce onwards, he was rarely solvent.

Still, in 1935 all that bitterness and indeed all the rest of Flynn's problems lay far ahead in the future. In 1935, in fact, things could hardly have been better for him. Robert Donat, who was to have played the title role in a swashbuckler called *Captain Blood*, withdrew at the last moment either through illness or a dispute over money and Warner Brothers, taking a considerable gamble, handed the active and adventurous role to the unknown Flynn whose Hollywood career up to this point, of course, had virtually consisted of lying motionless on the floor.

The result both made and, it could be argued, destroyed Flynn. The film, directed by the Hungarian Michael Curtiz, made its leading man, in true Hollywood fashion, a star overnight and immediately typed him in the kind of role that he played so well and that he came to regard with something very close to contempt. Nobody is ever going to accuse Errol Flynn of having been a great actor, though he always thought he could have been one if only he'd been given the opportunity. But he was undeniably a superstar and although he attained that status partly because his private life was bigger, wilder, bawdier and more scandalous than any role he ever played on screen, one must also take into consideration the not insignificant fact that when you think of the great swashbucklers of the movies there's no need to think any further than Douglas Fairbanks Senior, and Errol Flynn.

It was one of the minor tragedies of Flynn's life that he never believed the ability to cut a dashing and romantic figure in costume, with a sword, on a horse or a pirate ship amounted to very much. He thought anybody could do it, but he was wrong.

That contempt stemmed perhaps from the attitude of the director, Curtiz, who had little regard for the actor and tended to describe him as "a beautiful puppet". Since the first part of that description was manifestly true and even Flynn — the least vain of men as far as his looks were concerned — must have been aware of it, it's not unreasonable to suppose that he was prepared to accept the second part as being equally true. When you add to that the fact that most of his early successes (*Captain Blood, The Charge of the Light Brigade, The Adventures of Robin Hood* and *The Sea Hawk* for example) were directed by the brilliant but disdainful puppet-master Curtiz, the result was always likely to be an actor with very little confidence in either himself or his work.

Captain Blood also set the pattern for Flynn's relationship with Warner Brothers. Halfway through the film he decided that he was being paid too little and refused to work any more until his salary was increased. With no real alternative but to agree, the studio raised his pay from 125 to 750 dollars a week, since it would have been far more expensive to scrap the film and start again with another and more biddable star. Encouraged by this success, Flynn used the same gambit again and again and, while his films were making vast fortunes for Warner Brothers, continued to get away with it.

Indeed at times it seems as though Flynn's entire career at Warners was a continuing battle against the company and in particular the head of the studio, Jack L. Warner. Vincent Sherman, who directed the actor's last major film there, *The Adventures of Don Juan* in 1947, said: "They had a kind of love-hate relationship. I'd hear them fighting terribly on the phone and then during the making of the film Warner must have called me twenty or thirty times saying, 'You tell that bastard so and so and this and that,' and finally I couldn't take any more and I said, 'Mr Warner, I have to work with him. I can't discipline him. You pay him, you discipline him,' and he said, 'Well, don't think that I'm afraid of him.' But I think he was a little afraid, though he also had a genuine affection for him, the kind of love for an errant son almost. I was at Errol's funeral when there was a far smaller crowd than was anticipated. A lot of Flynn's so-called friends stayed away. But Warner was there."

Warner's paternal attitude towards Flynn, such as it might

have been, was not returned in the same coin. Nora Eddington, Flynn's second wife, says her husband arranged for her to have a bit part, virtually her only acting experience, in *Don Juan* simply to spite the studio chief. "He said, 'If you do this little bit they won't pay you for it but I'll get Jack to buy you a new wardrobe.' He was always looking for a way to screw Jack Warner."

Flynn's and Nora's daughter, Deirdre, remembers that her father had a house in the hills looking down on the studio and she said he used it "as a place to hide from Jack Warner. He wasn't afraid of Warner and I don't think he liked him very much, although he did have a great deal of respect for him. He used to say he liked to sit up on the hill there in the house knowing he could throw rocks down on Jack Warner."

It's worth remembering, however, that both Nora Eddington and her daughter were talking about the period in the late 1940s, when Flynn's association with Warner Brothers was coming to an end, a time when fashions were changing and his particular kind of swashbuckling could no longer be guaranteed to draw huge audiences. It was perhaps the time when, most of all, he felt the need for change, to break away from the parts in which he had been typecast but while he was still at Warner's the chance of doing that was remote. His few attempts to play something other than an adventurer of one sort or another had not been particularly successful and the studio was not noticeably keen for him to repeat them. As Deirdre Flynn said: "He blamed Jack Warner for a lot of his problems, careerwise, and the relationship between them was cat and dog most of the time."

In the early days, though, Flynn's attitude towards Warner was wary and grasping but not especially bitter, probably because his first seven years at the studio were quite the most successful of his life. In the period between *Captain Blood* in 1935 and *Gentleman Jim* in 1942 he made twenty films, including all those for which he is best remembered, *The Charge of the Light Brigade*, *The Adventures of Robin Hood* (quite the best picture of its kind ever made), *Elizabeth and Essex, The Sea Hawk, They Died with Their Boots On* and, of course, *Captain Blood* and *Gentleman Jim* themselves. He also made a couple of comedies, *The Perfect Specimen* and *Four's A Crowd*, a weepie, *The Green Light*, and a love story, *Another Dawn*, but, although he did well enough in all of them, Flynn in modern dress was never so popular at the box-office as Flynn in costume with a sword or a six-shooter in his hand.

On eight occasions during that fertile and prosperous period his co-star was Olivia de Havilland of whom Bette Davis recalled in her memoirs: "It was Olivia whom he truly adored and who evaded him successfully in the end. I really believe that he was deeply in love with her." These days Miss de Havilland herself puts it rather less passionately. There was, she says, a deep and abiding affection between them and, at one point, there was even talk of marriage, an improbable eventuality, as they both knew, since he was still securely, if not very happily, married to Lily Damita. "I suppose you could say I had fallen in love with him," she said. "It seems an inadequate sort of term, perhaps not quite accurate. I developed a very deep crush, shall we say."

She was twenty at that time and he was twenty-seven and he wooed her with some ardour, being temporarily separated from his wife. Miss de Havilland suggested that they should keep apart until he had decided what he was going to do about his marriage and, although Flynn hardly took this seriously and continued to call her and ask her out, she insisted on sticking to the arrangement until some firm decision had been made. This was wise of her, as it turned out, because within a few weeks Flynn and Damita were back together again and that was more or less the end of the matter, although Miss de Havilland admits that had he been single, "I certainly would have wanted to marry him". But whether that would have been a very good idea she is not at all sure. "He was very young. A number of pathways lay open for him in terms of a style of life. I don't know . . . he would have been a handful and I'm not sure that I was experienced enough to deal with that."

Not only was Flynn very young; he was also very immature. His method of attracting Olivia de Havilland's attention, for example, was to slip a dead snake into her knickers — not, I must add, the knickers she was actually wearing at the time but the knickers she was about to put on for her role in *The Charge of the Light Brigade*. Since they were large and roomy, nineteenth-century pantalettes rather than twentieth-century briefs, she didn't realise there was a snake in them until she had them on, whereupon, thinking the creature was alive, and acting with great presence of mind, she plunged into a deep pond in order to drown the thing. Flynn thought this was hilarious though, not surprisingly, Miss de Havilland failed to see the joke for some time and still feels it was an odd way for a grown man to declare his affection, which is what Flynn was undoubtedly trying to do. But she believes that at that time and probably until his death there was a strong element of the small boy about him and perhaps it was that, along with his remarkable good looks and more charm than was good either for him or the people on whom he used it, that explained the immediate attraction almost everybody seemed to feel for him.

Until the looks and the luck deserted him and the drugs began to take a hold, he could get away with almost anything. Hal Wallis, a senior producer at Warner Brothers, said that even when Flynn was behaving atrociously and refusing to continue with a film until his salary was raised he was "the same likeable rogue. He would make these demands, he'd disappear, he'd come back to work and he would have the top brass in the studio apologising to him for having inconvenienced him."

But inevitably it was women upon whom Flynn's combination of looks and charm had the greatest effect. Olivia de Havilland said that on first meeting him she felt "instant attraction. I thought he was the most beautiful-looking man that I'd ever seen in my life and I suppose he's still the most beautiful-looking man I have ever seen in my life." Nora Eddington, recalling her introduction to him beside the pool at his home, said: "I decided he was the most beautiful thing I'd ever seen. He had marvellous green eyes and a deep tan and his hair had lightened — it was a sort of ruddy blond. And he couldn't have been more charming."

Many years later Flynn came to England to film *Lilacs in the Spring* with Dame Anna Neagle. He was in his middle forties and the ravages of time and his own destructive way of life had left their marks, but nevertheless Dame Anna found that "he was all the things the legend had said about him. He was a marvellous-looking man, full of charm and he just knocked one sideways."

Yet, despite all that, or possibly because of it, his relationships with women were never particularly happy. He was said to be an ardent pursuer of women and perhaps he was (though more often, I think, he was the prey rather than the predator) but if he did pursue them it was noticeable that they took great care not to run so fast that he couldn't catch up. His attitude to women was always ambivalent and many people were not at all sure that deep down he even liked them very much.

Deirdre Flynn is one who thinks he did. "He'd have to," she said, "considering all the time he spent with them. Some part of him liked them anyway. But then again he wanted to spend time with his buddies, his drinking partners and he didn't feel women should be included on those occasions."

Nora Eddington, on the other hand, believes he was "really a man's man. He liked some women but he wasn't all that sexually driven that he had to seek women all the time. In fact, they sought him out — they sought after him and he'd say, 'Well, why not?'"

Against that, Vincent Sherman talked of Flynn's "constant pursuit of women" and felt it was "some unconscious desire to debase them or to reassure himself of his own manhood and vitality. He was very complex; not just an ordinary woman chaser. Errol liked men, not in a sexual sense, but he liked men much better than women. He could love a man but he couldn't love a woman. I think he was distrustful of them, maybe he was afraid of them."

Olivia de Havilland said: "He enjoyed the idea of conquest but that doesn't mean he was capable of a very deep love and of sustaining it, does it? It means the opposite if anything."

In discussing Flynn and his attitude towards women it's difficult to ignore his relations with his mother. Miss de Havilland said: "You often wonder about a man who had complex feelings about his mother, which Errol did. I think most men who have perhaps been ridiculed by their mothers are never quite sure of themselves with women." Vincent Sherman said that one day during the filming of *Don Juan* Flynn "made a remark about his mother, a very distasteful remark about his mother. He didn't like her at all: he loved his father."

What significance there may have been in this "distasteful remark" it's now impossible to say; but it is unusual to find a romantic movie star of thirty-eight or thirty-nine, twice-married and the father of three children (which was Flynn's marital and parental state at that time) discussing his mother with a film director. It's certainly unusual in the case of a heterosexual movie star and Flynn was surely that, even though it has been suggested that he had occasional homosexual relationships too. If he did they were very discreet and not, apparently, of any great importance to him.

But it does seem likely that the mutual suspicion and antipathy which existed between himself and his mother had a lot to do with his largely unhappy experiences with women in general and his tendency to treat them as sexual toys to be acquired on a whim and discarded when he was tired of them.

When they were filming *Don Juan*, Vincent Sherman said, there was "a very beautiful little girl who played one of the small roles and Errol came over to me and said, 'Why don't you tell her how much I'm interested in her and that I've persuaded you to give us close-ups and so on. That'll sort of pave the way for me.' I was absolutely shocked. It was like asking me to do a little pimping for him. But to him it seemed perfectly legitimate."

On another occasion, said Sherman, "There were two girls he called up — prostitutes. I was a little surprised. It was the first time I'd known him bring prostitutes on the set. They were sitting over in the corner waiting for us to finish the day's work and he said to me, 'What are you doing after we've finished?' I told him I was going home and he said, 'Well, I thought maybe you'd like to come up to the dressing-room afterwards.' I said, 'Errol, I don't know how you can do it. You work all day here and then go up to the dressing-room with these women . . .' He said, 'Oh, it's nothing. I just lie there reading the trade papers while they work on me.'"

Neither anecdote is much to Flynn's credit (though there is a disgraceful touch of humour in the second) and both do tend to suggest, to put it mildly, a basic disregard for women.

All this time he was still married to Nora Eddington and she was well aware of his extra-marital activities but knew there was little she could do about them. Her one stipulation was to say to him, "I know the kind of life that you like. I know what goes on at the studio and I know you can't pass a pretty face. But just don't bring it home to the dinner table and don't ever humiliate me." And with these extremely lenient rules, she said, he complied. It was probably the closest approximation to fidelity that Flynn could make. He often said that he never wanted to marry but women wouldn't let him stay single and Deirdre Flynn thinks he was probably right. "I don't think a man like that really should be married," she said. "He's just not the type."

In 1942, just before the film *Gentleman Jim* was released, Flynn had an experience with two young women that was surely calculated to leave him with a highly jaundiced view of the entire sex, even assuming that he had had an unjaundiced view previously. In November of that year he was arrested and brought to trial on two charges of statutory rape, the allegation being that he had had unlawful sexual intercourse with two girls who were under eighteen, the legal age of consent in California.

One of them accused him of having assaulted her on board his yacht. Fortunately for Flynn both girls had very dubious backgrounds and he was acquitted, but he always believed that the trial was a political manoeuvre, an attempt by the Los Angeles district attorney's office to make a public attack on the morals of Hollywood generally by using him, probably its least moral citizen, as a scapegoat.

It does seem at least possible that neither girl would have brought charges against him unless she had been encouraged to do so. One result of the trial was that Flynn gained an imperishable reputation as a satyr; the phrase "in like Flynn" took on a specific and very lewd meaning and although all the unwelcome publicity helped the box-office receipts of *Gentleman Jim* (the story of James J. Corbett, the heavyweight boxing champion) — much to Warner Brothers' surprise and gratification — it also caused Flynn to believe, bitterly, that he had come to be regarded as little more than an ambulatory phallic symbol.

What with this and the fact that, from time to time, various women whom he had never met would accuse him of being the father of their children and, by threatening to "tell all" to the Press, would try to shake him down for maintenance, it's hardly surprising that henceforth such respect as he had for women was not altogether uncritical.

But the trial had one other and more pleasing result. Because of it he met Nora Eddington, who was then working in the tobacco kiosk at the Los Angeles County Court. She was only seventeen and dangerously, considering what he was charged with, Flynn arranged through an intermediary to meet her. Bearing this in mind and remembering too the taste for teenage girls that he indulged in till the end of his life, the nagging, though unfounded, suspicion arises that he possibly was guilty, technically anyway, of statutory rape despite the verdict of the jury. In any event, within a year he and Nora were married.

They actually married not because either of them thought it was a particularly good idea at the time, but because Nora was pregnant. She was a Roman Catholic, didn't even consider an abortion and wanted her child to be legitimate. She said: "When I told him, the first thing he said was, 'You know, I just don't want to get married. I care about you. I love you, but I don't want to get married.' And I said, 'Well, I can't force you to marry me but I'm going to have this child anyway and I would like it to be legal.' I said, 'Just give the child a name and you can have a divorce immediately afterwards; I'll sign any papers that you want and that'll be the end of it.' So we agreed to it. But then I couldn't get rid of him for seven years.''

Flynn, who was reluctant to abandon his bachelor image and way of life, kept the marriage a secret and sent Nora to Mexico under an assumed name to have the baby. She was there for six months, during which he telephoned and visited her so often that by the time Deirdre was born the fact that he had married again was common knowledge.

Nora said: "The day after the birth I said, 'What about the divorce papers?' and he said, 'We'll talk about it later.' And he put me off and put me off and then he said, 'I don't want a divorce but I'm also not ready for marriage and a child.' And I said, 'All right, fine. What do you want me to do?' And he said, 'Well, I'll get you a separate house; whatever you want.' In other words he wanted to keep me on the side and still have his bachelor life. So I went along with it for about six months and then I rebelled. I'd sit in that house with the baby and my parents and the nurse, and Errol wouldn't let me date anybody, although he was going out with other girls. Oh yes, certainly. He was having a ball, are you kidding? But he'd say, 'I'd rather you didn't go out right now.' And what he would do is, he'd have his weekend orgy so to speak and then he'd call me from his house and say, 'Come on up, I want to see you,' and I'd be running back and forth and between and all of a sudden I thought, I don't want this. You know? This is ridiculous, what am I doing?

"We had a lot of publicity and I met a lot of his friends and I started getting phone calls and so I began dating other men and this made him absolutely furious. So when he called to tell me to come on up I'd say, 'Well, I'm sorry, I'm not running up there at the drop of a hat. If you want to see me you'd better call me at the beginning of the week.' And when he saw it could be serious between me and someone else, he said, 'Well, I think we'd better move you up here.' So I moved in because that's what I wanted to begin with. I wanted a family, I wanted a home and I was in love with the man.''

Also by the time she and Flynn settled down to a more conventional married life she was pregnant again. Her move into her husband's house in the hills was the beginning of the happiest period of their time together. He was still a big star, earning a great deal of money, and he had a wife who was tolerant of his sexual adventures so long as he was discreet about them. The only thing that really bothered him at this time was the fact that the

Second World War was going on without him. He had become an American citizen and when the United States entered the war he was keen to do his bit, but his draft rating was 4F, he had an "athletic heart", suffered from recurrent malaria and also had a touch of tuberculosis and he was rejected by every branch of the armed forces.

David Niven, his friend and companion of earlier days in many a drinking and womanising bout, said: "Here was this huge man, a great boxer and a great tennis player, but he had all the things wrong for getting into the army. Here was this great hero-type fellow who was not in the war and I think it really destroyed him. I think he was lucky as hell myself, but anyway it destroyed him, poor old boy."

There are those who tell a different tale, who say that Flynn never had any intention of joining up but that would seem to be out of character. His early adventures in New Guinea, his love of boxing, riding, sailing and scuba diving and the fact that he had taken some brief and obscure part in the Spanish Civil War (admittedly to get away from Lily Damita and not for any particularly noble reason) indicate that, whatever his other faults, he was not a physical coward. Any impression that he might have been one stems from his own self-mockery, his habit of coming off the set of some swashbuckler mopping his brow and saying, "By God, that's the bravest I've ever been," and his suggestion in *My Wicked, Wicked Ways* that he had scampered out of Spain at the mere suggestion that he might be called upon to do a little fighting. But people who brag about their own cowardice are not usually cowards and there's no reason to suppose that Flynn was an exception.

It's most probable that David Niven was right and that rejection by the forces helped to destroy him. In the Second World War nobody sent white feathers to apparently able-bodied men who weren't in uniform but they were still subjected to a certain amount of derision. And, significantly or not, it was during this time that his drinking became heavier and he began to experiment with drugs. Nora Eddington said he had started taking them when she first met him, the time of the rape case and his rejection by the services.

"He started taking them on a low key, you know? I was horrified by it; I'd never been around drugs. But he said that he'd never tried it and he didn't want to leave this world without trying everything. So what could I do? We were only just married. But then it got progressively worse."

In the end it was Flynn's drug-taking which caused the break-up of the marriage after seven years. Nora said: "He went from one drug to another until finally he was a mainliner. And if you've never seen anybody on narcotics, they're in another world. They go crazy, they don't know what they're doing. He whacked me around a couple of times and when he came out of it he didn't know what had happened to me or how it came about. It got progressively worse and I must have left him, I don't know, half a dozen times and then I'd go back to him because he said he wouldn't use drugs any more and he'd try to stop but that was worse. And you know you can live with it for just so long. He didn't want me to leave him and when I finally did he said he would go into a sanitorium and take the cure but by then it was too late.

"You can take just so much. I adored the man but it wears away at you and wears away and the thing that was really bad was that he drank with it and you're not supposed to do both. You know, he always said he'd never get hung up on it but he did. Those are the famous last words — 'It won't get me: I can quit when I want to' — but he couldn't. That's what killed him."

By the time Nora filed for divorce in 1948 Flynn, though still less than forty years old, was already more or less finished in Hollywood. He had worked steadily through the war years and after but his films had made little impression at the box-office and one, *Objective Burma* in which he and a handful of other Americans appeared to have won the Burma campaign without any sort of assistance from the British, caused so much outrage in London that it was withdrawn from British cinemas.

His reviews were generally less than complimentary and the criticism hurt him. He took to drinking on the set, at first secretly by squirting oranges full of vodka with a hypodermic syringe and sucking them constantly as though he were desperate for Vitamin C, and then openly, although from time to time he would try to stop. Vincent Sherman recalled that for the first week of shooting on *Don Juan*, Flynn's behaviour was impeccable. But then the New York reviews of his previous film *Escape Me Never* were delivered to the studio. They were scathing. Flynn tried to laugh them off but the next day he began drinking again.

In October 1950, while on a trip to Europe, Flynn married the actress Patrice Wymore, then a twenty-four-year-old starlet at Warner Brothers, in the Lutheran Church at Nice and on the same day was charged yet again with rape and ordered to answer the allegations in the Town Hall at Monte Carlo. The plaintiff this time was a young French girl and once again the offence was said to have taken place on Flynn's yacht. But, just as on the previous occasion in California, the charge was decidedly flimsy and the judge had no hesitation in throwing it out of court. Once again Flynn had been proved innocent, at least of rape. But even so the Monte Carlo incident added yet another murky chapter to a life story that was beginning to read like a modern, grown-up version of *Eric, Or Little by Little*. In any event it was a pretty inauspicious start to a marriage which, like the previous two, soon began to fail.

Two years after the wedding Flynn's contract with Warner Brothers and the major part of his career in Hollywood came to an end. As a big star he was clearly finished and he was in desperate financial trouble with huge income tax demands and back-alimony suits brought against him by Lily Damita. Exactly how broke he was it is hard to tell because as Deirdre Flynn said: "He was always stashing money here and there and pleading poverty at the same time, hoping to get himself off the hook."

Certainly he must have had a fair bit tucked away — though perhaps not enough to meet his crippling obligations in America — because he put up $430,000 of his own towards an Italian co-production of a film about William Tell, for which he himself had written the script. But very soon his money ran out and so did that of his partners and the enterprise resulted in only thirty minutes of film which have never been shown. This put him into even greater financial trouble because he found himself being sued by various members of the cast and production crew of the abortive picture for $840,000 and at the same time his Hollywood business manager died leaving behind evidence of, to say the least, gross mishandling of Flynn's affairs.

Before the *William Tell* fiasco he had made a couple of swash-bucklers, *The Master of Ballantrae* in Britain and *Crossed Swords* with Gina Lollobrigida in Italy, but neither of them had worked and his reputation was at an extremely low ebb when he returned to London in the mid-fifties to co-star with Anna Neagle in *Lilacs in the Spring* and *King's Rhapsody*, the first of which was not particularly successful and the second a disaster.

And so he drifted on with two more indifferent movies, until in 1957 by an irony which I don't imagine he would have appreciated (or on second thoughts perhaps he would), he began to achieve recognition as an actor when it was too late to do him much good. Even more ironically he did it by playing drunks. First he received excellent notices in an adaptation of Hemingway's *The Sun Also Rises* and then turned in a most acceptable performance in *Too Much, Too Soon* in which he played his idol John Barrymore, another actor of astonishing good looks who had ruined himself with booze. It was almost type-casting, a role for which Flynn might have been preparing himself all his life. The film earned mostly downbeat reviews but Flynn was good and he was good again in John Huston's *The Roots of Heaven* in which he played his third successive drunk. By then, however, the drink and drugs were destroying him fast and, as Jack Warner was to describe him later in his autobiography, he was already "one of the living dead".

The Huston film was not well received and interest in Flynn's comeback swiftly waned. In the summer of 1958 he went to Cuba to make a semi-documentary of his own, a cheap and shoddy production called *Cuban Rebel Girls*, inspired by his interest, not so much in the girls, as in the young Fidel Castro. It was Flynn's last film. As he grew old not gracefully but disgracefully his last few months were spent in the company of a seventeen-year-old film extra called Beverley Aadland. He had been introduced to her by Ronnie Shedlo, who was his secretary at the time, while he was filming *Too Much, Too Soon*. She had been working on an adjoining set and Flynn, typically, had first been attracted by her legs. It was because of his association with Miss Aadland that he fled to Vancouver to escape the law and she was with him when he died.

After his death the unfortunate girl was the victim of a great deal of snide and even vicious publicity in the American papers but her relationship with Flynn, shattered old roué though he may have appeared, was not the sordid affair that the Press made it out to be. Ronnie Shedlo said: "To him, being with her was a re-affirmation of his own youth. I think he knew his life was ebbing and he hoped to recapture a youthful glow in himself. He described himself once to me as 'A bright fragment in a drab world' and I think he knew the bright fragment was slowly discolouring."

Deirdre Flynn, who was only eighteen months younger than Beverley Aadland, said: "Why does any man at that age start looking at young girls? I guess it was to reaffirm himself as a man, perhaps to boost his ego, aside from the fact that he always liked young girls anyway. I think it was a happy relationship. It certainly wasn't a rollercoaster for her. My father at that time of his life wasn't an easy man to live with but I know that she cared for him. I didn't think it was lurid or anything terrible. I liked Beverley very much. I thought the whole thing was great. Of course, now it would be nothing. I mean, people don't think twice about anything like that. Beverley was terribly maligned by the Press, which I thought very unfair. She was good to my sister and me and never interfered in our relationship with our father."

When the affair with Beverley Aadland began Flynn had been separated from Patrice Wymore for some time and she and their daughter Arnella were living on his estate in Jamaica, the only piece of property he owned in those final years. Nora Eddington said: "I certainly preferred Beverley to his wife. Beverley was kind to him. She wasn't out for anything, she didn't ask for anything. She took care of him. She used to pour his drinks and she'd tell me — and I believe her because she cared about him — that she would water them down, but he was too smart for that."

By then, in any event, there was little anyone could do for him. Nora still remembers her last meeting with him a month before his death and her horror at the way he looked. She said: "Oh my God, I almost died. I started to cry. He'd told me on the phone that he'd been to two specialists and they'd given him a year to live. When I saw him at the airport I just couldn't believe it. He was like a caricature of himself, a clown. That marvellous nose that he'd had, it was, oh God, it was so huge, it was like from here to here, you know? And his eyes were very small, you could hardly see his eyes. It was . . . it was just very sad."

Errol Flynn wanted to be buried in Jamaica but instead Patrice Wymore buried him at Forest Lawn, the graveyard of the stars and the one place in which, quite literally, he would have hated to have been found dead. Because at the end of his life he was a loser and hardly anyone in Hollywood wishes to be associated with losers, very few people attended his funeral. One of those who did was his old director and drinking companion, Raoul Walsh, and legend has it that as the body was being lowered into the grave — a grave still unmarked by any headstone — Walsh put half a dozen bottles of scotch in with it to keep his old friend well lubricated on his journey to wherever it was he finished up. Of course, it's probably an apocryphal tale but I like to believe it's true. I also like to believe that Walsh, who knew Flynn's tastes as well as anybody, would just as soon have slipped six nubile girls in there if only he could have found any willing to make the trip.

The picture which the Walsh anecdote conjures up of Flynn, indeed the general picture one receives of him, as a man who was reckless and self-indulgent, who was humorous, dashing and libidinous, who hurt others as well as himself though probably not intentionally, who was in the end his own worst enemy, may not be especially noble but it is at least more attractive than the reality of his last few years. The end of Errol Flynn was pathetic rather than tragic, the end of a man who seemed to have been bent on self-destruction. Olivia de Havilland remembers him as "unmatchable, full of warmth and charm. There was something affectionate about him, so that when he did unaffectionate things it was such a shock and so distressing because you knew he was capable of the opposite."

Deirdre Flynn remembers him as a strict but affectionate father who demanded courtesy and good manners of his daughters. He was a father who, just before his death, wrote his son Sean a letter expressing paternal concern that the boy didn't seem to have been to bed with his girl friend yet and ending with the postscript: "You needed a hundred dollars. I added an extra twenty-five for condoms and/or flowers."

Jack Warner wrote of him as "one of the most charming and tragic men I have ever met".

Flynn himself once said: "Hollywood is a lovely place to live. It's comfortable, it's warm, it's sunny but it's filled with the most unutterable bastards." He blamed those unutterable bastards for the fact that his career, in his own opinion anyway, never amounted to much, but the fault really lay within himself. He was a dreamer who was dissatisfied with what he had and always felt he might achieve greatness at something else — at archaeology, for instance, or writing. But something invariably distracted him from these lofty ambitions, the offer of another drink, perhaps, or the sight of a pretty girl passing by, and he settled for the easier options that Hollywood offered.

Deirdre Flynn believes he was not a happy man, but "I don't know that even he could say what it was exactly that made him unhappy, what drove him to do this or that, or act in such and such a way. Why the drugs? What did they do? Obviously he used them, turned to them, to escape from something within him."

Vincent Sherman said: "Something was bothering him because when you go to such extremes of drinking, when you are running from one woman to another, you're looking for something. Maybe he himself wasn't aware of what he was looking for but obviously something was bothering him to cause him to waste his life as he did."

On that last point Deirdre Flynn takes issue with Sherman. She doesn't believe her father did waste his life and she doesn't believe he would have thought so either. "I think in fact," she said, "that he probably led two lifetimes in one. It was very free, his life. And he actually did what he bloody well wanted to do. I don't see that as a waste at all."

At his peak Flynn, more than any other film star, was probably the man that every woman wanted and every other man envied. The implacable moralists among us never approved of that and no doubt derived grim pleasure from the tatty bathos of his end. But if he had an epitaph — and he hasn't because, of course, he has no headstone at Forest Lawn to engrave it upon — I suspect he might well have chosen that final statement of his daughter's. "He did what he bloody well wanted to do."

Spencer Tracy

The Metro star, in the middle years of his career.

Tracy with his wife Louise.

With his children, Susie and John.

above : Tracy and Hepburn in "The Desk Set".

opposite : "The actor's actor" — the greatest, perhaps, of them all?

S1403-9

Spencer Tracy was the actor's actor, a performer of such consumate skill that he was admired, almost without reservation, by his contemporaries, even Gable with whom he shared for many years the Number One spot at MGM. Indeed it was Gable who said of him: "This guy's good. There's nobody in the business who can touch him. And don't be taken in by all that humble stuff either. The bastard knows he's good."

Tracy's trick, if it can be so described, was to shun all tricks except the most difficult trick of all, that of appearing to be totally natural. He wouldn't wear make-up unless it was quite unavoidable and he refused to join in any intellectual debate about the nature of acting. It was, after all, Tracy who, when asked what advice he would give to a young actor, replied: "Tell him to learn his lines and try not to bump into the furniture." Perhaps the only other time he was known to hold forth on the subject of his craft was when a graduate of The Method school of acting, for which Tracy had profound contempt, was having much trouble with a scene and complained to him: "I haven't the motivation to come into the room and cross to the table." Tracy gave the matter considerable thought and then said: "Well, you come in the damn door and you cross the damn room and you go to the damn table because that's the only damn way to get into the room and that's your motivation."

He was an actor who prided himself on his professionalism and yet frequently decried his own profession. He once said: "There are things lower than acting — not many, mind you, but politicians give us something to look down on from time to time."

Nevertheless, no matter what he may have felt about the suitability of acting as a career for grown men, he took it seriously enough and was shrewd enough to let the roles he played grow older with him. Gable and Cooper, Bogart and Flynn were all guilty occasionally of playing parts that were too young for them but Tracy never made that mistake. He matured from leading man to dominant character actor and so remained at the top of his profession for the best part of thirty years, which is no bad achievement for an actor whose initial screen test evoked the comment: "He's not much good and he's ugly."

Many actors, of course, have suffered such one-line condemnations early in their careers and managed to triumph over them. (Gable, after all, could hardly have been much encouraged by the reference to his "sugar-bowl ears".) But Tracy's longevity as a star is the more surprising because it was achieved despite an even graver, self-imposed handicap. He once told a friend, the writer Garson Kanin, that he had spent twenty-five years of his life drunk. Even that admission, alarming though it was, barely told half the story, for Tracy, as a drunk, was in a league of his own, and this in Hollywood, a place that has created some of the most awe-inspiring drinkers of our time.

John Sturges, who directed him in what I believe to be one of Tracy's finest pictures, *Bad Day at Black Rock*, told me: "He was the first to admit that he was absolutely head of the unpleasant drunks of all time. He was a charming man, normally, as I'm sure you know. But when he was drinking people saw him coming and they'd run or hide or jump out the window. If you said, 'Hello' he'd say, 'Who the hell are you?' And if you ignored him he'd say, 'So you don't talk to me, huh?' He had fearful fist fights — he was beat up all the time. He worked at drinking for long periods of time until exhaustion overcame him. He didn't know why, of course. Who does?"

It says much for the man that he not only survived twenty-five years of that kind of behaviour with his faculties intact but that for the last twenty-five years of his life he gave up alcohol almost entirely and died with the reputation, that still has never been seriously challenged, of being the finest screen actor America has ever produced. As to why he found it necessary to anaesthetise himself with booze for such a very long time, his friends, as we shall see, had their own theory but Tracy himself never proffered an explanation. When challenged directly he was always evasive, as for example when John Sturges had asked why he kept going on those enormous benders. Tracy replied: "Oh hell, why do you keep pushing your glasses up?" Sturges replied: "Because they slip down," and Tracy said: "Well, I don't know why I slip down," and there the conversation ended.

Spencer Tracy was born into an Irish-American family in Milwaukee in April 1900. His background was Roman Catholic and comfortably middle-class, his father being the sales manager of a prosperous truck company. Young Tracy himself appears to have been a bright, pugnacious and difficult boy, who created some kind of Wisconsin state record by attending about fifteen different schools, performing indifferently in each and getting himself expelled from some, usually for fighting. "If there'd been any other way of learning to read the sub-titles on silent films," he said later, "I wouldn't have gone to school at all." If this showed an early interest in the cinema it was not altogether a serious one and certainly not evidence of any consuming childhood desire to become an actor, for his earliest known ambition was very different.

At seventeen he was sent to Marquetta Academy, a Jesuit preparatory school in Milwaukee and there, for the first time, he settled down and began to think about his future; and what he wanted to be, according to Garson Kanin, was a priest.

"That," said Kanin, "was what he wanted to do in life and he once said to me, 'I've had a lot of good parts. I've been so fortunate in my roles but I never get a feeling so satisfying as when I play a priest. I put that collar on and I get into a thing like *San Francisco* or *Boy's Town* and that's heaven for me.' He was a deeply religious man. I would say off-hand I think he was probably the most devoutly religious man I ever met in my life."

But in 1917 this deeply religious young man, this putative priest, potential drunkard and eventual great actor moved off in another direction. With his friend Bill O'Brien, who was later to achieve movie stardom himself as Pat O'Brien, he joined the US Navy and though his brief service ended soon after the Armistice it was sufficient to turn his thoughts away from the priesthood. He went to Ripon College with vague ideas of becoming a doctor and there, probably influenced by O'Brien who was already determined to be an actor, he drifted, quite successfully, into student drama and, enjoying both the satisfaction it gave him and the attention it brought him, began to think seriously of the stage as a career.

His father was helpful but not impressed. George Cukor, who in later years was Tracy's friend, landlord and director in such superb comedies as *Adam's Rib* and *Pat and Mike*, said: "When he first told his father that he wanted to be an actor, the father, who was a very nice businessman, looked at this kid — this skinny kid with big ears — and said, 'Oh, you poor son of a bitch, you're going to have a terrible time.'" Undeterred by these parental misgivings, Tracy, now twenty-two, followed Pat O'Brien to New York where they both enrolled at the American Academy of Dramatic Art and shared digs in a lodging house. Tracy's career at the Academy was satisfactory but not spectacular. His looks were generally considered to be against him, for in those days actors were expected to be exceptionally handsome and the thin, red-headed Tracy was hardly that. Later, yes, his face was to develop a strength and beauty of its own. But not in his youth. As his father remarked: "Can you imagine that face ever becoming a matinée idol?" Young Spencer's friends and family, loyal though they were, searched their imaginations hard but had to confess themselves defeated.

Thus, since New York's casting directors felt much the same way, Tracy the actor made only painful progress. Between attending auditions he took odd jobs, as door-to-door salesman, as bellhop, as a janitor, to support himself. Finally he joined a touring company, specifically to play small parts, and found that he and the leading lady, Louise Treadwell, were mutually and equally impressed by each other.

By the time the first tour ended and the second had begun Tracy had been promoted to leading man and in September 1923 he and Miss Treadwell were married. For the next two years they struggled along in summer stock (though Tracy did land a small part in a play starring Ethel Barrymore that flopped on Broadway) and around the middle of that period — in June 1924 — their son John was born. A year later they discovered that he was deaf.

John Sturges said: "They gave him a little birthday party. They were living in an apartment and they put him on a sofa with his back to the kitchen, I think blindfolded, and they had a cake with one candle on it and they all came marching in singing 'Happy birthday, dear John' and about the second trip round they saw he wasn't responding and at that time they realised he was totally deaf."

People said that when Louise found out about John's handicap she worried and took him to a doctor and that when Tracy found out he worried and went out to get drunk. John Sturges said: "Pat O'Brien, who is John's godfather, says that Tracy went on a gigantic bender, which doesn't necessarily lead to alcoholism of course, but Pat felt that his heavy drinking stemmed from that time."

Tracy was already a practised drinker — most actors were in those days — but it does seem likely that if any one event triggered off the exceptional consumption that led to dependence and alcoholism it was the discovery of his son's deafness. Certainly both Tracy and Louise took it very hard indeed.

"I think he was like any father, you know?" said Pat O'Brien. "You're trying to solve a problem and you want to blame yourself for it. And I imagine Spence probably blamed himself for John's trouble. They used to take him up in aeroplanes and then fly down to see if anything would happen. But . . . well, it was just one of those things and every doctor they went to said, you know, this happens to other people, too. I think one of the most tragic things that occurred was when we were both playing on Broadway and we'd meet every night after the theatre and walk to a restaurant for griddle cakes and coffee. Well, this particular night I noticed he was under some emotional strain and he actually started to cry. This was while we were walking up Broadway, and I stopped and said, 'What's the matter?' And he said, 'Well, you know every night when I come back home to the apartment after the theatre I go in and I pick Johnnie up and I kiss him goodnight. But . . . I don't know what happened; it was one of those things . . . last night I came home and I was terribly tired and I went directly to bed. In the middle of the night — God knows what time it was — I awoke and I always leave the door open into the little room with the crib and I looked in and Johnnie was standing in his crib. I'd forgotten to kiss him goodnight. The ordinary, normal child would call "Daddy" but he couldn't. God knows how long he'd been standing there. I got up and I went in and gave him his teddy-bear and he went to sleep.' "

Memories like that may not be a justification for taking heavily to drink but they are at least an understandable reason, especially perhaps for a man like Tracy whose love for his children and loyalty to Louise — even after their marriage had finished in everything but name — were not to be questioned. Not that alcoholism was the only result of the family tragedy. A far more constructive aftermath came in 1942 with the creation in Hollywood of the John Tracy Clinic for the Deaf. It was founded basically by Louise with the financial help of her husband who, over the years, poured about half a million dollars into the enterprise. From a modest beginning in two cottages in the grounds of the University of California, Los Angeles, the John Tracy Clinic has since grown into one of the most respected establishments of its kind in the world.

In the late 1920s, despite his family problems and his increasingly heavy drinking, Tracy's career as an actor began to prosper. He found work on Broadway and producers and public started gradually to notice him. In 1929 he landed the role of Killer Mears in the play, *The Last Mile*. It was to change his entire life, although he personally thought little enough of it. But then, on his own admission, he was always a surprisingly bad judge of a role; those he believed would make an impact rarely did and those of which he thought little were often his biggest successes.

"I remember Spence coming back to New York after the

opening of *The Last Mile* in New Haven," said Pat O'Brien. "He was sort of immersed in despair and said, 'We've got a flop. I wish I could get out of it.' But I went to the opening, sat up in the gallery, and it was the biggest smash in years on Broadway."

Tracy's performance in *The Last Mile* was impressive enough for John Ford, the film director, to offer him a screen test and to bring it about against considerable odds. The studio concerned was Fox and Tracy had already tested there once before, only to be dismissed with that damning comment: "He's not much good and he's ugly."

With Ford's influence to help him, however, Tracy succeeded this time and after his first film, *Up the River*, which also marked the debut of one Humphrey Bogart, he was signed to a five-year contract and moved his family out to California. Will Rogers, actor and cracker-barrel philosopher, who rapidly became a close friend, gave him this advice: "Take the part of Hollywood that you like and leave the rest alone." What Tracy didn't like were nightclubs, parties and general socialising. What he did like was the Riviera Country Club where he played polo with great enthusiasm until the late 1930s when his studio — by then MGM — made him give it up for fear that he might damage his increasingly valuable self.

In the first three years of his contract with Fox, Tracy made sixteen films, well up to par for the course for a promising young newcomer, but they did little to imbue him with confidence. In the first place he was afraid he might fail as a screen actor. "This mug of mine," he said, "is as plain as a barn door. Why should poor people want to pay thirty-five cents to look at it?" From this distance that might seem an over-modest assessment but at the time such doubts must have appeared justified.

Contracts were being dropped every day, among them that of his fellow-debutant Humphrey Bogart, another whose looks would have qualified him for acceptance among the "barn door" school of actors. And in the second place Fox had failed to comply with its promise to him. Tracy's second film, *Quick Millions*, had featured him as a truck driver corrupted by money and the prospect of power during the Depression and as a result Fox had sworn to build him up as a tough guy. Tracy had approved of that, believing no doubt that his general appearance made him most suitable for such casting. But his next eight films or so were all romantic comedies and he began to wonder bitterly, "Whatever happened to the tough guy?"

Coincidentally, or perhaps not, it was about now that he began to earn his label as "the bad boy" of Hollywood. On the day he was due to start shooting on a picture called *Helldorado* he simply vanished, almost certainly on a drinking spree, and when he reappeared several days later he was sent to Honolulu to pull himself together. Tolerantly, his employers failed to hold this particular lapse against him and he returned to make a great impact in *The Power and the Glory*. His reviews were excellent but he was still in conflict with the studio. Fox Films said they were unhappy with Tracy because he drank too much and Tracy said he drank too much because he was unhappy with Fox and the roles they gave him.

In any event he also had other problems on his mind. Soon after their daughter Suzie was born in 1932, he and Louise announced formally that they had separated. Tracy moved out of the family home and rapidly became involved in a celebrated love affair with Loretta Young, his co-star in *A Man's Castle*. With her, and probably for the only time in his life, he did the usual Hollywood round of premieres, nightclubs and fashionable restaurants. The affair was extremely well publicised, not to say eventful, being punctuated by dramatic scenes in which Tracy rowed fiercely with the Press, kicked at least one reporter, wrestled frequently with photographers and smashed a few cameras. But in October 1934 it all came to an end when Loretta Young issued a statement saying that, as she and Tracy could not hope to marry because they were both Catholics, they had agreed not to see each other any more. Putting that another way, Joseph L. Mankiewicz, who was a close friend of Tracy's during the 1930s, said: "I wouldn't say he was a closet Catholic but he had the fear of Catholicism in him. He and Loretta Young were very much in love but they were both called in by one of the studio inquisitors out there and told they were threatened with excommunication if they didn't stop at once. So they did."

Tracy then returned to Louise and was loaned out by Fox to MGM to make a domestic comedy called *The Show-Off*, in which he greatly impressed the studio's production supervisor, Irving Thalberg. Tracy enjoyed the experience too, and the contrast when he returned to Fox to make five more unmemorable pictures was such that he sought refuge ever more frequently in alcohol. Finally, one of his bouts landed him briefly in jail and Fox gave him his cards. The same afternoon Irving Thalberg signed him up for MGM in the belief that it was dissatisfaction with his work that had caused his drink problems and that better roles would produce a more sober Tracy. It was a nice idea but it was wrong.

Still, Tracy did settle down well at MGM. He made three suspense films — *Murder Man*, *Whipsaw* (with Myrna Loy), and *Riffraff* (with Jean Harlow) — which suited him better than romantic comedies and his personal life improved too. There was one minor, but much-publicised, brawl in a nightclub when the director William Wellman made an ill-considered remark about Loretta Young, blows were exchanged and Tracy retired with a black eye, but otherwise he and Louise seemed happy enough. They bought a twelve-acre ranch on which he housed his stable of a dozen or more polo ponies. He was extremely fond of his horses and refused to give them up even after they and he had become too old for the game.

From the start of his association with MGM Tracy's career began to blossom. Films like *San Francisco* (in which he played the battling priest, Father Mullin, and won the first of his nine Oscar nominations), *Libelled Lady* and *Captains Courageous*, the screen version of Kipling's story in which his performance as the Portuguese fisherman won him his first Academy Award, brought him the kind of status at Metro that otherwise only Gable had enjoyed. Tracy missed the Oscar ceremony itself because he chose that time to go into hospital for a hernia operation which, though necessary, was by no means urgent. Louise picked up the award on his behalf, even though their marriage was again in trouble and he was soon to move out of the family home and take up residence in the Beverley Hills Hotel.

Joe Mankiewicz, who was by then one of his closest friends, believes that Tracy deliberately ducked the Academy Award presentations because he was afraid he might not win and had no taste for the role of good-natured loser. Mankiewicz, however, also believes that the prospect of winning frightened him almost as much. "He couldn't handle open approbation and he couldn't handle being rejected. He was embarrassed when people told him he was a good actor but he was terrified by the idea of people not telling each other he was a good actor."

In order to guard against this latter eventuality he would take enormous care to prepare his roles and then pretend that he had done no preparation at all. In those years of their friendship when Tracy frequently stayed at his house, Mankiewicz says, "I would come home at night and pass his bedroom door and he'd be working. He'd be working extremely hard. I remember when he was making *Test Pilot* with Clark Gable I heard a lot of noise going on and I opened the door of his bedroom and there he was rehearsing, working on the next day's dialogue, and cracking nuts. He cracked the nuts over Gable's dialogue, not his own. But, anyway, he'd come to the set the next day and say to the continuity girl, 'What are we shooting today, kid?' and she'd say, 'Oh my God, he doesn't know his lines.' But in fact he'd worked all night long. He was fully prepared."

Yet despite the fact that he worked so hard for the success and esteem that he was soon to enjoy, Mankiewicz believes that when they came they embarrassed him more than they pleased him. "You see," he said, "Spence essentially trusted very few people and limited his friendship to very few people because he was walking the tightrope of the alcoholic. He did it magnificently. He went for long, long periods knowing he literally mustn't touch a drop of alcohol but there would come a time when he would announce that he was going away for a couple of weeks and he would take a hotel suite and a couple of cases of booze and lock himself in.

"He never explained to me why he did that. I think he just reached a certain point when he simply had to do it. He knew how important it was for him to work, how important it was to be Spencer Tracy, and yet the urge would come on him to drink. So he'd worked this thing out of going away and having the drinking bout over with and sweating it out and coming back. It couldn't have been pleasant because he locked himself in his room and could literally not get out of a chair for two weeks. All he could do was drink. And yet in between those bouts, when I knew him, he was an incredibly funny and charming man."

John Sturges, who knew Tracy only later when he was on the wagon and able to reminisce without too much pain about his earlier days, said: "He told me that he went at it in a very methodical way. He would hire a limousine and a driver and put four or five cases of cognac in the back seat and take off."

Stanley Kramer, who directed Tracy's last few films and also got to know him well and knew the stories of his drinking days, said: "People talk about modern drinkers and guys who are fire-balls in terms of the way they react to the syrup but Tracy was head and shoulders above all of them. That was in the days before I really knew him, but when I was an assistant cutter at MGM he would leave a film set, drunk, and break store windows, throw chairs through them and generally create disturbances that were fantastic. It's said with some truth that Katherine Hepburn would go with the studio ambulance and pick him up some place and bring him back."

But the Katherine Hepburn days, the days that were to end Tracy's drinking, were still some way ahead in 1937. After *Captains Courageous* he made *The Big City*, in which he played a taxi driver opposite Luise Rainer, appeared as Joan Crawford's love interest in *Mannequin* and teamed up with Gable again for *Test Pilot*. His role was very much secondary to Gable's but already *Time* magazine was calling him "the cinema's number one actor's actor", a title he was never to lose. For all that, he was still a tricky man to handle, as MGM discovered when they wanted him to play the role of Father Edward Flanagan in *Boys' Town*. Dore Schary, who had written the script, remembered that episode well.

"Tracy turned it down at first. He'd made *San Francisco* in which he played a priest and he said he didn't want to play another part with his collar turned round. He'd had enough of that. So he went on one of his, at that time, periodic benders, and no one was able to find him, till it occurred to somebody to look in the polo stables that he kept and they found him there asleep and quite under the weather. They took him to the hospital and Tracy came out of it and immediately said he wanted to go back to work. He said, 'Whatever script you've got, I'll do it.' And they told him they'd only got one script, which was *Boys' Town* and reluctantly, but nevertheless sensibly, he said, 'All right, I'll play that.'"

That it was indeed an eminently sensible decision became clear when the film was released and promptly won him his second Oscar. By now he ranked equal with Gable as the most popular male star in Hollywood and the studio had more or less come to terms with his drinking bouts. Since they knew they couldn't stop them, they did their best to control them.

Dore Schary, who succeeded Mayer as head of production at MGM, said: "Whenever he'd get into one of these moods the studio would assign somebody to kind of stay with him and watch him. And he would travel around — he might go to some town in Arizona or Mexico and this person would always go with him and watch him and this would finally irritate Tracy. I found out from someone who knew about these events what he would do when, eventually, he wanted to break loose. He'd cosy up to the man and say, 'How are you, my buddy? Wonderful being with you,

you're a nice fellow to be with. Come over here. How about another drink?' And they'd have another drink and he'd say, 'That was great. Let's just have one more and then we'll get on the road, eh buddy?' And he'd get the buddy closer to him and then suddenly he'd go like that — bam! — just coldcock him stiff and then he'd get up and walk out of the bar and the fellow could never find him again."

This kind of ruthlessness and drunkard's cunning could hardly have been endearing and yet Tracy obviously had great charm and other amiable qualities or good friends like Mankiewicz and Pat O'Brien would not have stood by him for so long. And they did stand by him until in the early 1940s a remarkable change came over him.

He had played Stanley to Cedric Hardwicke's Livingstone in *Stanley and Livingstone*, he had appeared in a flop called *I Take This Woman*, with Hedy Lamarr, he had done well in *Northwest Passage*, based on Kenneth Roberts' novel, not so well with Gable in *Boom Town*, had then appeared in *Men of Boys' Town*, a predictably disappointing sequel to his earlier success, and had made rather a fiasco of *Dr Jekyll and Mr Hyde*. (George Cukor took W. Somerset Maugham on to the set of that one day and, after watching for several minutes with some interest, Maugham said: "Which one is he playing now?")

And then, in 1942, Tracy met Katherine Hepburn. Garson Kanin had provided a script for her and says, incidentally, that it was his idea to team her with Tracy. Joe Mankiewicz disputes that, claiming instead that it was his idea, not that it really matters much either way, I suppose, though it was indeed Mankiewicz who introduced them.

He said: "Kate came to me with this screenplay — the title was mine, by the way, *Woman of the Year*; originally I wanted to call it *Katherine of Arrogance* — and I read it and, of course, it was a very funny script and she sold it to MGM. Before we made it Spencer and I went to the commissary one day for lunch and we ran into Kate. I had cast Spencer, naturally, as the man in the story and I said, 'I think the time has come for you two to meet.' And Kate looked at him and said, 'Mr Tracy, you look a little short for me,' and I said, 'Honey, don't worry. He'll cut you down to size,' which he did."

Now by then, Tracy had been living away from home for some time. Except in a legal sense his marriage was over, although for the rest of his life he remained devoted to his children and friendly with Louise and frequently spent his weekends at the family home. But apart from that he lived alone, first at the Beverley Hills Hotel and later in a cottage on George Cukor's estate in Beverley Hills.

So in 1942 then Tracy was, as it were, fancy free and during the making of *Woman of the Year* he struck up what was to become a loving, lasting and remarkable relationship with Katherine Hepburn. Mankiewicz, who produced the picture with George Stevens directing, said: "One knew towards the end of the film that they were cosy with each other and when they had to come back and shoot a new ending it was quite obvious that they were in love."

As Stanley Kramer said: "This was probably one of the great love stories of our time" but, though it lasted twenty-five years until Tracy's death, the relationship never attracted gossip or scandal and that, in Hollywood, is to say the least unusual if not unique. Not even the formidable and much-feared columnists — the likes of Louella Parsons and Hedda Hopper — sought to make capital of it and such delicacy of feeling on the part of such people was surely without precedent. It could be that the Press respected their privacy because, largely if not entirely thanks to Miss Hepburn's influence, Tracy became a much more manageable and far less cantankerous fellow.

He stopped fighting, he stopped drinking. He wasn't cured of alcoholism, of course, but he did go almost permanently on the wagon and became more or less addicted to coffee rather than booze. He also broke with nearly all his old friends and became instead, and rather surprisingly, a member of Miss Hepburn's set — rather surprisingly because her set was very different from his. It consisted of far less rowdy and much more theatrical people like George Cukor and Garson Kanin by whom, initially, the tough and bellicose Tracy must have been received somewhat uneasily, like a cuckoo in the nest.

Joe Mankiewicz said: "I've never been able to see the Spence I knew so well participating in that group. I used to go to the fights with him. He lived the life of a sports writer, a sort of New York sports writer — really tough. He liked going to the fights. He liked reading. We used to spend evenings together, reading. It was an extremely close relationship, so close that Spence was my eldest son's godfather, but after Kate sort of enfolded him I saw nothing of him. He used to keep sending the same doll to Chris, his godson, when the boy was well into the

age of puberty. Everything just stopped between us and I didn't
see Spence at all. I think I got a phone call when I hit the jackpot
— I got four Academy Awards or something — and Kate called
and said how pleased they were but Spence never got on the
phone."

Tracy's introduction to the Hepburn set was probably completed when they made the second of their nine films together,
The Keeper of the Flame. It was directed by George Cukor, an
old friend of Miss Hepburn's and a man with a reputation as a
"woman's director". This didn't mean he was unable to direct
men but merely that he had a greater rapport with women than
some of his more male chauvinist colleagues. Nevertheless, there
was much speculation in Hollywood as to how the painstaking
Cukor would get along with the notoriously impatient Tracy.
In fact, the two rapidly became firm friends. Cukor found him a
modest but very intelligent man, "very sharp, very acute, very
knowledgeable".

One day on the set when Cukor was directing him as the father
in *Edward My Son*, Tracy said: "You know, I'm a better actor
than I think. This comes awfully easy to me, playing someone
who's mean." Cukor felt that Tracy did have a streak of hardness
— in that American sense of the word mean — within him.
"He wasn't always little Mary Sunshine, you know. And he was
a very private and reticent man. But he could be very funny
when he wanted to; he could be a great clown."

John Sturges, too, noticed the hardness in him. "He was a
very violent man intrinsically. I've had actors tell me they were
terrified playing a scene with him when they thought he was
going to kill them. Of course, this was simulated violence for the
purposes of a film but with him the difference between real and
simulated would be hard to detect. He could create an almost
psychopathic aspect of himself if he chose to."

The contrast between the reticent, pugnacious Tracy and the
enthusiastic, intellectual Hepburn made their relationship and
their closeness even more surprising. The attraction of opposites,
perhaps. Why they never married is entirely their business, but
it might be pertinent to recall that Tracy and Louise were both
Catholics and had the Catholic abhorrence of divorce and that
Miss Hepburn was on record as saying that she did not believe
in marriage and had never felt it necessary. But certainly she and
Tracy seemed to complement each other. Garson Kanin said:
"The success of their relationship was founded on many things:

a mutual respect and high regard for each other's talent; a total lack of possessiveness and perhaps more than anything else a gloriously shared sense of humour." Furthermore, and this is a point mentioned by everyone who observed them closely together, Tracy was able to bring Miss Hepburn down to earth; as Mankiewicz put it "to cut her down to size".

George Cukor said: "They were a very amusing combination. She says that he helped her very much and he didn't spare her, you know. If he thought she was grandiose he could be terribly funny about her. She talked in a certain rather elegant way and there was nothing la-di-da about him so, chemically, they were very amusing together."

Stanley Kramer, director of Tracy's last film, *Guess Who's Coming to Dinner*, says that Hepburn took more from Tracy in the way of teasing than she ever took from anyone else. "With Tracy it was a special relationship, personal and professional. We'd be rehearsing a scene for example and she'd suddenly come in and kneel down alongside him. She was always watching her neckline, you see; she liked to be low down. So he'd look at her and say, 'What the hell are you doing there?' And she'd say, 'Well, Spence, I just thought . . .' He'd say, 'You just thought. You always talk as though you've got a feather in your anus. Now for God's sake get up out of there and let's do what the feller wants to do. Come in like a normal human being.' And she'd do it."

Joe Mankiewicz believed that Tracy and Hepburn were well-matched because "if you were going to be in an intimate relationship with Spence it had to be one where essentially you took care of him, waited on him, cleaned up after him. Spence was in your care. On good psychological grounds the alcoholic is in that infantile position. He renders himself helpless, which is a state of infancy and which is the most powerful position that the human being is ever in. He has to be taken care of as an infant. He has to be wiped and dried and fed and dressed and cleaned as an infant. And Kate I think wanted to do that."

But that can have been so, assuming that Mankiewicz is indeed right, only in the early days of the relationship. It's not known exactly when Tracy stopped drinking heavily but it was certainly within a few years of meeting Miss Hepburn. On the other hand, there is no doubt that, in one way or another, she did take care of him until the end of his life. Stanley Kramer remembered that when he and Tracy went to Berlin for the premiere of their film *Judgement at Nuremberg* in 1961, Hepburn went too and "she used to feed him pills. His health was not too sound and she had set up this little pill rack for him and was popping him with pills regularly and putting on his slippers. I mean, this was one of those real one-in-a-million relationships. Sometimes I felt she was even a little jealous of me because I got on very well with Spence."

That, however, is very much a one-dimensional view. Another dimension was added by Garson Kanin who said: "Kate brought a wonderful sense of ambition, aspiration, to Spence because it seems to me that before that time Spencer was quite content to be a big Metro star, report to the studio, learn the lines and do the picture. If you look at the whole list of films that Spencer did before he met Kate and then at the list he did afterwards, I think there are more distinguished things afterwards."

This, of course, is an arguable point because Tracy's whole career was liberally sprinkled with distinguished performances both pre- and post-Hepburn. Indeed, the early Hepburn days, the 1940s, were the least satisfactory professionally of Tracy's three decades of stardom, with the exception of the films he made with her, chief among them *Adam's Rib*, one of the most stylish of all comedies. The 1950s brought a noticeable resurgence and an improvement in the scripts that came his way, starting with *Father of the Bride* and progressing through *Pat and Mike* and *The Actress* to *Bad Day at Black Rock* in 1955.

By the time he made the latter film, Dore Schary had become head of production at MGM and had discovered what he called "the Tracy syndrome". It manifested itself like this: Tracy would be offered a role in a film and would accept it and go away and mull things over. Then a few days later he'd come back with all manner of reasons, some serious but most of them rather trivial, as to why he couldn't play the part after all. Schary would calm him down, ease his fears, convince him all over again that the role was ideal for him and send him away happy and wait for him to come back again, which he invariably did a few days before shooting was due to start, with some bizarre explanation of how the entire project was utterly impossible and they would have to find somebody else. And then, of course, he would have to be persuaded all over again.

Bad Day at Black Rock provided a splendid example of the Tracy syndrome at work. "We were supposed to start shooting on location in the desert on a Monday," said Dore Schary.

"Tracy came in on the previous Friday. We'd built the set, everything was cast and he said, 'Daddy, I got news for you. I'm not going to play it.'"

This time, instead of giving the customary quiet pep talk, Schary used a different tactic. He said: "That's okay with me."

Tracy said, a little surprised at the ease with which he'd apparently won his point: "Is it?"

"Sure," said Schary. "Makes no difference to me. I'm supposed to make about thirty-seven pictures a year. If I make thirty-six nobody's going to squawk. So it's okay with me."

Tracy (doubtfully): "Really?"

Schary (expansively): "Sure. Maybe there'll be a problem for you, Spence, because . . . well, it's New York. You know? The New York office? They'll understand but they'll want you to pay for the set and for the commitments of the other actors and the wardrobing and, you know, the director — he has a commitment, too — and I'd guess, all told, you'll probably get stuck for, oh, about 350–400,000 dollars."

There was a moment of horrified silence. And then Tracy said: "You'd do this to me? You'd be part of this? You'd really sue me?"

"Yeah," said Schary. "I would."

"You son of a bitch." He brooded a while and said, bitterly: "Well, that's typical. I'll be out there in the desert, sweating like a pig, and you'll be sitting here in this air-conditioned office." And that, apparently, was his main gripe: the fact that he would be working in about 110 degrees of heat.

So Schary said: "If that's your only problem, Spence, I'll go with you."

And Tracy said: "That's my only problem and I want you to go with me."

John Sturges, who directed *Bad Day* said: "Spence was a very metropolitan man. He was an actor who was willing to do anything to make a picture but certainly at the bottom of his list was going on location. It was very hot out there, nothing but motels, and he didn't like it. When he wasn't working he filled his time trying to create crises. He was a man who loved to have something going on and he'd be at his happiest when a disaster occurred to some other organisation in films. That would keep him in great spirits for a couple of days. Freddie Zinneman was making *Oklahoma* in Arizona, a place Spence was very familiar with, and his happiest two days on location for *Bad Day* was when there were some flash floods and Freddie's whole group was isolated somewhere. Spence went around saying, 'I could've told 'em. They didn't ask. I could've told 'em.'"

Generally speaking, however, the cause of the Tracy syndrome seemed to lie a great deal deeper than mere resentment at having to go out on an uncomfortable location. Dore Schary and Stanley Kramer both believed that it stemmed from insecurity — a fear that he wasn't prepared enough, despite all the homework he had done, or, even worse, that he simply wasn't good enough.

Kramer, the director of Tracy's last four films — *Inherit The Wind*, *Judgement at Nuremberg*, *It's a Mad, Mad, Mad, Mad World* and *Guess Who's Coming to Dinner* — said: "He was always insecure, particularly in the later years. At the start of *Inherit the Wind* he said, 'I can't do it,' and I said, 'Well I won't do it without you.' I think I would have done really but he said, 'My God, if you feel that way let's go.' He needed to be told that he was really that substantial, that important."

In 1955, however, for the first time in many years the reassurance he needed was not forthcoming from MGM and the Tracy syndrome, or a variation upon it, proved his undoing. Tracy was due to shoot a western called *Tribute to a Bad Man* with the director Robert Wise. This time he really didn't want to make the film. He turned up six days late on location, behaved abominably and created all manner of problems for Wise. After several fierce rows it became clear that MGM and Dore Schary had to choose between the director and the star and this time they chose the director. After more than twenty years at Culver City, Spencer Tracy was fired.

He had not expected this kind of treatment but perhaps he should have done. Clark Gable's contract had been terminated the year before and it was becoming increasingly clear that the days of the star system and the all-powerful studios were coming to an end. Nevertheless, MGM's decision was a bitter surprise to him and he wept when he heard the news. After all, he had made a great deal of money for the studio and, besides, fifty-five is no age for anyone, even a superstar, to be thrown onto the streets. For the first time in a quarter of a century Tracy was obliged to go out and hustle work for himself.

He went first to Paramount to make *The Mountain*, in which he played a grizzled Alpine guide, and then to Warner Brothers for a trouble-ridden screen version of Hemingway's *The Old Man and the Sea*. Neither was really satisfactory and, after playing the wily politician on his final campaign in John Ford's *The Last Hurrah*, Tracy announced his retirement. He went to live in a cottage on George Cukor's estate just off Sunset Boulevard where he led a quiet, almost solitary, existence for the next two years. But in 1960, to the general surprise of Hollywood and at the prompting of Stanley Kramer, he emerged from his brief retirement to make *Inherit the Wind* and thus to start on the last phase of his career.

Kramer said: "He was already ill then. He was ill during the making of every one of our films together and also in between making them. Not seriously ill, we thought, but ill all the same. He could be quite cranky and disturbances would throw him off his lines because he really wasn't feeling at all well. He had a great many troubles physically. But he wasn't drinking. He hadn't had anything to drink really in years because he'd pretty well battered those organs that are affected by alcohol in his earlier days."

The films he made with Kramer were not among Tracy's best, though his own performances were as convincing and immaculate as ever. In between working, and perhaps to nurse his health, he lived an almost reclusive life at his cottage in Cukor's grounds. He was rarely seen in public and spent most of his time with Miss Hepburn (and at the weekends with his family) and their own small group of friends and, according to Kramer, developed a love of gossip.

Kramer said: "You know, he had a peculiar group of people around him. At the very end there were people who just reported gossip. There was a director, Jean Negulesco, who used to tell him who was with whom at Ciro's or the Trocadero or whatever nightclubs were still open then. And Negulesco would say, 'Now who do you think was at Ciro's last night? Well, there was Loretta Young with Eli Wallach . . .' And Spence would say, 'No?' And he'd say, 'You hear that, Katie? Who do you think was at Ciro's last night? Loretta Young and Eli Wallach. What do you think of that?' You see, he never went out. He was always sitting up on the hill there in that house and he never went out and he loved to hear the gossip."

In 1963 Tracy was taken seriously ill. He retired again, his career as an actor apparently finished for good. But like the first, his second retirement, too, was premature, for he had in fact one more film to make. In 1967, at the age of sixty-seven and despite chronic ill-health, he appeared in *Guess Who's Coming to Dinner*, directed again by Stanley Kramer and co-starring, for the ninth and final time, Katherine Hepburn.

"Katie got him to do the job after we'd all talked about it, because she thought it was better for him than just sitting at home vegetating," said Kramer. "Columbia Pictures to this day do not know that he worked only in the mornings from nine till twelve thirty. In the afternoons he was never there because he didn't have the energy. We couldn't get insurance for him because of his health and Columbia wanted to pull out of the picture but Hepburn and I put up our salaries in lieu of insurance in case the film couldn't be completed. Three days before the shooting was over Tracy came to me and said, 'You know, kiddo, I've been looking at the script and if you never shoot these last three days it won't matter; you can still release the film.'"

The last three days were completed — but only just. Three weeks after it was all finished, on June 11th, 1967, Spencer Tracy died of a heart attack. His performance in *Guess Who's Coming to Dinner* seems to me to be a worthy memorial to him.

He and Katherine Hepburn played the wealthy, apparently liberal parents, of a young girl who has suddenly announced that she is going to marry a black man, Sidney Poitier, and from then on the story deals with the way in which the parents face, and conquer, the racial prejudice that has unexpectedly stirred into life within them. The film has been much criticised on the grounds that it was a cop-out, that it would be comparatively easy to come to terms with a black son-in-law who, apart from being as handsome as Poitier, was also — as shown in the script — a brilliantly successful scholar. But that, I believe, is to miss the point. Had he been loutish and boorish there would have been many reasons to object to him without ever touching on colour. But since he was portrayed as an eminently desirable son-in-law in practically every way, the only possible objection to him was his race and it was the way that Tracy grappled with this realisation that made his final performance particularly memorable and deservedly won him the British Film Academy award for best actor, the first time a major film award has ever been given posthumously.

It was an appropriate ending to a career that had never really done anything but climb. In his thirty years of stardom Tracy had occasionally stumbled a little but, unlike nearly all his contemporaries, he had never really slipped.

Yet if he was acknowledgedly the actor's actor and by any

standards a great screen actor, there is still a certain amount of doubt and debate as to the scope of his greatness. Among those who were close to him and knew his work well, Kramer, Cukor, Kanin and O'Brien were unstinting in their praise.

George Cukor said: "He touched the people's hearts. They felt that they knew him. There was something average about him and yet he was very versatile. He could play comedy, he could play serious parts and he was enduring. I can't compare him with anybody because he was unique. He was very distinguished and very strong and his reputation is that he was a first-class actor."

Pat O'Brien said: "I think he was the greatest. I really do."

Garson Kanin said: "His range was absolutely enormous. I think he had a greater range than any other actor I've ever known. He seemed to be able to play anything that was put before him."

And Stanley Kramer said: "Tracy brought something different to it every time. He was *the* character actor, character star, of motion pictures. There wasn't anything he couldn't do."

But against such paeons of praise it's perhaps worth pointing out that he never tested himself against the great roles. The English classics he shied away from on the grounds that "you can't mumble Hamlet" and the one obvious part that might have been the ultimate test of his greatness, that of the father in O'Neill's *Long Day's Journey Into Night*, he refused to undertake despite repeated urging.

Thus John Sturges said of him: "I thought he was superb. But he had a very wide range playing one kind of person. Within that range it was impossible to think anyone was better — but he would always be Spencer Tracy."

And Joe Mankiewicz said: "As an actor I think Spence set up boundaries for himself. He said, 'Within these boundaries I'm safe; I'm not going to be afraid.' The idea of going to work in new territories or territories he couldn't handle safely would have terrified him."

Mankiewicz also said: "As a man he was a wonderful companion — I wouldn't say friend in the sense that I don't think you could count on Spence in an emergency. I think Spencer was afraid of emotion beyond a certain point and even devotion beyond a certain point. I think he distrusted himself because he was afraid of what might happen if he took a drink."

On the other hand his undoubted devotion to Katherine Hepburn and, in its unconventional way, his continued devotion to his family tend to gainsay that opinion. And in his later years at least he clearly had a commendable degree of strength and self-discipline. John Sturges recalled that the first time he met Tracy, to discuss *Bad Day at Black Rock*, it was at Romanoff's bar, at that time the traditional meeting place for the upper echelons of Hollywood. Sturges was with Tracy's agent and they were both drinking martinis. Tracy was also offered one but declined and drank coffee instead. "Five years later," Sturges said, "we were talking about alcoholism and I asked him how long it had taken him to get over the urge to drink. He reminded me of that moment at Romanoff's and said, 'You know, at that time I hadn't had a drink for five years but I wanted that martini and I looked at it with as much longing as the day I quit.' So that's what the man lived with."

"At the very end," said Stanley Kramer, "he didn't have a vast circle of friends and there weren't a great many people at his funeral service. But there was one incident at the funeral which I think is worth mentioning because I've always felt that Tracy would have loved it. I was near the back and John Ford, an elderly man with an eye patch, was a few pews in front of me and when we knelt to pray — he was on the aisle — he fell off the kneeling platform into the aisle and I've always been able to imagine Tracy, wherever he is, saying, 'Hey, what do you think happened at my funeral? John Ford fell on his butt right in the middle of the service.' That would really have appealed to Spence."

Gary Cooper

"Just an average Joe from the middle of the U.S.A."

above : With his mother.

opposite : Cooper and Rocky — the wife he got to know when he locked himself in the lavatory.

707-42

*above : With his daughter, Maria. Cooper was already seriously ill
with cancer when this picture was taken in September, 1960.*

*opposite : With Patricia Neal in "The Fountainhead", the film on
which they met.*

Just before Gary Cooper died the poet Carl Sandberg described him as "one of the most beloved illiterates America has ever known." On the face of it such a description seems extraordinarily apt; not all that complimentary perhaps, but certainly understandable. If, with this line of Sandberg's in mind, you think of Cooper as he appeared in his best-remembered films you can easily find yourself nodding in agreement and murmuring, "Yes, that's about right." Except, of course, that it isn't right at all or, more accurately, it's only right in part. The image of Cooper as the shy, pebble-kicking cowboy whose conversation never extended much beyond "Yup" and "Nope" and occasionally, in moments of deep thought, "Mebbe", existed only on the screen. In fact, he was an intelligent and sophisticated man, as much at home in a salon or a boudoir as he was on a horse.

It can be said of Cooper, the actor, as it can be said of all the other enduring stars of Hollywood, that he always played himself but that, too, is only part true. In his ninety-five films, most of them made for Paramount, he actually played a wide variety of roles — from Beau Geste to the sheriff in *High Noon* and the architect in *The Fountainhead*, for instance — and it would be underrating the man to maintain that in each of them he was merely playing Gary Cooper. It would be more accurate to say that he only played a certain kind of role but within that range there was scope for a good deal of variety and subtlety and Cooper was a good enough actor to provide those qualities.

He only liked to make films which, as he put it, "had something to say". One might add something positive to say, for both professionally and otherwise he took an optimistic view of mankind. And once the film he was offered had met this basic criterion he devoted a great deal of time and thought to the character and development of his particular role.

No illiterate, however beloved, would have gone to so much trouble or been clever enough, as Cooper was, to keep his deliberations and his philosophising from the public. Cinema audiences don't particularly like their heroes, their men of action, to be smart and sophisticated. They like them to be ordinary, down to earth, modest; they like them, in fact, to be "just folks" and Cooper, being smart and sophisticated, was aware of that. So the Hollywood publicity people played up his rural Montana background and he let them get on with it. Thus his admirers, Carl Sandberg among them, were left with a satisfying, though slightly distorted, picture of Cooper as the archetypal, all-American pioneer, an uncomplicated fellow whose cerebrations took him no further than recognising and accepting the difference between right and wrong.

Cooper once described himself as "Mr Average Joe America". But in fact he was only a first-generation American. Both his parents came from England, although his father, Charles Cooper, had emigrated from Bedfordshire to the United States in the true spirit of the western pioneer, looking for land to settle and Indians to fight. In 1885, however, there was a scarcity of both and he became a lawyer instead. He had been married for some years to the former Alice Brazier, lately of Gillingham in Kent, when their second son, Frank James Cooper, was born in Helena, Montana, in 1901.

At that time Helena was still a fairly rough town, much patronised, especially at the weekends, by boisterous and hard-drinking cowboys and miners and by 1910 Alice Cooper had come to the conclusion that her sons needed a more civilised atmosphere in which to grow up. She therefore took them back to England where they were enrolled at Dunstable School, which their father had also attended, and stayed there until shortly before America entered the First World War.

It has been said that Frank Cooper was actually expelled for fighting and this may even be so, though it's noticeable that expulsion from school for this sort of misdemeanour figures in the official — which is to say, studio-issued — biographies of quite a number of film stars of Cooper's generation. This could be merely a coincidence, indicating that actors tend to be of an independent, rebellious and pugnacious nature, but equally it could be that, during a time when acting was widely supposed to be an unsuitable job for a real man, the studios were anxious to establish, truthfully or otherwise, that movie stars were and always had been from childhood onwards tough and virile persons, well able to take care of themselves in a brawl.

But whether Frank was expelled or not, Mrs Cooper and her sons returned to Helena where Charles had now acquired a ranch and had also become a justice of the Montana Supreme Court.

The elder son, Arthur, went off to join the army and so did most of the Coopers' ranchhands and it was left to Frank and his mother to look after the family spread. When the war ended young Frank spent three years at Wesleyan College, an agricultural school, and then in 1921 he went to Grinell College in

Iowa to study art. By the time he had completed a three-year course there and had had some slight success drawing political cartoons with a Republican slant for various Montana newspapers, his father had resigned from the Supreme Court and returned to private law practice.

This was a decision which was to have considerable bearing on Frank's future career, for Mr and Mrs Cooper went to California on a business trip that took considerably longer than they had expected and, at his father's urging, their younger son travelled to Hollywood to join them.

He was now twenty-three years old, a long, lean fellow, well over six feet tall, not aimless exactly but with no clear idea of what he wanted to do with his life. He tried to find work as a newspaper cartoonist and failed. He also failed as a door-to-door salesman, trying to hustle young mothers into having their babies photographed.

So he was simply drifting from one unsatisfactory job to another when he bumped into a couple of old friends from Montana who convinced him that there was money to be made from working as an extra in the movies. They took him to Poverty Row, a ramshackle stretch of old Hollywood which, in those comparatively early days of the silent pictures, was where the makers of quickie westerns maintained their headquarters.

By virtue of the fact that the years on the family ranch had made him an excellent horseman, Cooper was rapidly hired and through 1925 and into 1926 galloped across the screen in countless westerns, sometimes falling off his horse as a mortally-wounded cowboy in the morning and then falling off a different, or even the same, horse as a mortally-wounded redskin in the afternoon.

Not surprisingly, however, this somewhat painful way of life had lost much of its magic after six months or so and Cooper decided that if he were to stay in the movies it would be sensible to seek larger, more lucrative and more sedentary roles. So with the aid of an agent and a demonstration reel of film showing highlights of his work as an extra, he began to hawk himself round the studios. By now, Hollywood being for some reason tolerably well stocked with aspiring young actors named Frank Cooper, he had changed his first name to Gary after the birthplace of his agent, Gary, Indiana. As a name it seemed as good as any other and was certainly more suitable than that of his own birthplace and it appeared on screen for the first time in a film called *Lightnin'*

Wins, a two-reeler in which the newly-dubbed Gary Cooper provided modest support to a wonder dog.

Soon afterwards, however, a far better opportunity presented itself. The actor who was to play second male lead in *The Winning of Barbara Worth*, which starred Ronald Colman and Vilma Banky, was delayed on another film and Cooper was standing in for him in the long-shots. Eventually the director, Henry King, decided he could wait no longer for his second lead to report for duty and handed the role to Cooper. Even though he had had no formal dramatic training of any kind, he turned in a useful enough performance to impress Paramount who offered him a contract. Cooper accepted and thus embarked on a career that was to last for thirty-five years.

Recalling those days later, he said: "When I started in pictures I think I started off something new in the way of leading men. All the leading men at that time were very, very handsome fellows. In fact I signed my big contract the year Rudolph Valentino died. Every leading man then was a real handsome son of a gun and then I sort of came along with, you know, my elbows not in the right place and I was reputed to be shy, awkward and bashful."

To some extent this rather self-deprecating assessment was reasonably accurate. He was not conventionally good-looking, though he was extremely handsome in a rugged, outdoor sort of way, and he was certainly gawky and, at first anyway, rather clumsy. But possibly because he was entirely a product of the cinema and, unlike nearly all his contemporaries, had never even set foot on the stage of a theatre, he brought to the screen a new kind of naturalism, a style of underplaying that seemed to reduce acting to total immobility and was to inspire John Barrymore to say: "This fellow is the world's greatest actor. He does without effort what the rest of us spend our lives trying to learn — namely to be natural."

This quality was summed up by Howard Hawks, who directed him in his Oscar-winning film *Sergeant York* in 1941, and who said quite simply, as he also said of Gable: "The camera liked him." This, though, is perhaps too simple because after all the camera liked a good many other stars whose styles were very different from Cooper's and indeed Hawks also said: "He worked very hard and yet he didn't seem to be working. He was a strange actor because you'd look at him during a scene and you'd think, this is never gonna do, this isn't going to be any good. But when you saw the rushes in the projection room the next day you could read in his face all the things he'd been thinking."

So in 1926 the relaxed and apparently effortless Cooper style appeared for the first time and was immediately recognised and appreciated. The following year he appeared in *It* with Clara Bow, after which she became known permanently as the "It" girl and he, briefly, as the "It" boy, thanks to a widely-publicised romance between them. As an affair it was nothing very serious and probably owed a lot to the studio publicity department but at that time Cooper did have a reputation as a pretty voracious ladies' man. Howard Hawks said: "If ever I saw him with a good-looking girl and he was kind of dragging his feet over the ground and being very shy and looking down, I'd say, 'Oh-oh, the snake's gonna strike again.' He found that the little bashful boy approach was very successful."

It also appeared to produce extraordinarily fast results. After the dalliance with Clara Bow, Cooper's next and far more tumultuous affair was with the Mexican actress Lupe Velez with whom he appeared in another silent picture, *Wolf Song* in 1929. On the first day of shooting Miss Velez was driven to the location by her current paramour, Tom Mix, the cowboy actor, in two Rolls-Royces; more precisely, perhaps, Mix drove her there in one Rolls-Royce while his man followed on with the lady's luggage in another. At the end of the day Mix was obliged to return to Hollywood and the next morning Henry Hathaway, who was then an assistant, and was later to become a noted director, went round all the hotel rooms waking up the actors for their early call. Cooper was always a notoriously difficult man to rouse in the mornings and after knocking on his door several times without evoking any response, Hathaway let himself into the room with a master key and found Cooper asleep in bed with Lupe Velez asleep beside him. Bearing in mind that they had met for the first time only the previous day, the snake (as Howard Hawks would have put it) had obviously struck with enviable speed.

The affair, though to say the least tempestuous, lasted for some time, greatly no doubt to the chagrin of Mr Mix. Delmer Daves, writer, director and friend of Cooper's, said: "Lupe excited him. She was like a wild cat and he'd never met anybody like that before. She would scratch him and bite him and do strange things but he'd laugh. She'd hit him and he'd laugh. He'd think this was the funniest thing that ever happened to a man. It's like, well you know how you get a pet dog that leaps all over you, well, Lupe would leap all over him. She was a little wild one. But when he got over that affair I don't think he ever had another one of that kind. I think you have one Lupe in your life and then you move on to calmer seas."

At this time, professionally as well as privately, Cooper was leading an extremely hectic life. Between 1927 and 1931 he appeared in twenty-five films, including his first talkie, *The Virginian* in which, confronted by a menacing Walter Huston, he delivered one of the classic (and incidentally one of the most misquoted) lines of the cinema: "If you want to call me that — smile!"

The introduction of the talkies destroyed the careers of many popular leading men but it merely enhanced Cooper's. Henry Hathaway believed that this was because Cooper was probably the first screen actor to use his own normal voice. Others, those trained in the theatre, would attempt to project their voices as they did on the stage and consequently sounded artificial. There's a saying in Hollywood that "A good voice has ruined more actors than whisky." Cooper, however, being ignorant of such technicalities as projection and hitting the back of the stalls, merely talked. As Hathaway said: "He used just his own voice. He talked as he talked normally and it sounded realistic and natural."

So he went on increasing his reputation and establishing himself as one of the leading western stars of the cinema. He was *The Virginian*, then he was *The Texan* and after that *The Man from Wyoming*, although by way of a change he also cropped up as a foreign legionnaire opposite Marlene Dietrich in *Morocco*. But the life he had been leading, though undoubtedly full, began to affect his health. He lost weight and contracted anaemia and jaundice. His doctors ordered him to rest and so Cooper took the first of what he called his "long walks". Throughout his life at times of stress he liked to go off on his own. As his daughter Maria said: "He was a very private person. He liked being alone. He liked just being with nature. Just sitting and sorting out such problems as he had."

Normally these "walks" would last a day or so, but in 1931 something more was obviously called for and he determined to go to Europe. He went first to Paris and then to Rome where he was taken up by the Countess Dorothy di Frasso, the daughter of an American millionaire who had married into the Italian nobility and, on the strength of her inherited wealth and acquired title, had become one of the pillars of Roman café society.

Cooper's affair with Lupe Velez was more or less over by now and he was clearly ready for some new adventure. Talking later about this stage of his career, he said: "When I went to Hollywood I had no talent for acting. I had gone there full of zip and energy, ready to take on any assignment no matter how rugged. Now I was approaching thirty — not really old — but what energy I had was gone. I felt like an old man. Hollywood had burned me out and I hadn't even begun to act. I felt like throwing in the towel. I was very depressed."

The countess, however, changed all that. After some weeks in her company in Rome, Cooper's health and spirits had recovered sufficiently for him to decide to go hunting in Tanganyika and the countess went with him. And when eventually he returned to Hollywood, largely because he was practically broke, she followed close behind.

Delmer Daves believed that di Frasso had a profound effect upon Cooper, that she gave him an edge of sophistication that had hitherto been lacking in his make-up. "She tried to re-make Coop," he said. "He was still very much a Montana man when she met him and she resolved to change all that. So the Coop who returned from Italy and the African safari was quite different from the man from Montana because Dorothy had sent him to the best tailors in Rome and from then on he dressed very well. I think he felt a little grateful to her because she was so generous with him and after travelling as much as he did with Dorothy I believe he now felt he could be a citizen of the world. I think it amplified his career. When he came back to Hollywood he no longer played parts just as Gary Cooper. He started to become an actor and so I think Coop began to grow at that time as an actor."

With the Clara Bow romance and the Lupe Velez affair still quite fresh in Hollywood's memory and with the sophisticated Countess di Frasso clearly much smitten by him, Cooper the ladies' man had now acquired an awe-inspiring reputation. Helen Hayes, who co-starred with him in *A Farewell to Arms* soon after his return from Africa and Europe, approached him, she said, "in terror".

"Oddly enough," she said, "before I did the picture with Gary I became the Mother Confessor of Lupe Velez when I was working at Metro. She liked to come up into my room and unburden herself to me. She was losing Gary at that time; he was getting tired of her fiery ways and all the shenanigans and nonsense that was going on. So she wept on my shoulder a lot about that. I didn't know Gary then and that also made him a little terrifying to me. A heart-breaker, that's what he seemed to be. And then when we were doing the film together the Countess di Frasso was on the scene. She'd taken him over. She was an older woman, very worldly wise. She invaded the set as much as she could because she knew the character of the picture, the passion in it, and she wasn't going to leave him loose with an actress to play that. So she kept coming around until the director closed the set."

None of which, however, is to suggest that Cooper was merely Dorothy di Frasso's creature. On the contrary, his attitude towards her was often more than a little cavalier. Henry Hathaway recalled that at one point during the relationship the countess left Hollywood to travel briefly to Europe on the *Queen Mary*. One day when Cooper was in the studio preparing to do a scene in an aeroplane suspended high up against a sky-blue backcloth a phone call came for him from the liner. Hathaway said: "It was about the first time there was a ship-to-shore telephone and, Christ, Dorothy had got through from the ship to New York, to Hollywood, to the studio and out to the stage. Cooper, between takes, was up there sleeping in the plane, so they got a ladder and climbed up and shook him and said, 'Dorothy di Frasso's on the phone; she's calling from the *Queen Mary*,' and Coop says, 'Tell her I'll call her back.'"

An added complication in Cooper's life at the time of the making of *A Farewell to Arms* was that Helen Hayes had also fallen in love with him. She was married, and had been for some while, to Charles MacArthur, the playwright and scriptwriter and joint author with Ben Hecht of *The Front Page*, and she had a young child but, she said, "if Gary had crooked a finger I would have left Charlie and my child and the whole thing."

She said: "Gary was no farm boy or anything like that. He was an artist. He was a darn good artist you know and he was a very sensitive man and a very sensitive actor. Our scenes were so wonderfully enacted by him and, I hope, by me that the inevitable happened and I fell desperately in love with him, I really did. If it hadn't been that I had a very sensitive and kind and understanding and wise husband my marriage might have ended in one of those crack-ups that are so much connected in one's mind with Hollywood."

What makes this a particularly interesting confession is that Miss Hayes also starred with a number of other romantic leading men, among them Clark Gable and Ronald Colman, but never felt much passion for any of them. Yet she couldn't, she said, get through that film with Cooper without "really tearing my heart out". On reflection she thought that perhaps the highly romantic nature of the story had much to do with her infatuation but she was also attracted by the fact that he didn't make passes at her and he "wasn't a professional Lothario". There was also, perhaps, the fact that her feelings were unrequited.

"I remember once," she said, "I tried to get a little flirtatious with Gary . . . I can't even remember what it was about but I know I was getting a little over the edge there and, whatever it was, Gary just looked at me very levelly for a moment and said, 'Helen, no. Naughty.' He knew that I had a fine husband and . . . well, after that I felt twice as desirous but I got a grip on myself finally."

In such circumstances it's perhaps understandable that Helen Hayes's opinion of Dorothy di Frasso is not particularly complimentary. "A very possessive and terrifying woman," was her description. "A rough sort of woman. As for the idea that she gave him polish, I seriously resent that. He could have given her a lot of style if she'd been receptive. After the romance with Gary broke up she had a fling with a gangster in Palm Springs. Bugsy Siegel. That doesn't reflect much style and taste, does it?"

It was about this time, however, with women apparently fluttering around him like autumn leaves, that Cooper met his future wife, Veronica Balfe, the daughter of a wealthy and well-connected New York family, who had vague ambitions to be an actress and had made two screen appearances under the name of Sandra Shaw. To her friends she was known as Rocky and Cooper met her through the good offices of Howard Hawks.

Hawks said: "He called me up one day and said, 'What are you doing?' and I said, 'Going out in my boat.' He said, 'Can I go?' and I said, 'Yes. Two girls who've just come in from New York are coming out with me.' And one of them was Rocky. Well, she and Coop started to fight immediately — just the kind of argument that people get into when they like each other on sight. And then he broke that up by getting locked in the toilet and she had to help get him out and so they became friends and pretty soon they decided they were going to be married."

By then, obviously, the attractions of the Countess di Frasso had started to pall because Rocky saw her off pretty briskly and she and Cooper were married in New York on December 15th, 1933. He was thirty-two and she was twenty and he said afterwards, "I was delighted to be rescued from my career as a playboy. Both of us were so pleased to settle down that we did it wholesale."

Cooper did indeed settle down, not only to his marriage which, except for one brief period, seems to have been one of the steadiest and most successful in Hollywood, but also to his career. From 1936 to 1957 he was only out of the top ten list at the box-office three times and, by that criterion, may well have been the most popular movie star ever. Certainly by the end of the thirties he must have been one of the richest. Indeed in 1939–40 he was the highest-paid actor in America with an income of half a million dollars a year.

But he worked for his money. Throughout the 1930s he was turning out films at the rate of three a year and, looking back on them now, looking back in fact on his entire career, it's easy to understand why he was so popular. There was a reliability and an integrity about Cooper that was never quite shared by anyone else. Whatever role he played, whether in a Lubitsch comedy like *Design for Living*, or Henry Hathaway's drama of war and heroism on the North West frontier, *The Lives of a Bengal Lancer*, or a thoughtful western such as de Mille's *The Plainsman*, or the social comment of Frank Capra's *Mr Deeds Goes to Town*, Cooper always portrayed the honest man. He was never the villain; there was never the remotest touch of the heavy about him.

It could be argued — and was by men like Henry Hathaway and Delmer Daves — that it would have been a ridiculous waste to cast him as a heavy anyway and they were right because the public simply would not have accepted him in such a role. His last film, *The Naked Edge*, which he made in England in 1961 had an uneasy response because, for most of the time, the audience and his co-star Deborah Kerr were wondering whether he was a murderer. It seemed unlikely and, of course, turned out to be a totally wrong impression but just for a moment there people were worried. Gary Cooper a murderer? It was against all the laws of nature. If you couldn't rely on Cooper to be the good guy, then what on earth could you rely on?

His daughter, Maria, believes that some heroes "are up on a mountain — you can't reach them. I think though there are other heroes who somehow give you the sense that you could be that man, too, and it seems to me that my father conveyed that to the public. He wasn't remote from them. He was the average man but maybe he was the best of what the average man could hope to be."

So I suppose the essence of Cooper's acting and the reason for the success he achieved was his inherent decency. A natural sincerity shone out of him. As his friend and fellow actor Richard Arlen put it: "He was just a nice guy." And, as a result, he became on screen a sort of glorified Everyman — the fellow who always stood firmly on the side of right, never wavering, no matter what the temptations or the odds ranged against him. He had the rare ability for an actor of being able to portray goodness, a laudable but not particularly exciting quality, without ever being dull.

By 1941, just before America entered the war, Cooper had made more than fifty films. He was forty years old and at the very top of his profession except for one thing — he had never yet won an Oscar. But even that was soon to be remedied. When the war came he was rejected for military service because he was physically unfit, the result of a badly-healed broken hip that he had sustained years before while riding herd on the family cows. But before either the war or his own exclusion from it, Cooper had undertaken what was to be his finest performance to date, that of the First World War hero in *Sergeant York*. It was a role that he embarked upon without much conviction and he was, in fact, talked into it by the director, his friend and hunting companion, Howard Hawks, as a favour to a mutual friend, Jesse Lasky Senior.

Lasky had been one of the founders of Hollywood but by 1941 he was badly in need of a successful film to re-establish himself and had come up with the story of Sergeant York, a devoutly religious man who had gone into the First World War as a conscientious objector, then changed his mind and ended up by capturing an entire German machine gun battalion of 132 men single-handed in the Argonne Forest.

Cooper had already turned down the role when Hawks phoned him saying: "Didn't Jesse Lasky give you your first part in pictures?" Cooper agreed that he had. Hawks said: "Well, he gave me my first job, too. I don't think it would hurt us any if we made that picture and maybe we could do him a lot of good." Cooper said: "Okay, I'll come over and see you."

When he arrived, according to Hawks, he shuffled around the place, talked of hunting for a while, asked if he could see Hawks' new rifle and generally evaded the subject at issue until the director said: "Look, Coop, we have to talk about this." And

Cooper said: "What's there to talk about? You know we're going to do it." So they did. And Gary Cooper won his first Academy Award.

During the next few years he continued to make highly successful films — playing the baseball star Lou Gehrig in *The Pride of the Yankees* and Robert Jordan in *For Whom the Bell Tolls*, for example — and also undertook a 23,000 mile tour of the South West Pacific to entertain the troops. Sam Wood, who directed him in both those pictures and also in *Saratoga Trunk* in 1946, said of him: "You're positive he's going to ruin your picture. I froze in my tracks the first time I directed him. I thought something was wrong with him and I saw a million dollar production go glimmering. But I was amazed at the result on the screen. What I thought was underplaying turned out to be just the right approach. On the screen he's perfect, yet on the set you'd swear it's the worst job of acting in the history of motion pictures."

Cooper's own opinion of himself, summed up on a BBC television programme in 1959, was as follows: "I just sort of concluded the only reason I got along in pictures was because I'm an average looking fellow and I've been mistaken, coming into strange towns, for the fellow somebody knew back in Podunk or any other town . . ."

At this point one of the female panel of interviewers broke in to say wistfully: "I wish some of the average men around looked like you, I must say." Cooper accepted this interruption with becoming modesty but hastened to add: "No, I really mean that. I looked like the fellow next door or down the block and stuff. You know. There's nothing spectacular about it." It was a somewhat ingenuous claim perhaps, but at least he was consistent about it for he repeatedly maintained that he merely represented the "average guy from the middle of the USA".

Unfortunately he rather tarnished this image in the mid-1940s when, to the disapproval of the general public, he dabbled briefly in politics, a thing any average guy from the middle of the USA is probably ill-advised to do, especially if he also happens to be an actor. He delivered, first on radio and then in the form of a newspaper advertisement, a faintly xenophobic diatribe against President Roosevelt and in support of the Republican presidential candidate, Thomas E. Dewey. The general tenor was isolationist with criticism of "the company Roosevelt has been keeping" and an expressed distaste for the idea that America should "borrow foreign notions that don't seem to work any too well where they come from". Millions of Americans, of course, agreed with him but millions of others were shocked and disillusioned, believing that this political outcry clashed oddly with the impression of Cooper received from films like *Sergeant York* and *Meet John Doe*.

Whether coincidentally or not, from this time onwards his success began to wane and perhaps it was inevitable that it should. He was now approaching his mid-forties, a difficult age for any romantic leading man, as Gable also found out. His long-term contract with Paramount had come to an end and, as an independent artist, he found it difficult to secure the right kind of part in the right kind of film. He made a pleasant enough comedy, *Casanova Brown*, again directed by Sam Wood, and then starred in and produced a western, *Along Came Jones*, which was neither a satisfactory film nor a happy experience for Cooper and he never attempted to produce a picture again.

Throughout the second half of the 1940s he worked more sparingly, averaging perhaps a film a year and never quite reached the pinnacles on which, hitherto, he had been wont to reside. Perhaps it was partly dissatisfaction with the way his career was progressing and partly the fact that he was approaching fifty that caused him eventually to embark upon what was, for him, a most eccentric course of action.

In 1949 he played the idealist architect, Howard Roark, in the screen version of Ayn Rand's *The Fountainhead*. It was a film that attracted little praise at the time but it improves with keeping and has since acquired a good many admirers. However, the most significant aspect of the production was that Cooper and his co-star, the twenty-three-year-old Patricia Neal, fell deeply and obviously in love. It was a development which astonished Hollywood. Cooper and Rocky had been contentedly married for sixteen years and not a hint of scandal had attached to either of them.

True, the marriage had for some time apparently been conducted on a philosophy of live and let live, with each of them pursuing their own social interests but the relationship had nevertheless seemed to be securely based. But in 1950 Cooper asked Rocky for a separation and told the newspapermen: "I can't say we haven't had a little difficulty but I can say that it isn't serious."

The separation became legal in May 1951. There was never any question of a divorce because Rocky was a Roman Catholic and indeed it seems that Cooper did not ask for a divorce anyway. Besides, by the time the separation papers were drawn up, the affair with Patricia Neal was almost over. It was Miss Neal who brought it to an end, not without causing herself a great deal of pain and suffering. She did so because she knew that marriage between them was impossible, even though she had never asked for it, and because she had begun to realise the grief which was being caused to Cooper's family.

In an interview in New York early in 1952 with the gossip columnist Hedda Hopper she said: "I will not see him when I go back to Hollywood. I have been very much in love with him and I'm sure he has loved me. But I saw that it wouldn't work, so I stepped out. Coop is wonderful. I never knew anyone like him. We last saw each other on Christmas Eve (1951) briefly. It is, I assure you, over and ended forever."

Speaking of that period, Maria Cooper said: "I didn't try to think too much about whether my parents would or would not come back together. As you get older what you really want most is to see the two people you love most being happy and not in pain, physical or emotional. I was lucky, I guess, in that I had a very solid sense of their love for me, whether or not my father was living under the same roof as us."

To suggest that Cooper's extra-marital romance had been prompted by what is known, loosely, as the male menopause would be insulting to Miss Neal and belittling to him. But by the time the affair came to an end he was nearly fifty-one and certainly afflicted by some form of middle-aged restlessness. His private life was in a mess and so was his career. The former he tried to straighten out, if only in his own mind, by taking the second of his "long walks" to Europe and the latter was totally restored by the film he made before he left—*High Noon* one of the best of all westerns.

The part of Sheriff Will Kane who, abandoned by his erstwhile friends in the town, is obliged to face four vengeful killers alone was, he said, "a part like in *Sergeant York* that took everything I had, and I gave everything I had". He even gave up much of his usual high salary to make the film, although in return he took a percentage of the profits which turned out to be an exceedingly wise move. He also, for the second time, took the Academy Award for best actor.

The trip to Europe, made before the Oscars were announced, had neither the healing effect nor the excitement of his earlier jaunt. He developed a persistent ulcer and went back to America for treatment.

The success of *High Noon* had both re-established him and to some extent typed him, for three of his next five films—*Springfield Rifle*, *Blowing Wild* and *Vera Cruz* — were westerns. None was outstanding but they all did well enough and, with his career now settled again, he turned to the task of repairing his private life.

In 1954, wearying of the unsettled bachelor existence he had been leading for the last four years, he was reconciled with his wife. By then he was fifty-three, his health was not particularly good and no doubt he felt that it was time for him to settle down at last. Rocky had, in any event, handled the whole separation with great wisdom. She had got on briskly with her own activities and, as Maria Cooper said: "She didn't mope. I think sometimes you get strength and create the thing you want most by just going and doing what you have to do, leading your own life and not just wringing your hands over a problem. She was very determined and intelligent and she knew what she hoped for ultimately — for the family to be together."

Reunited with his wife and daughter, Cooper settled back into the routine of making one film a year, *The Court Martial of Billy Mitchell* being followed by *Friendly Persuasion* and *Love in the Afternoon*, in the last of which he co-starred with the eighteen-year-old Audrey Hepburn. Even his most loyal admirers felt this was a mistake. A romance between a man of fifty-six and a teenage girl left the audience feeling uneasy and embarrassed. Cooper himself couldn't quite understand why people should find such a story distasteful. "Is it impossible," he asked a friend, "to believe that a young girl could fall in love with a man like me?" And, of course, it wasn't but still the cradle-snatching aspect of the film roused a good deal of indignation, not least, possibly, among other middle-aged men who didn't look like Cooper and resented the fact that, unlike him apparently, they would never again be able to fondle a nubile teenager without grave danger of ending up in court.

Perhaps as an over-sensitive reaction to all the criticism, Cooper had his face lifted in 1958, the year after *Love in the Afternoon* was released. It was an unexpectedly vain thing for him to do and maybe there was a touch of desperation in his decision to have the job done — a reluctance to face the fact that he was now too old to play romantic leads. The same year he was treated again for a stomach ulcer but he eased up neither in his work nor in his social life, which tended to be very busy both in Hollywood and New York.

The following year, somewhat to the surprise even of his own family, he was converted to Roman Catholicism. Hitherto he had been a fairly easy-going Episcopalian, not noticeably religious, and Howard Hawks, Henry Hathaway and Delmer Daves all believed that his conversion was less the result of any deep conviction than of a desire to please Rocky and Maria, who were both devout Catholics. However, Maria Cooper said: "It certainly wasn't because of any pushing or prodding from our side. He'd always been very nice and come to mass with us at Christmas and Easter, that sort of thing but generally he looked on the Church as our affair. But suddenly, one Sunday, he just sort of said: 'Hey, let me come along with you' and I guess that maybe on some of his many drives or walks or times alone in the mountains he began to feel there was something that the Catholic religion had to offer that he wanted. He didn't talk about it very much to us. Again, he was a very private man and it was his private affair but I know he did get a lot of strength and comfort from it."

In an interview soon after his conversion Cooper himself said: "I'd spent all my waking hours, year after year, doing almost exactly what I, personally, wanted to do and what I wanted to do wasn't always the most polite thing either. I've had a lot of good things in my life — maybe too many of them — fame, success, money and of course love. It's true I've had some of the other things, some disappointments, some despair, some worry. I've had some moments of swollen-headedness too, moments of horrible conceit. But on the whole it's been good for me and then this past winter I began to dwell a little more on what's been in my mind for a long time. I began thinking, 'Coop, old boy, you owe somebody something for all your good fortune.' I guess that's what started me thinking seriously about my religion." He also said: "I'll never be anything like a saint, I know. I just haven't got that kind of fortitude. The only thing I can say for me is that I'm trying to be a little better. Maybe I'll succeed."

Whether he knew it or not — and the probability is that he didn't — Cooper was already ill around the time of his conversion. That year he made a film called *The Hanging Tree*, an offbeat western directed by Delmer Daves and for the first time in his life he found it painful to sit on a horse. The pain was in the lower part of his back and the problem was temporarily resolved when Daves had a special saddle made for him so that he could sit with his legs practically straight. During the rest of the film, Daves said, "he was never bothered by the pain again. But when he went to Europe to do his last film, in England, that hurt that he had in his back was cancer. He died of cancer of the spine."

By the time he came to London in 1960 to star with Deborah Kerr in *The Naked Edge*, Cooper had already had two operations for cancer. At that time he was not told the nature of the complaint but soon after he returned to California he knew. "He wasn't a man to be lied to," said Maria Cooper, "particularly about something like that. And he reacted as you would expect. He was very accepting. He said, 'Well, I'd like it to be different but if that's God's will, that's the way it's meant to be.' He had tremendous courage. After the initial moment, when we all knew the score, we didn't talk about it. We just went on and lived our lives and did what we could. He was in a lot of pain but he went to New York and did a programme for television about the American Indians. He was always very concerned about them long before it became a fashionable banner to carry. He really wanted to do that programme. He was suffering a lot but he didn't want people to know he was ill because he thought it would just make a lot of unnecessary talk so he simply went ahead and did the show. He lived right up to the last minute. That was a marvellous thing to see because his wasn't an easy way out."

Cooper's last public appearance was at a testimonial dinner given in his honour in Hollywood in January 1961. (It was at this dinner incidentally that Carl Sandberg described him as a "beloved illiterate"). At the Academy Award presentations several weeks later he was due to be given a special Oscar for services to the movie industry but by then he was too ill to attend.

James Stewart, an old and close friend, accepted the award on his behalf and was so obviously close to tears that it became clear that the news of Cooper's terminal illness could no longer be kept secret. It was announced to the Press a couple of days afterwards.

Ten days before his death he asked Henry Hathaway to come and see him. Hathaway said: "We sat down and talked and he had a hatband that was a little sliver of silver and leather with a silver buckle and I'd always admired it. I'd also asked him once where he bought a leather wallet that he had for carrying foreign money. So that last time I saw him he had the hatband and the wallet on the table and he never said, 'I'd like you to have these' or anything like that. We were sitting there and he just kept shoving the hatband and the wallet a little closer to me and a little closer and he said, 'You like these.' And he just shoved them closer again until I took them. There was nothing sentimental in what he did and that's a real test of a man, I'll tell you."

On May 13th, 1961, six days after his sixtieth birthday, Gary Cooper died. He was buried at the Holy Cross Cemetery in Beverley Hills. His pall-bearers included James Stewart, Jack Benny and Sam Goldwyn.

Arthur Jacobs, the producer, later described him as "the greatest film star there's ever been — and that includes Gable". Maybe he was at that. Yet despite the fact that he made ninety-five films no cult or mystique has built up around him. Perhaps the roles he played were too diversified for that or perhaps what he represented was too obvious to need the constant reappraisal and theorising which go hand-in-hand with the cults that surround other movie stars. Whatever part he played he was always essentially the same character, the quiet American hero striving to remain a hero in a world growing ever more cynical and corrupt. The values he epitomised, honesty, decency, integrity, loyalty, are those which everyone professes to admire but which, nevertheless, are not so easily found in modern life.

He once said: "I looked at it this way. To get folks to like you — as a screen player, I mean — I figured you had to be sort of their ideal. I don't mean a handsome knight riding a white horse, but a feller who answered to the description of a right guy."

That certainly is what he always was on the screen and I think it inconceivable that a man could consistently play "a right guy" in ninety-five films for thirty-five years without being something of a right guy himself. I suppose if you'd suggested to Gary Cooper that his motto might have been the motto of the mythical West, that "a man's gotta do what a man's gotta do", he might quite possibly have looked down at the ground for a long time and shuffled his feet and scratched the back of his head and then, adopting the role of the beloved illiterate, have nodded bashfully and said, "Yup".

Humphrey
Bogart

The perfect hero
for an age of disillusionment.

above : Bogart, the one with the "old-shoe face" hugging Mary Phillips in the Broadway play "Nerves" in 1923. She was to become his second wife.

opposite : Mayo Methot, his third wife, who stabbed him with a knife.

above : With fourth wife Lauren Bacall and their son, Steve.

opposite : Bogie and Bacall. In private life he never would wear his "rug".

When Humphrey Bogart left his hand and footprints in the wet cement outside Graumann's Chinese Theatre on Hollywood Boulevard, he wrote: "May you never die till I kill you." This message, at once tender and strangely menacing was addressed to his fourth wife, Lauren Bacall. It was typical of a man who was always something of a paradox.

Bogart was the screen hoodlum with the rasping voice and sinister lisp who actually came from an impeccable social background. He had the hard, cold-eyed look of a professional hit man but inside the shell he was slightly softer than a three-minute egg. He was an actor of narrow range who yet became perhaps the most enduring of all Hollywood stars, a man who was snapped up by the movies in his early thirties and then took eleven years to become an overnight success.

He is revered and even idolised by the cinema-going youth of America and Europe and, at the same time, the story of his life and his career offers warm reassurance to all middle-aged men who still believe, wistfully and in defiance of the general evidence they see around them, that life can begin at forty. Bogie was the nineteenth-century baby who, somehow, grew up to be the personification on the cinema screen of mid-twentieth-century attitudes. Lauren Bacall says he always called himself "the last century boy" because he was born on Christmas Day in 1899.

"He was very old-fashioned in many ways," she said, "and he was very much a gentleman." His friend and biographer, Nathaniel Benchley, describes him as "a puritan who found himself in a business where such a thing is a rarity, so I think he very often covered up with tough talk". Bogart was married four times, which seems excessive (though not, in Benchley's view, contradictory) for a puritan and he met Miss Bacall, his final wife and the one who could accurately be described in the language of the fan magazines as "his last and true love" on a film set. What, in Hollywood, could be neater or more appropriate than that? When you consider Bogart the screen tough guy who, as director Stanley Kramer once said (and he meant it affectionately), was just "a big sloppy bowl of mush" inside, the cynic who was truly a romantic at heart, there is little wonder that a cult has sprung up around him that is stronger than that which surrounds any other film star. In Bogart there was something for everybody.

"The last century boy" was born in New York, the son of Dr Belmont DeForest Bogart, an eminent physician who, as Joe Hyams says, "was in the social register at a time when the social register really meant something". Hyams, incidentally, is another friend and another biographer and on balance it seems to me that Bogart had even more of the latter than of the former, which is a further indication of the appeal he has for movie buffs. His mother was an artist, Maud Humphrey, a famous illustrator in her day and a leader of the suffragette movement. One way and another the Bogarts, five in all (for along with their son they had two younger daughters, Frances and Kay) were a well-to-do, upper-class family. Young Bogie went to the best primary schools in New York and then to Phillips Academy at Andover, Massachusetts, which was possibly the best private school in America. "He grew up," said Joe Hyams, "with, if you will, a silver spoon in his mouth."

More than that, really. You might almost say with a silver pusher and spoon, for when he was only one year old his face — already, it seems with hindsight, curiously sardonic and knowing for one so young — was a familiar sight in Mellins Baby Food advertisements. That Bogie was chosen for this dubious honour was due to his mother's connections and until he was eighteen it was the only thing which set him apart from other children of similar backgrounds who were clearly destined for an Ivy League education and a life of well-connected affluence in New York business circles. But when he reached the age of eighteen, the path chosen for him by his parents took a sharp deviation because he failed his examinations and could not be accepted by Yale University. His father was greatly annoyed and made no secret of the fact and young Humphrey ran away to join the navy. The war was actually over by then but nevertheless he returned with a wound about which a small legend was later to be spun.

The legend has it that the wound, which resulted in the famous scar on his lip, was acquired when he was hit by a splinter of wood while his ship was under attack by a U-boat. In fact, according to Nat Benchley, the whole affair was rather more prosaic. "Bogart was doing shore patrol duty between assignments," said Benchley, "and he was taking a prisoner to Portsmouth Naval Prison. The man was manacled and when they changed trains at Boston he asked Bogie for a cigarette. Bogie reached into his pocket to get him one and the man pounded the manacles across his face, tearing it open, and ran. Bogie just couldn't get rid of the scar. Some navy doctor, apparently a frustrated sail-maker, got to work on it and he had three plastic surgery operations, but it didn't clear up." An interesting enough anecdote in itself, though less glamorous than the legend. Bogart never actually confirmed the war wound story but, on the other hand, he never said anything publicly to deny it.

However, home again and slightly mutilated after his brief service, Bogart became friendly with the daughter of William A. Brady, a famous theatrical producer, and through her found work on the stage. It was something into which he simply drifted, largely because after trying one or two jobs on and around Wall Street he was frankly bored by the prospect of a business career.

In those early days, from 1920 onwards, Bogart said later, he would literally bound on stage shouting "Anyone for tennis?" This is probably quite untrue, since there are very few, if indeed any, plays in which anybody actually says "Anyone for tennis?" but, even though he seemed to find regular employment as a small-part actor, his was a fairly inglorious start.

Helen Hayes, who knew him at that time, said: "We were all youngsters together in New York. He was one of a vast crew of juvenile actors playing in silly comedies. We didn't think much of Bogie. He just wasn't anything very much and he was cursed with a rather plain, old-shoe face. There was nothing romantic or attractive about it. We were anxious for him. We didn't think he was worth anything."

For a long time that view, perhaps not quite so candidly expressed, was shared by Hollywood, although in fact Bogart was not even to arrive there until 1938. In the meantime, in 1926, he married an actress named Helen Mencken, who was considerably older than he. By all accounts he didn't really want to marry her at all. It was far more her idea than his but he seems to have agreed in an unguarded moment and then, not wishing to reject her, determined to see the business through. Perhaps this was where the old-fashioned gentleman came in; or again, perhaps not. Miss Mencken was a very powerful lady around Broadway and he had serious, and probably well-founded fears, that, if jilted, she could do his career a lot of harm. On the whole he probably married her partly through a misplaced sense of chivalry and partly through prudence.

Still, as it turned out, the marriage was a brief hiatus for both of them. It didn't work at all well and within two years they were divorced. A year later Bogart was married again, to another actress, Mary Phillips, whom he had first met in 1924 when they both appeared in a play called *Nerves*. Nathaniel Benchley believes that Bogart was genuinely in love with Mary Phillips, in a way that he was not with Helen Mencken, but "their various careers pulled them apart". Joe Hyams, while not disputing that, ascribes Bogart's first two marriages, and also his third, to the fact that he simply "got involved".

"It was another time and another period," Hyams said. "People didn't live together the way they do now. He began to go with someone, he began to have an affair with her and he was a gentleman of the old school. We're talking now about the twenties and thirties and it was expected that if you slept with someone you married her and I think that's what led him into marriage."

A logical and even gallant explanation, if not particularly flattering to anyone concerned and perhaps not the whole truth anyway, because Bogart and his second wife were happy enough at first while they were both working on Broadway.

But in 1930, after a decade which had seen him achieve steady progress as an actor, though not exactly stardom, Bogart was summoned to Hollywood for a screen test by Fox, which later became Twentieth Century Fox. His wife refused to go with him because she was working in a play and thus his first venture into the movies was also the first of several separations which, eventually, were to end the marriage.

Bogart's screen test was declared "magnificent" and he was immediately cast in supporting roles in six films, all made in rapid succession and all equally indifferent. He played a cowboy in one and a bright young socialite in a couple of others; nobody thought of him as a hard man or a gangster in those days — certainly Bogart himself didn't. And he obviously didn't impress anybody much because in 1931 the actor who was thought "magnificent" only a year before had his contract dropped by the studio and, greatly discouraged, returned to Mary and Broadway.

He did not, however, stay very long for, early in 1932, Columbia offered him a six-month contract and he headed west again to appear in three more indifferent pictures before returning, no less discouraged than before, to New York. Indeed, this time he swore he would never go back to Hollywood and for six years he kept this vow, a fairly easy thing to do because in that period Hollywood didn't approach him again.

The years of the Depression were a hard time for stage actors, just as they were for anyone else and Bogart, particularly, and. Mary had much difficulty in finding work. Quite often the only way he could make a contribution to the family budget was by playing chess (at which, apparently, he was rather good) for sidestakes in New York cafés and clubs. But among the many "downs" in his life at this time there were also a few "ups" and the greatest of these occurred in 1936 when, somewhat to his own disbelief, he was cast as the gangster Duke Mantee in the Broadway production of Robert Sherwood's play, *The Petrified Forest*. Sherwood thought the idea of Bogart, a specialist in playing rich young men about town, in that part was ridiculous and in this Bogart heartily supported him. The play and Bogart, however, were a great success and Warner Brothers promptly acquired the film rights.

Now the star of *The Petrified Forest* was the English actor, Leslie Howard, and he had sworn that when the film was made he would insist that Bogart be invited to recreate the role of Duke Mantee on screen. Such promises are frequently made by actors and seldom kept, but Howard, like Bogie, was a gentleman of the old school and was therefore as good as his word. Warner Brothers were most put out because they had earmarked Edward G. Robinson for the part, but eventually and reluctantly they acceded to Howard's stubborn demands and so Bogart went to Hollywood for the third time, never to leave again.

When the film was released Bogart was hailed as a new star by everybody except his employers, who had taken the precaution of signing him to a not very expensive contract and to whom anyway he was something of an embarrassment. What did Warner Brothers want with another heavy when they already had Cagney, Robinson and George Raft on the payroll? The studio could see very little future for him except as a kind of supporting gangster, the one that Cagney, Robinson or Raft could shoot as and when the occasion demanded, and so his career was settled for the next few years.

Indeed, in his first two years at Warners he appeared in eleven films, eight times as a gangster or some other sort of criminal, and in four of them he was killed. In fact his overall track record was even more dismal than that. "In my first thirty-four films," he said, later on, "I was shot in twelve, electrocuted or hanged in eight and was a jailbird in nine. I played more scenes writhing around on the floor than I did standing up."

It was the duration and the difficulty of his struggle to better himself that gave Bogart a decidedly jaundiced view of the Hollywood establishment, which he later blamed for the lack of opportunity he was given during all those years as a minor heavy on the Warner Brothers lot. Jack Warner, the head of the studios, certainly had very little faith in him except as a criminal type. Indeed, the nearest thing to a compliment that Warner ever paid him was when he said: "Nothing can happen to your face that will hurt it a bit."

In an age when leading men were invariably handsome and sometimes downright pretty, Bogart was an obvious misfit, an actor doomed to play unsympathetic supporting roles. One of the very few who could see beyond that rugged and not especially prepossessing exterior to something finer and potentially more exciting was Sam Jaffe, the man who became Bogart's agent after the third coming to Hollywood and who remained his agent and his friend until Bogie's death.

Jaffe said: "When he was playing heavies and gangsters I thought he could become a leading man and many people laughed at me. I thought he could be a different kind of leading man. He wasn't a good-looking boy or as handsome as Robert Redford is today but he was a marvellous actor and I thought he had great potential as a character leading man."

At that stage, however, it was simply Jaffe and Bogart and, for a while, Mrs Bogart (Mary had joined him from Broadway) against the rest. In the five years after *The Petrified Forest* he was constantly working, becoming increasingly familiar to cinema audiences but always, except in the odd B-picture, in secondary roles.

Meanwhile his second marriage went the way of his first. Mary Bogart was bored by Hollywood and, to her husband's resentment, went back to New York to resume her stage career. And while she was gone Bogart met and was ensnared by yet another actress, Mayo Methot, a voluptuous and alcoholic blonde with whom Bogart shared not only a love of the bottle but also a love of the sea. She moved into his apartment to keep him company while his wife was away and was discovered there by Mary on a flying visit from New York. That was the end of that marriage. Mary sued successfully for divorce and in August 1938 Bogart, trapped again, did the honourable thing and married Miss Methot.

This marked the beginning of the booziest period in his career. He always prided himself on being a great drinker and once gave it as his considered opinion that he, Errol Flynn and Winston Churchill, three very ill-assorted bar-flies, were the biggest and finest drinkers of their time. He also insisted that the whole world was permanently three drinks below par — that if each of us took three quick belts we would be much nicer people. Somehow I don't think medical opinion would support that theory, though I dare say the distillers might. Until the day he died Bogie was partial to the odd snort (or two, or three) but during the years with Mayo Methot his alcoholic consumption must have been awe-inspiring.

Their whole marriage seems to have passed in a drunken haze, punctuated by fierce, frequent and potentially lethal fights. On one occasion she stabbed him with a carving knife and on another she threw a heavy soda-water bottle at him, missing him so narrowly and frightening him so much that he called Sam Jaffe and instructed him to take out a 100,000 dollar insurance policy on his (Bogie's) life. What he said to Jaffe was: "You see this seltzer bottle? She threw it at me but she was drunk and she missed me. If she ever connects, if she ever hits the bull's-eye, she'll kill me." So the insurance policy was taken out, with Jaffe as beneficiary, in order that he should not be the loser, after all his hard work on the actor's behalf, if Bogart should one day be murdered in a fit of drunken rage by his wife.

By all accounts Mayo Methot was a most formidable woman. When I talked to him at the "21" restaurant in New York (one of Bogart's favourite drinking haunts) Nat Benchley said: "She was a savage drunk. I've seen her throwing crockery in here just for the hell of it. Get a little scotch inside of her and she was terrible." And the barman at the same restaurant revealed that, on one occasion, Mayo created such a scene there that Bogart went and ate his lunch in the men's room, that being the one place where she couldn't get at him.

Joe Hyams said: "Mayo was very sexy, very pretty and I think he was physically attracted to her. He was drunk when he met her and they stayed drunk throughout their entire marriage. They had a tremendous drunken brawl on their wedding night and she chased him out of the house. The wedding itself was one of the classics in Hollywood history with Mischa Auer dancing nude on a table top. Bogie once said to me that Mayo got him drinking and kept him drinking because that was the only way she could hold him. They boozed a great deal and they fought a great deal and once I asked him why he enjoyed fighting with her so much and he said, 'Because the making-up was so pleasant,' which makes sense, too."

While this was going on, while life with Mayo was punctuated by drinking bouts and quarrels, reconciliations and nights of violence when she would lock her husband out of his own house so that he had to sleep on the lawn, Bogart's career was simply marking time. He knew that most of the roles he was asked to play were worthless but, though he complained about them, he took them nevertheless. As he explained to Nat Benchley: "The only way to learn is to do it. If you're going to become an actor, then you just act. Never mind what it is, get it right, get your lines right and don't louse up the scene."

Vincent Sherman, who directed him in 1939 in *The Return of Dr X* in which Bogart played a vampire, of all improbable things (a vampire with red lips and dark eyes and a white streak down the middle of his hair), says that nobody on the Warner's lot could with any honesty claim to have regarded Bogie at that time as star material and that Bogie knew it. "There's no question," said Sherman "that he felt he was being wasted. He knew he wasn't held in any great esteem."

But though they could hardly have known it, the very people who treated him so dismissively were probably doing him a favour because it was this cynicism, this sardonic disbelief in the words and actions of the Establishment that became the Bogart trademark in his most notable films and appealed so strongly to the scepticism of later generations. But his immediate and most material reaction to the struggle he had to establish himself was that he began to look after his money, because he believed that only in financial security lay the freedom he wanted if his bosses should ever seriously displease him.

Thus, from what amounted to a lengthy and sometimes painful apprenticeship in Hollywood, there emerged the familiar Bogart character — a wary man, not easily gulled; something of a loner who despised the social conventions of Film City, the big, back-slapping parties, the ostentatious visits to fashionable night spots. He became a deflator of pomposity, a needler who, when the whim took him, would mercilessly pick upon a complete stranger for the pleasure of seeing how far he could provoke him.

Sometimes, though not very often, this led him into trouble. Bogart, after all, was a comparatively small man — less than medium height and no more than 150 pounds in weight — and he was no fighter. So, as he once explained to Joe Hyams, he devised a certain procedure to protect himself from the deserved aftermath of his verbal excesses. He said: "If you're in a club and a fight's about to start and you're going to be part of it, you throw the first punch and then run like hell to the nearest, biggest waiter and stand there and he'll break up the fight for you."

Occasionally even this ingenious plan failed to work. "There was an agent," said Nat Benchley, "called Paul Small. A very big man. One night Bogie needled him and Paul slapped him, right in the face. Well, they were pulled apart and people took Small into another room, calmed him down and said that needling was only Bogie's way of having fun and they told him so much that he became enraged all over again and went back and slapped him a second time."

But this waspish behaviour was simply part of a dangerous game that Bogart liked to play. After a particularly fraught scene in Romanoff's restaurant in Hollywood, Lauren Bacall told her husband: "One of these days, you're going to get your head blown off." And he replied: "You don't understand. The trick is to get a guy just to the point where he's about to slug you and then you either lie down, put on your glasses or take a drink. Just get it to that point and stop. That's the essence of the game."

To his credit, however, it wasn't only agents and other comparatively small fry that he picked on. Sam Jaffe recalls that one day he had an irate phone call from Jack Warner himself.

"Jaffe," said Warner, "your star behaved very badly last night."

"Really, J.L.?" said Jaffe, understandably anxious, for the great man was extremely cross. "What happened?"

"Well, I was at this party, everybody was dressed up and Bogart walked up to me and said, 'J.L., you know you're a creep?'"

Jaffe made the required solicitous noises. "Well, Jack, what do you want me to do about it?" he said, "I mean, I just manage his career. I don't manage his personal life. I don't have anything to do with what he says at night."

"Well," said Warner, "you ought to talk to him about it. I think it's terrible."

The next day Jaffe phoned Bogart. "Bogie," he said, "I had a call from J.L. He says you called him a creep."

"Yes," said Bogie, "I did."

"But why?"

"Well, he is a creep," said Bogie.

And that was the end of the matter, though perhaps it needs to be said that this attack on the mighty Warner was made when Bogart was a hugely established star. It was, in fact, simply a touch of revenge for the humiliations he had suffered in the past. Those humiliations were exemplified by the way he was cast in *The Return of Dr X*. Vincent Sherman said: "Warner called me up to the office and said, 'I'm going to give you this guy Bogart.

For Christ's sake, see if you can get him to play something besides Duke Mantee.' ''

Bogie was, in fact, forty-one years old before anything resembling stardom was visited upon him and even then the opportunity came to him quite by chance. James Cagney was offered the role of the ageing gangster brought back from prison to take part, reluctantly, in one last raid in *High Sierra* but turned it down. The part was then offered to George Raft but he didn't want it because he didn't like the idea of dying at the end of the picture. Paul Muni didn't want it either because it had previously been offered to George Raft and Edward G. Robinson would have nothing to do with it because all those other people had been asked before him. So Bogie, the reserve heavy, got the job instead and turned in a performance of such sensitivity that at last the studio began to take him seriously.

Sam Jaffe said: "Bogart's whole career was made possible by other people turning down roles. He got the breaks because, first, there was the *High Sierra* business, and then George Raft turned down *The Maltese Falcon* because he said he wasn't going to work with an unknown director, John Huston. It was just a series of coincidences that made Bogart a star."

But even with the coincidences it wasn't easy. The role of Sam Spade in *The Maltese Falcon* was the prototype for the later Bogart roles and screen persona — the archetypal city man, tough and knowing, honourable but ruthless, brave but not foolhardy, sexual but not romantic, a natural survivor in the urban jungles. Jack Warner, however, was still not convinced about Bogart's potential. Valiantly resisting any impudent suggestion that he had been mistaken about this unlikely new star for more than a decade, he announced: "Bogart's a tough guy, not a lady's man." It was not until *Casablanca* and the odd chemistry produced by the blending of the apparently ill-assorted Bogart and Ingrid Bergman that even Warner had to admit grudgingly and no doubt only to his closest confidants, that he might have been a bit wrong.

Bogart's new-found luck — the right parts in the right films at the right time — held firm throughout the making of *Casablanca* which, strictly speaking, should have been a disaster since the script was being written as they went along and nobody, not even the director Michael Curtiz, knew until almost the end whether Bogie or Paul Henreid would finish up with the girl.

As an example of the haphazard way in which the film was shot, there was one occasion when Curtiz told Bogart to go on to the balcony of Rick's café and nod.

"Okay," said Bogart, "but what am I nodding at? What's my attitude?"

"Don't ask so many questions," said Curtiz. "Get up there and nod and then go home."

Bogart did as he was told and didn't discover until a long time afterwards that his nod had triggered off the famous scene in which Henreid led the other clients of the café in singing the "Marseillaise" and drowning out the Germans who had been chanting aggressive Nazi war songs. Whether or not he ever quite knew what he was supposed to be doing, Bogart nearly won the Oscar for *Casablanca*, losing out in the end to Paul Lukas for *Watch on the Rhine*.

So at the age of forty-three Bogie had finally arrived. He and Mayo went to Africa to tour the Allied bases — causing German radio to announce that American morale was so low that a notorious gangster had been sent out to entertain the troops—and then, on his return to Hollywood, he starred for Howard Hawks in Hemingway's *To Have and Have Not*. His co-star was an unknown nineteen-year-old actress named Lauren Bacall.

The start of the film was less than auspicious. On the first day of shooting Bogart returned to the set after lunch slightly drunk from far too many martinis. Hawks promptly hauled him out in front of the entire crew and said: "Right, we're going to Jack Warner and see whether I get a new star or you get a new director."

Bogart said: "I don't want to do that."

"Okay," said Hawks, "what are we going to do instead?"

Bogart said: "I'm going to stop drinking at lunchtime."

And so it was resolved. In any event he soon found something far more interesting than booze to help him while away his spare time. He fell firmly in love with Lauren Bacall, despite the fact that he was twenty-five years older than she was.

This made life more than a little difficult for him because he was still married to the intensely jealous and increasingly alcoholic Mayo Methot. Inevitably there were fights when Mayo discovered what was going on. Howard Hawks recalled that one night, early in the filming, the Bogarts came to dinner at his house and started brawling. Hawks told them: "Look, first of all, whoever tries to punch the other one, I'm going to punch that person. This is my house and I don't want any fighting in it." After that, he said, they were "as nice as anybody could be . . . but I don't think it was

Bacall who broke up the marriage, you know. I think it was breaking up long before that.''

In the event, the divorce was surprisingly amicable for two such volatile people. It was finalised in May 1945, and afterwards Mayo went to live in Oregon with her mother. Six years later she died of an illness brought on by acute alcoholism.

Eleven days after the divorce, while they were making their second film for Howard Hawks — the classic screen version of Raymond Chandler's *The Big Sleep* — Bogart and Lauren Bacall were married. Bogie was gravely concerned about this step, feeling that a marriage between a man of forty-five and a girl of twenty could hardly last very long. It was his friend Peter Lorre who helped him make up his mind to go ahead with it, saying, philosophically: ''It's better to have five good years than none at all.''

Therefore, consoled if not exactly inspired by this thought, Bogart entered upon his final marriage. He was aware of the age difference, as any sensitive and intelligent man would be, but, according to Nat Benchley, he more or less solved the problem by telling his wife that ''if she ever saw anyone she preferred to him, she should simply say so and Bogie would get lost.'' Happily, this never happened. Delmer Daves, who directed Bogart in *Dark Passage* and had known him for a long time before that, said: ''Betty Bacall was a blessing after Mayo.'' And indeed Lauren Bacall effected, intentionally or not, a great difference in Bogart's life. The heavy drinking, which had brought him to the verge of alcoholism with Mayo, came to an end partly, in Miss Bacall's view, because he now had security, not only professional but also emotional security. He had no need to drink heavily any more, although he never renounced the stuff completely. Towards the end of his life Nat Benchley was with him when somebody asked: ''Have you ever been on the wagon?'' and Bogart replied: ''Yes, I have and it was the most miserable afternoon of my life.''

To some extent the marital relationship was that of mentor and pupil. Miss Bacall has frequently mentioned the debt she owed to Bogie for what he taught her about acting for the cinema and about how to find her way around Hollywood. But it was also a deep and genuine love affair and what she gave him was stability — not, one would think, before time. He began to regard himself, at last, as a securely married man, and potentially a family man. For someone who had been married so often, this would seem to be a radical change in character, since a man with four wives could usually be classified with some confidence as promiscuous and a womaniser. Nat Benchley says that Bogie was neither of those things. It was the puritan streak, he says, the feeling that he should make an honest woman of the lady he had compromised that led him into his first three marriages and "he never had any action on the side, which in Hollywood is unheard of".

The desire to be a family man, which came upon him decidedly late in life, had a distressing side effect. In 1947, while he was filming *Dark Passage* with Delmer Daves he embarked upon a course of hormone pills to make him more fertile, as a result of which his hair started falling out. Daves said: "He came down to work one morning in San Francisco and said, 'Del, have you ever found a lot of hair on your pillow when you woke in the morning? Because I did.' The next day it was worse and very soon he went quite bald. I started having pieces of wig made for him. At first he needed only a little piece and then he needed more and more. In the end he lost all his hair, although a few months after we'd finished the picture it came back again."

More accurately, it came back as it had been before he started taking the hormones, which is to say that, even when restored, his hair had receded enough to necessitate the use of a toupee, an invaluable deception for an actor but one which he regarded with scorn.

Joe Hyams said: "He hated the toupee, although I don't think he was embarrassed by the baldness. I never saw him wear the toupee except on a film set and then he'd snarl about that 'goddamn rug'."

Despite their embarrassing side effects the hormone pills must have worked because, when he was nearly fifty, Bogart became a father swapping, as it were, his hair for an heir. Sentimentally he named his son Steve, after the character he had played in *To Have and Have Not*, the film on which he met Lauren Bacall. And when, in 1952, the Bogarts had a daughter, he called her Lesley, in honour of Leslie Howard whose help and loyalty had brought him to Hollywood to make *The Petrified Forest*.

Generally speaking, however, Bogart's early reaction to parent-hood was distinctly uneasy. He had never been particularly comfortable with children, as witness an anecdote retailed by Nathaniel Benchley. "He had a twelve-year-old godson in New York and one day, when Bogie was in town, the kid's mother called him up and suggested he take the boy out and give him some religious instruction, the way a godfather should. So Bogie, who couldn't think of anything else to do, took him to the '21' restaurant for lunch. Well, they sat there, making some kind of stilted conversation, and then suddenly Bogie said, 'Listen, kid, one thing you must remember — there are twelve commandments. Waiter, where the hell's my drink?' And that was the boy's religious instruction."

Initially he was no more at ease with his own children. Benchley believes that because he "came into the parenthood game late" he looked upon his offspring almost as "characters from another world. He was rather in awe of them." Nevertheless, although both of the children were still very young when their father died, Bogart had obviously got to grips with fatherhood and started to enjoy the role, because other people tell of finding him in the nursery, devotedly snarling baby talk at the infant Steve.

Meanwhile, as Bogart began to enjoy the unfamiliar fruits of a happy marriage and a thriving career that was bringing him not merely fame, which many actors enjoy, but also admiration, which is given to few, a kind of hysterical fascism, eventually to be orchestrated into mass paranoia by Senator Joe McCarthy, began to grip the American people. A grim national sport called "hunt the Reds" became more popular than baseball and a great deal nastier. In 1947 a Federal Grand Jury indicted ten Hollywood writers as alleged Communists for refusing to answer, as was after all their constitutional right, when asked if they were now, or had ever been members of the Communist party.

In protest at this witch-hunting, John Huston gathered together a planeload of stars and other prominent members of the Hollywood community and took them to Washington to campaign in support of the so-called "Unfriendly Ten". Among these indignant and notable citizens were the Bogarts. It was a brave gesture — braver perhaps than any of them knew, when you consider that within a very short time the merest suspicion of the slightest taint of Communism would be enough to ruin a man's career and even drive people to suicide.

Bogart's participation in this act of protest did not, however, last very long. When the going became tough and public opinion started to turn against the protesters, he backed away, dis-associating himself from the whole business. A lot of people, though not his friends Joe Hyams and Nat Benchley, believed that this was a cop-out, that he had lost his nerve. Hyams prefers to see it as "a re-thinking of his position and a re-estimation of what he had done". Bogart himself said later on that, initially, he had believed he was defending the Bill of Rights but then came to the conclusion that the Communist Party, which was striving to make martyrs of the "Unfriendly Ten", was using him and the others.

"We went in there green and they beat our brains out," he said, in an interview with *Newsweek* magazine. "In the shuffle we became adopted by the Communists and I ended up with my picture on the front page of the *Daily Worker*. I detest Communism just as any decent American does—the trip was ill-advised, even foolish. I am an American and very likely . . . sometimes a foolish and impetuous American."

No doubt his recantation was sincere, but it was also prudent, just as his first marriage had been prudent. When he was thinking of pulling out of his proposed wedding to Helen Mencken his brother-in-law, Stuart Rose, told him: "You're in too deep now. If you don't marry her, you'll never get another part on Broadway." And in the same way it must have been quite clear to him in 1947 that, successful though he was, any further association with alleged Communists could seriously damage his career. If, in addition, he was indeed a "decent American" who detested Communism then his withdrawal from the scene was only sensible, no matter how many people might call it a cop-out. Certainly it would be unfair to suggest that Bogart lacked moral courage. In the 1930s he appeared on the radio in support of Franklin Roosevelt, despite the fact that Jack Warner was implacably opposed to Roosevelt and had made it known that anyone at the studio who came out publicly in favour of the President would have his contract torn up and be barred from the lot.

Neither of these dire threats was carried out in Bogart's case but, at the time he made his broadcast, he had every reason to believe they might be. He was never afraid to swim against the tide as he showed in a different context in 1954.

At that time, Joan Bennett's husband, Walter Wanger the producer, shot her agent, Jennings Lang, in a car park in a fit of jealousy and in the groin. Though Lang, happily, recovered, Wanger was jailed and Miss Bennett found herself the object of scandal and professionally ostracised. "I was more or less black-listed," she said. "I wasn't being offered any pictures. Well, the Bogarts were very close friends of ours and at that time Bogie was making *We're No Angels* and he went to the head of Paramount and said, 'I'd like Joan Bennett in the picture.' And the man said,

'Oh no, we can't have her. She's been involved in this dreadful scandal,' and Bogie said, 'If you won't have her, forget it — I won't do the picture.' So I got the part. I don't think you can have a better friend than that."

One final testimonial to Bogart's integrity and perhaps another reply to the "cop-out" school of thought, came from Adlai Stevenson, whom the Bogarts supported fervently in his presidential campaign of 1952. "Bogie," Stevenson said, "never seemed to give a damn for what people said or thought. And it was quite perilous in those days to be a Democrat, especially one partisan to me."

However, once the controversy over Bogart's aborted Washington protest had died away, he swiftly resumed the successful path he had been treading for the last few years and furthermore he now had the confidence, from time to time, to step out of the familiar Bogart character. He did so initially in *The Treasure of the Sierra Madre* which, Sam Jaffe insists, he made for the sake of Walter Huston.

Jaffe said: "Bogie came to me and said, 'Sam, there's no question that I'm going to have to support Walter Huston and I think this is the only chance Walter will ever get to do that kind of role. So I'm going to support a character actor, but a brilliant one, and I don't think it'll hurt my career.' There's no doubt that, if Bogart hadn't played in it and so guaranteed a box-office attraction, this picture might not have been made because Jack Warner wasn't that enthusiastic. But Bogie did it because he had a great admiration for Walter."

He was also quite right in his assessment of his own role. He did, in effect, play a supporting part and Walter Huston won the Academy Award.

After *Sierra Madre* Bogart returned to his more traditional character in *Key Largo* with Lauren Bacall and Edward G. Robinson and then, in 1949, disillusioned with the sort of scripts that Warner Brothers were offering him, he set up his own production company, Santana, for which he made four films, the best of them being the first, *Knock on Any Door*, in which he appeared as an attorney defending a young hoodlum played by John Derek. The Santana experiment was short-lived because the results were disappointing and most disappointing of all was Bogart's realisation that he was no better at picking roles for himself than Warners had been at picking them for him.

Nevertheless, in 1950 he ended his contract with the studio and thereafter worked as a freelance. At once he landed another, out-of-character part — probably the best of them all. One day John Huston called him and said: "I have a great story. The hero is a low-life. You're the biggest low-life in town and therefore the most suitable for the part." Wooed by these soft words Bogart went to Africa to play Charlie Allnut, the seedy, wingeing, down-at-heel skipper of *The African Queen* and so at last won an Oscar of his own.

From then on, however, his films and the roles he played were mostly routine; a newspaperman investigating a vice ring in *Deadline — USA*; an officer at a field hospital behind the lines in Korea in *Battle Circus*; William Holden's stuffy elder brother in *Sabrina Fair* and so on. There were exceptions such as *Beat the Devil*, a comedy thriller that didn't really work at all but has since attracted a small and perverse cult-following, and *The Barefoot Contessa*, wherein he appeared as a once-drunken Hollywood director.

But after *The African Queen* his most notable performance was as Captain Queeg in *The Caine Mutiny*. This, too, was not an entirely successful film ("It was crapped up with an unnecessary love story," as Bogart put it) but he himself was excellent as the mentally sick and twisted Queeg and was again nominated for an Oscar. This time he lost out to Marlon Brando in *On the Waterfront* which was, perhaps, only fair because it was Bogart's successful nomination for *The African Queen* which had almost certainly robbed Brando of the award for *A Streetcar Named Desire*.

In the last years Bogie reverted to type. In *The Desperate Hours* he was virtually an older version of Duke Mantee from *The Petrified Forest* — a psychopathic hoodlum holding a family as hostage. And in his final picture, *The Harder They Fall* he was the cynical ex-sports reporter exposing the racketeers in boxing.

This film was made in 1956 and by then Bogart was already gravely ill with throat cancer. Soon afterwards he had an operation on the oesophagus and then went home to convalesce. For more than nine months he tried to believe, or at least to convince others, that he would recover.

Sam Jaffe said: "It's hard to tell whether he was aware that he was dying. He didn't look sad, he didn't act sad. I don't know whether people who are dying of cancer ever accept the fact that they're going to die because he said to me, almost in the last stages, he said, 'What about it, bud, are there any scripts around?'

136

I was shaken up. I couldn't believe it. His body was withering away; he must have been down to about eighty pounds then. But I said, 'Well, sure there are scripts,' and I called up the studios and said, 'You know, I think Bogart'll get well,' because I didn't want to play games and ask them to just give me a script, any kind of script. Anything I gave him I knew he'd read and if it was no good he'd know I was just playing games, pretending. So I said, 'Look, I think Bogart's going to recover,' and, of course, the studios had a lot of scripts, good ones, and I'd take them to him and he'd read them and he was very much interested. He loved life and he wasn't about to give up."

Nat Benchley, on the other hand, believes that Bogie knew he was dying. He said: "Betty (Lauren Bacall) says he didn't know but that was because he was a very good actor and he managed to hide his knowledge. He just fought it as long as he could and tried to pretend that the next week was going to be all right."

But, of all these tributes to Bogart's physical bravery, the most moving description of the end of his life comes from Joe Hyams, who was perhaps the only journalist he fully trusted and probably the only non-drinker (Hyams is teetotal by choice) ever admitted to his small and very select circle of friends.

"In the last, oh, three months of his life," Hyams said, "you could see him kind of slowly disappearing. He was just wasting away. He went from 150 to ninety pounds and he was little more than a genial skeleton after a while. But he had tremendous courage and I remember once that I went upstairs and his valet was dressing him — Bogie was lying in a big double bed — and he put Bogart's trousers on him and then he put on his smoking jacket, Bogart lying in bed all this time, and then he lifted him up gently, put him in a wheelchair, pushed the wheelchair over to the dumb waiter shaft, which was used to haul food up, put Bogart in the dumb waiter and lowered him slowly to the floor below. Then he went downstairs, carried Bogart and the wheelchair out and wheeled him through the house to the bar/sitting room where he entertained guests and propped him up in his favourite chair and put a martini in one hand and an unlit cigarette in the other.

"All this took maybe twenty-five minutes. At about five minutes to five guests started to arrive — all the people in Hollywood who were his friends and the idea was to fill him in on what was going on, give him the gossip, bring him up to date, cheer him up and in that sense it was a very social gathering and he would sit there like this for an hour or two, without really sipping because he didn't have the strength to lift the glass or light the cigarette and then, after about an hour, Betty Bacall would say it was time for everyone to go home and everyone would leave and they'd reverse the procedure — pick him up, put him back in the wheelchair, push him over to the dumb waiter shaft and take him back to bed.

"So he really had enormous courage because his doctor told me that he was going through the most agonising pain since the cancer was literally eating him up inside. But he was able, until almost a week before he died, to put on this kind of brave front — and it was never depressing. No one ever talked about the imminence of death, though it was there like a shadow in the room. Richard Burton would come, David Niven, Frank Sinatra, Spencer Tracy, Katherine Hepburn, everyone who was anyone at that time in Hollywood would be there during one of these sessions and I don't think any of us knew until almost the very end what courage it took for Bogart to get there, sit in that chair and, for an hour, try to be a host."

One Saturday night as Tracy and Hepburn were leaving the house Bogart watched them go and, instead of saying "goodnight" as usual, he said: "Goodbye, Spence." The next night, on January 14th, 1957, Humphrey Bogart was dead.

The funeral took place three days later at All Saints Episcopal Church in Beverley Hills. At Bogie's request the priest read the Ten Commandments — no doubt he would have read twelve if he could have found the extra two that Bogart once commended so warmly to his godson — and also Tennyson's poem, "Crossing the Bar" . . . "I hope to see my Pilot face to face when I have crossed the Bar . . ."

Afterwards the mourners returned to the family home for a drink, the sort of touch that Bogie himself would have applauded, while the body was cremated at Forest Lawn. Mythology has it that the gold whistle which he gave to Lauren Bacall after *To Have and Have Not*, the film on which he first met her and in which she said to him, "If there's anything you want, just whistle," was placed in the urn with the ashes. The story is probably apocryphal but felicitous. Bogart, the sentimental tough guy, the "big bowl of mush inside" would probably have liked to have that whistle with him.

Later on Lauren Bacall said: "Bogie is the only man I have ever known who truly and completely belonged to himself." And Richard Burton, whom Bogart befriended and introduced to the right kind of people when the young Welshman first arrived, virtually unknown, to seek his fortune in Hollywood, said: "His was the first theatrical death that deeply touched me. Hollywood has never been the same since he died."

Indeed the tributes to, and eulogies of, Bogart are endless because they continue to this day. He is the only star of the thirties and forties around whom a cult has sprung up since his death and there are many reasons for that. In the first place he was distinctly ahead of his time. In a period when most cinema heroes were basically Establishment figures, simple, straightforward and handsome, Bogart was none of those things.

On screen he was small and slight and brave and honest — the kind of man we all feel that we might have been, or be, or become. Watch him on screen in his classic roles, being Bogart, and you wish, as you rarely wish with other actors, that you had actually known him. In his professional persona — as, I suspect, in his private life — there was about him the wary, decidedly mocking, air of one who knew that the world, and especially its ruling bodies, was full of hypocrisy. Towards rigid authority he had a sardonic and rebellious attitude that reflects far more the 1960s and the 1970s than the thirties and forties, the eras which a man born when he was might have been expected to represent.

Most of all, though, it was that sense of unwavering honesty which, in the twenty-odd years since his death, has endeared him to new generations of young film-goers. It was an honesty that once made him suggest to his agent, Sam Jaffe, that at 250,000 dollars a picture he was being overpaid. (Jaffe countered this remarkable, if not unique, complaint by saying that Spencer Tracy received 250,000 dollars a picture and, if Tracy was worth that, then so was Bogart. Bogie, satisfied by such irrefutable logic, never raised the subject again.) So with his honesty and his toughness, his refusal to kow-tow or to be bullied he created a canon of work, a cadre of films which have often been imitated but never equalled because, at the heart of them all was the incomparable Bogart himself, gritty, scornful, world-weary but never so cynical as to be bitter: the ideal hero or, if you prefer, anti-hero for an age of disillusionment.

Joan Crawford

The starlet with her first husband, Douglas Fairbanks Jr. — "the prince and Cinderella".

Crawford, aged five and before her teeth were fixed, with her mother.

With Franchot Tone, husband No. 2, who rather wearied of being
"Mr. Crawford".

above : Her third husband was Philip Terry. She felt she owed him an apology for marrying him.

opposite : "The Mother of the Year" with her adopted family.

above : Mr and Mrs Al Steele on their wedding day.

opposite : Crawford in the later years and still plugging Pepsi-Cola.

A couple of nights before they were due to start working together on a film called *Torch Song*, Joan Crawford summoned the director, Charles Walters, to her home for drinks and a talk. It was a summons and not an invitation because Miss Crawford was much in the habit of issuing commands to her colleagues.

When he arrived Walters found her looking, as ever, as if she were about to make a public appearance, the hair and the make-up immaculate. There are those, such as Radie Harris, the Hollywood columnist, who maintain that even in her bath Crawford probably looked as if she were about to make a public appearance, just in case a crowd happened to drop by. However, on this occasion Crawford introduced a note of informality by wearing a housecoat which, once the drinks had been served and Walters was comfortably settled, she proceeded to throw open, revealing that underneath there was nothing but raw Crawford in prime condition.

Walters was simultaneously astonished, hugely flattered and somewhat embarrassed. "Well, I mean," he said, "at a time like that where do you look?" But once he had solved this not particularly difficult problem and looked his fill, the housecoat was closed and the show was over. "There was absolutely nothing sexual in what she did," he said. "It was purely professional. This was our first film together and what she was saying was, 'Okay, you'd better see what you've got to work with.' She simply wanted to show me the equipment."

Crawford was understandably proud of her equipment because she made it all herself. When she arrived in Hollywood in 1924 as Lucille le Sueur, a name so theatrical that it could only be genuine, which it was, she was a plump little thing with a round face; pretty enough, certainly, but in no way outstanding. Had you thrown a stick on the back lot of MGM you would probably have hit a dozen of her.

She was a dancer then, a talented and energetic exponent of the Charleston and the Black Bottom at such fashionable night spots as the Coconut Grove where Scott Fitzgerald, surveying her no doubt through the bottom of his martini glass, was moved to describe her as "the best example of the flapper". Flattering, to be sure, but nothing more than that. To be a flapper, even the best of flappers, in Hollywood in the 1920s was nothing extraordinary, especially as the flapper in question was also by profession a dancing girl and dancing girls in Hollywood at that time were only a step or so up the social scale from hookers. Indeed, it has been suggested that Crawford herself was not, in those days, averse to a little honest hooking on the side; it has even been suggested that she appeared, cavorting lewdly, in a stag movie. But there is no evidence to substantiate either of these allegations, common though they still are in Hollywood and it seems reasonable to attribute them to malice — and she attracted a lot of that.

Certainly it was as a dancer that MGM discovered her on Broadway and signed her to a contract and it was as a dancer that she won her first important film role in *Sally, Irene and Mary* in 1925, the director Edmond Goulding having been as impressed by her exploits at the Coconut Grove as Scott Fitzgerald was. That picture was one of twenty that she made before the end of 1928 and by that time she was no longer recognisable as the Lucille Le Sueur who had come to Hollywood in 1924. She was no longer Lucille Le Sueur for a start. The studio had decided she must have a new name and had organised a contest in a fan magazine to find one for her. For a week she went about as Joan Arden until MGM discovered they already had a Joan Arden on their books and so the alternative choice of Joan Crawford was adopted.

But her name was not all that was new. She had altered the shape of her face by having her back teeth removed to give herself cheekbones and she had changed her figure by drastic dieting or even by surgery. A popular operation among women in Hollywood at that time was to have excess fat cut away from their thighs and their calves and it has been suggested, though again without any evidence to substantiate it, that Crawford, too, had this operation. Equally to the point the familiar Crawford look — huge, heavily-emphasised eyes, square, scarlet letter-box of a mouth and square shoulders to match — was already in evidence. And most important of all, as far as her career was concerned, she had entered Hollywood society as the fiancée of Douglas Fairbanks, Junior.

Now it has been said that in Hollywood the aristocrats are those who can trace their ancestry all the way back to their own fathers. But in the 1920s a rigid social system existed there and at the top of it were Douglas Fairbanks, Senior, and his wife, Mary Pickford. The height of every social climber's ambition was to be invited to their home, Pickfair, a palatial house in Beverley Hills. As a dancer and a starlet, Crawford would have been lucky to get past the gate but as "young Doug's" fiancée she was accepted, albeit with some reluctance on the part of Miss Pickford.

Crawford had met young Doug after seeing him in a play in

Los Angeles. She sent him a telegram of congratulations, that telegram led to a meeting and the meeting led to their engagement, just after Christmas 1927, and eventually to their marriage in June 1929. Douglas Fairbanks, Junior, maintains that his wife was accepted cordially enough by his father and stepmother but Crawford claimed that she was greeted with hostility by Mary Pickford.

She once told Charles Walters of an early meeting which, she alleged, took place in Mary Pickford's bedroom during which Miss Pickford, not looking at her directly but staring at her in a mirror, said: "If you ever dare to make me a grandmother, I'll kill you." Whether this dramatic encounter ever took place it's impossible to say but it does seem likely that Mary Pickford disapproved of Crawford, if not on social grounds then certainly on grounds of age.

At the time of the engagement, young Doug was eighteen, while Crawford could have been anywhere between nineteen and twenty-three. Most reference books give her year of birth as 1906 but this is perhaps a compromise between the birth date she claimed, March 23rd, 1908 and the more probable March 1904. Mary Pickford certainly seems to have favoured the latter and therefore believed that Crawford was too old for her stepson. Nevertheless, and whatever the differences between the two women, as the fiancée and then the bride of young Doug — "the Prince and Cinderella" they were called by the Press — Crawford had found a happy short-cut into the upper echelons of Hollywood society, to which position she clung tenaciously for the next forty years.

In any event, and no matter how old she was, she had come a remarkably long way in a very short time. She was born, probably illegitimate, in San Antonio, Texas, and her parents had separated before her birth. She never knew who her father was until many years later and in fact for some time she believed herself to be the child of another of her mother's men friends, Henry Cassin. Indeed, for much of her childhood she was not even aware that her name was Lucille Le Sueur; she thought she was Billie Cassin.

At one stage during her youth she attended St Agnes Academy in Kansas City and when Cassin, too, deserted his family, leaving them destitute, she was allowed to stay on at school only on condition that she helped to clean the rooms, make the beds and wait on other children. Vincent Sherman who, much later, was to become her friend and director, believes that she always had an innate hostility to the world because of this mortifying experience. Whether this was so or not, it was clearly a hard childhood with no father, no money to speak of and her mother working in a laundry to scrape a living.

In time, when her mother found yet another man friend, things became a little easier, but at sixteen Billie Cassin, or Lucille Le Sueur as she now knew herself to be, ran away from home to become a dancer. Eventually she found her way into the chorus of a Broadway musical where she was seen by an MGM executive and offered a film contract.

What sort of wounds such a childhood left on her it's difficult to assess. But, in retrospect, it does seem that those early experiences instilled in her an almost terrifying ambition — an ambition to make herself into something very special, no matter what the price she had to pay. And in the end the price was the complete burial of Lucille Le Sueur in a figment of the imagination called Joan Crawford.

Today, again with hindsight and admittedly without the benefit of ever having known her, it appears to me that Joan Crawford was totally unreal. Joan Crawford was a film star and that's all she was. That was all she ever wanted to be. She was the very epitome of a film star, the most durable of all the female stars in Hollywood and she played the part with relentless dedication for twenty-four hours a day, every day of her life.

She had, for instance, a fan club. Now, every star has a fan club but nobody ever had a fan club like Joan Crawford's. In 1938 when her career was on the slide — and it slid many times — the American film exhibitors described her as "box-office poison". Crawford promptly countered this deadly accusation by claiming that she had just received her 900,000th fan letter; apparently she had retained and counted them all. Other stars would keep their activities secret from their fan clubs so that they could enjoy a little privacy, but not Crawford. Wherever she went she gave her fans a complete itinerary of her movements in order that they should turn up at the hairdressers, the restaurant, the theatre or wherever to adore her. She remembered her fans' birthdays and the birthdays of their children — many of whom, inevitably, were named after her — and at Christmas she sent out anything up to 7,000 cards. When the tour buses trekked round Beverley Hills with the guides pointing out the homes of the famous for the benefit of the rubbernecks, the other stars would retire indoors and close the curtains. But Crawford would regard the arrival of the tour bus as one of the important appointments of her day and she would instal herself, immaculately turned out of course, in some prominent place in her garden so that she could look up from her apparent task of doing a little light weeding and wave to the fans. "They made me," she said. "I owe it to them."

Such loyalty to people who were, after all, complete strangers was no doubt commendable but again a little unreal. As she grew older the fans became more important to her than the people she knew, more important even than her husbands and lovers, certainly more important than her adopted children, and at the end of her life they were all she had left.

But in the late 1920s the fan club was only in its infancy, even though the young Crawford's career was already flourishing. In 1929 she received the bizarre but much-appreciated accolade of being asked to leave her hand and footprints in wet cement outside what was then Graumann's, and is now Mann's, Chinese Theatre on Hollywood Boulevard. This is a privilege accorded only to major stars and Crawford had reached that eminence extremely fast. The same year, when she was heard singing with more enthusiasm than talent in *The Hollywood Revue of 1929*, she made the transition from silent to talking pictures without any apparent difficulty and thereafter her career soon outstripped that of her husband.

In her silent films she had mostly played bright young things, what she called "dancing daughter" roles, but in 1930 she appeared in *Paid* as a department store girl who was sent to jail, wrongly of course, and was then bent on revenge and thenceforth, either by chance or more likely by shrewd casting, she acquired a special niche for herself in the movies. Throughout the thirties and into the forties she epitomised every shop assistant's and every factory girl's dream. She was tough, hard-boiled and glamorous, a working-class girl on the make. And naturally she suffered. Suffering, sometimes relieved by a happy ending though frequently not, was the hallmark of a Crawford film. Nobody suffered as much in movies as Crawford did, though Bette Davis and Barbara Stanwyck sometimes came close, and it was the suffering that the fans enjoyed. When she was young they liked to see her suffering in poverty or similar adverse circumstances and clawing her way to the top, and when she was older they liked to see her suffering in mink while caught in an unhappy marriage or love affair. Quite often, as in *Harriet Craig,* a film in which, though she was unaware of it, she virtually played herself, the suffering was brought about by her own unreasonable actions but the fans didn't care. For them nothing in the world could beat the ecstatic pleasure of settling back in a darkened cinema with a bag of popcorn and watching Joan Crawford suffer.

There is no doubt that she tried very hard to master the craft of acting and to extend her range but she never really managed it. All her life she played that one particular kind of American woman, a dominant, irresistible woman, a born matriarch and in a matriarchal society that was enough to establish and maintain her as a star.

But the acting equipment that she took with her into each role was minimal. She could cry at will with both eyes or, if the director preferred it, with one eye at a time and she had an instinctive rapport with cameras. George Cukor, who directed her in *The Women* and *A Woman's Face*, said: "The closer the camera came the more relaxed she was, the more she showed her seductive side. She showed her heart, she showed everything to the camera and I said some place when working with her, 'You know, no lover or husband ever saw that side. In there she's more melting, more interesting than anything she ever showed in real life.'"

She had the priceless gift of touching the imagination of the audience but that was a matter of star quality and little to do with acting. Scott Fitzgerald said of her: "She can't change her emotions in the middle of a scene without going through a Jekyll and Hyde contortion of the face, so that when one wants to indicate that she is going from joy to sorrow one must cut away and then back. Also, you can never give her such a stage direction as 'telling a lie' because if you did she would practically give a representation of Benedict Arnold selling West Point to the British."

Still, in the early 1930s before this kind of detailed criticism was levelled at her, her career followed an upward graph although her private life was considerably less successful. Her marriage to Douglas Fairbanks ended in divorce in 1933, probably because what had been a very youthful romance had simply run its course. Also the fact that he was sophisticated and highly educated and she was neither of those things and that his background was wealthy while hers was poor may have made it difficult for them to achieve any lasting compatability.

Long before the divorce the two had drifted apart and she had become involved in a celebrated and passionate affair with Clark Gable, her co-star in *Laughing Sinners* and *Possessed*. As an affair it was ardent, clandestine and brief. They talked about marriage, she wrote much later on, but added in the kind of hot, breathless prose that so admirably suited her style: "I dared not ruin the dreams. I'd rather live with them unfulfilled than have them broken." In any event, the break-up with Gable and indeed with Fairbanks hardly seems to have shattered her because, even before she was divorced, she was already involved with Franchot Tone, an actor she first met in the film *Today We Live*.

Like Fairbanks, Tone came from a wealthy background, being the son of an industrial magnate and a graduate of Cornell University. He was an actor of no little talent but as "Mr Crawford", which he became in 1935, he found his own career suffering and he had to make do with supporting roles in several films which starred his wife. She, on the other hand, had now reached perhaps the peak of her success at MGM despite the fact that the critics dismissed her as "a clothes horse de luxe".

Until 1937 indeed very little went wrong for her — professionally at least. But in that year for some reason — not necessarily to do with her work because *The Last of Mrs Cheyney* in which she co-starred with William Powell and Robert Montgomery had done well — her popularity began to wane and, remarkably, she failed to appear in the list of the biggest money-making stars.

In 1938 an even worse fate befell her because that was the year when she was included among a list of stars declared in a full-page advertisement in the trade paper *The Hollywood Reporter* to be box-office poison by a group of distributors who announced that they were "tired of losing money on the glamour stars detested by the public". By now her box office rating had plunged from third to anywhere between twenty-fifth and sixtieth place but MGM continued to show faith in her by signing her to a new five-year contract, which at least gave her a measure of security.

Crawford herself, however, was not unnaturally worried at the turn her professional fortunes were taking and, with typical resolution, set out to re-establish her position at or near the top. "At this critical moment," she wrote, "I set my sights on the part of Chrystal, the hard-boiled perfume clerk who uses every wile to catch another woman's husband in *The Women*." If she wanted the part that badly quite obviously nobody was going to stand in her way and she duly got it. According to the American critic Bosley Crowther, she hurled herself into the role of a bitch with such enthusiasm that she continued it off-screen and when sitting beside the camera to read her lines back to Norma Shearer for Shearer's close-ups she knitted distractingly all the time, never once looking up at her co-star. George Cukor says he believes this was done unthinkingly and unmaliciously but it could equally have been done out of sheer spite because Shearer, as the wife of Irving Thalberg, the production supervisor at MGM, had always been given the pick of the roles in the studio's biggest films. And in any case Crawford was not above perpetrating acts of petty malice on any actress.

When Natalie Schafer came from Broadway to appear with her in *Reunion in France* in 1942 Crawford virtually ruined her first big scene by continually moving so that her shadow always obstructed Miss Schafer's face. To this day Miss Schafer is convinced that she did it on purpose because it was followed by another act of apparent spite. During the making of the same film, Miss Schafer went into Crawford's trailer dressing-room, which was at that moment empty, to look at herself in the full-length mirror. When Crawford discovered what she had done she summoned the studio policemen to guard the door and prevent her from repeating the offence.

However, *The Women* went a fair way towards re-establishing Crawford as a top box-office star and in the same year that she made the film she divested herself of Franchot Tone. The marriage had never been much of a success partly because his career had been secondary to hers and partly, perhaps, because Tone could never properly adjust himself to living with a star who could never forget that she was one. Also it was during this marriage that she had taken to alerting the fans as to her movements. (Spencer Tracy once said: "She likes to have them follow her when she goes shopping.") And Tone could never find a way to compete with this hydra-headed rival that turned up clamouring for his wife's attention whenever he appeared with her in public.

Around this time Crawford's egocentricity took her off in an unexpected direction. She decided to become a mother. Nobody knows why she had never had any children of her own. Some said that eventually she was unable to conceive because she had had several miscarriages. Others maintained that she simply couldn't bear to lose her figure for a year while she had a baby. But whether because she was unable or unwilling to have children of her own, she decided to adopt a couple — first a girl called Christina, then a boy named Christopher.

For a while she continued as a single parent, but in 1942 she met a rather obscure young actor named Philip Terry (best remembered for his role as Ray Milland's brother in *The Lost Weekend*) and six weeks later she married him for reasons which were totally obscure even to Crawford. She often said, when the marriage had come to its inevitable end, that she owed him an apology, adding: "I've never really known why I married Philip. I guess I mistook peace of mind for love and at the time believed it with all my heart."

But married again for the third time she adopted two more children, Cathy and Cynthia, whom she described as twins, even though they came from different families and were born a month apart. Why she ever resolved to take on these unfortunate children is a matter for conjecture for, by all accounts, she was an extremely harsh mother with not the slightest aptitude for the role. Even discounting the more horrendous tales of her treatment of the brood, the discipline she imposed upon them was, to say the least, excessive.

She insisted on tidiness to such an extent that, according to Radie Harris, there was never a sign of a child in the house; never a doll or a toy to be seen. On one occasion Christopher was shut in his room all day because he had forgotten to clean his shoes. On another — and this anecdote Crawford herself recounted to Natalie Schafer with pride — he asked if he could take a chocolate from a huge box on the coffee table. Crawford said he could but he was only to have one. A little later she caught him taking another and, by way of punishment, insisted that he eat the entire boxful while she sat and watched him. When he had finished he was, not unnaturally, violently sick. "He won't do that again," said Crawford to Miss Schafer. "My children must obey me."

Gregory Bautzer, the Hollywood lawyer who was close to Crawford between her third and fourth marriages, remembers being at her home one Sunday for family dinner. Christopher was left-handed and Crawford disapproved of that and insisted that he eat with his fork in his right hand. At one point the boy forgot and used his left. Crawford immediately leaned across the table, knocked the fork and the food out of his hand and hit him across the face. "He started to cry," said Bautzer, "so I immediately went over and put my arms around him and as I was holding him — we were having a roast leg of lamb — I got it right in my face . . . There was a strictness with those children

I think was probably the primary cause of the estrangement that occurred with them."

Vincent Sherman believes she wanted to be a good mother but since she appears to have shown no warmth towards the children one wonders what her definition of a good mother was. Somebody perhaps whose children reflected credit upon her. Sherman would remonstrate with her about the rigid discipline she imposed upon them and say: "Joan, they're going to hate you when they grow up. You shouldn't do this." And then, he said, "Her jaw would get tight and she'd say, 'I'm going to raise my children to be ladies and gentlemen.'"

Christopher finally rebelled and several times ran away from home. Crawford used to complain to Radie Harris that her fourth husband, Alfred Steele, the chairman of Pepsi-Cola, had spent more than $40,000 on psychiatric treatment for the boy "trying to straighten him out". Miss Harris commented: "A lot of people thought a psychiatrist should have tried to straighten Joan out in her relationship with the children."

As they grew up the children virtually lost contact with her. Christopher married and had a family of his own whom Crawford refused to see and when Christina, who had been divorced, was married again, Crawford would not attend the ceremony. In her will she disinherited the two older children, although she did leave money to "the twins".

It could be, I suppose, that something in her own childhood — a lack of discipline or an excess of it — accounted for her treatment of her adopted family. But the coolness she habitually showed towards them would suggest that, in adopting them, she was merely playing another role — Joan Crawford, mother, and that she swiftly tired of it. When she married Al Steele and moved to New York they took on an immense apartment, big enough for a very large family, but Crawford so redesigned it, knocking down walls to make several rooms into one, that there was no place for the barely-teenage twins. They had to live with a nanny in a nearby hotel and see their mother more or less by appointment. But no doubt Crawford herself regarded the adoptions as successful and certainly thought of herself as a very good mother. She even had an award to prove it, for one year — with huge but unconscious irony — an American women's organisation voted her "Mother of the Year".

But back in 1943 when the children were still young and her marriage to Philip Terry was hardly a year old, Crawford's professional life arrived at a crisis. Her ·contract with MGM expired and, by mutual consent, was not renewed. Her last few pictures had not done well and she was tired, she said, of the parts they offered her. "If you think I made poor films at MGM after *A Woman's Face* you should have seen the ones I went on suspension not to make." Possibly, too, injured pride entered into her decision to leave. Popular though she was, she had never been the number one female star at MGM. In the early days she had been pushed into third place by Norma Shearer and Greta Garbo and later she was kept there by Greer Garson and Lana Turner.

Ironically enough, however, on leaving MGM she immediately signed a contract — at a third of her former salary but with more script approval — with Warner Brothers where once again she found herself firmly installed at number three in the pecking order behind Bette Davis and Barbara Stanwyck. In fact for the first two years of her contract at Warners she didn't work at all but simply stayed at home playing the role of Joan Crawford, housewife-superstar, while she waited for the right part to come along.

It was a difficult period for her since Warners seemed to have little idea what to do with her. Once, she told Vincent Sherman, after she'd turned down a particular script she was summoned to the studio to discuss it. She bought a new hat and a new dress for the occasion but when she arrived she was kept waiting for twenty to thirty minutes before the producer admitted her to his presence and told her, in effect, that she'd better take what she was offered because it was hard to find work for her and nobody wanted her. She told Sherman that she went home and cried all afternoon.

But finally her patience paid off. In 1945 she gained the role of the waitress who killed for her unpleasant and undeserving daughter in *Mildred Pearce* and won the Oscar for best actress, the only Oscar she ever did win. It was after this that a new ingredient, neurosis, was added to the other characteristics of a typical Crawford role. For the rest of her time at Warners she appeared mostly as a neurotic, and of course suffering, career woman of a certain age, a woman whose affluence and apparent success barely disguised her inner discontent. It was in this sort of role that she was loaned out to Columbia in 1950 to make *Harriet Craig*, directed by Vincent Sherman. In this she played a particularly house-proud wife and Sherman introduced many of the idiosyncrasies which Crawford displayed in her own home, where everything had to be in precisely the place she had assigned for it.

By all accounts she had an obsession with cleanliness. If she stayed in a hotel, no matter how many stars it had, she would scrub the bathroom herself before using it and in at least one instance she covered all the furniture with cellophane. But then she covered all her own furniture with cellophane as well, so that she and it would look equally immaculate.

Everything in her house, according to Vincent Sherman, was "just proper". At dinner parties the table was set like an illustration from a book of etiquette. Guests who smoked would find themselves carrying ashtrays about for fear of incurring their hostess' displeasure by dropping ash on the carpets. And since the carpets were white visitors were frequently expected to take their shoes off before entering. Charles Walters remembers being invited for Sunday brunch and arriving to find Crawford in jeans on her hands and knees scrubbing the black and white marble floor in the hall and saying: "I'll be ready in five minutes. I've just got to clean up. I can't trust anybody any more."

Another time when he turned up to take her to a party he was summoned to her dressing-room where he discovered her in full make-up, her hair done and wearing a smart little hat with a veil, long black stockings, high-heeled shoes, bra and pants while she moved around the room constantly readjusting the curtains to make them look tidier. Vincent Sherman always felt that there was something unnatural about the orderliness and the elegance of her surroundings, as if she had no taste of her own but had learned from the advice columns what a film star's house should look like.

And yet no other film star lived quite like Joan Crawford. Her dressing-room was enormous, bigger than most people's living rooms, and the walls were lined with shelves and drawers holding her shoes and gloves and hats, hundreds of shoes and gloves and a hundred hats. Another, smaller room, just off it, housed her furs, minks and sables, perhaps seventy to eighty of them, for every possible occasion on which a fur might be worn. The total effect was less that of a woman's dressing-room than of a wardrobe department of a film studio. And Crawford knew precisely where everything was. If a friend asked for the loan of a handbag for the evening she would walk into the room in the dark and find exactly the right bag, and there were scores to choose from, without a moment's hesitation.

Well, none of this is at all blameworthy or risible. Clothes, after all, are a film star's vital accessories — or were in Crawford's day when the public expected their movie stars to be larger than life, more beautiful, more elegant, more ostentatiously wealthy than anyone else. And yet, as with much else in her life, there is an impression of excess, of close attention to detail magnified to obsession. What she was seeking perhaps was perfection — perfection in her surroundings, perfection in her children, perfection in her appearance. But perfection is an impossibility and the pursuit of it is chilling and inhuman.

In her career, as she sought to improve herself, the idea of perfection forced Crawford while she was shooting a film to move into her dressing-room at the studios. True, the dressing-room was positively luxurious, a kind of three-roomed apartment a great deal more splendidly appointed than the average home but a dressing-room in a studio, however grand, is no place to live. Yet Crawford would retire there each night when everyone else had gone home and, having scrubbed and cleaned and prepared herself a meal, would stay there alone, studying her script.

Increasingly, as I spoke to people who knew her, it seemed that there was little about her that was spontaneous; everything was subjugated to the needs of the role she created for herself. Whatever was left in her of Lucille Le Sueur might — or, on the other hand, of course, might not — have wanted occasionally, let us say, to let her hair down and get a little drunk. But that would not have suited the image of Joan Crawford and so it never happened. Not, at least, in public. Even when she was in love she appeared to be playing a part. Her comments on Gable, for instance — "his nearness had such impact that my knees buckled . . . a magnetic man with more sheer male magic than anyone in the world" — sound contrived and manufactured as though she were reacting according to some strict unwritten code of behaviour to which a woman in love was obliged to adhere.

When she was in love she was possessive and predatory and conducted the affair on rules established by herself. Her escort was expected to drive to her house and leave his car there while she drove them to their destination. This always worked according to plan because she had two Cadillacs, one specifically held in reserve in case the other should fail her. When they arrived at their destination, a restaurant perhaps, or a party, the ritual would always be the same: Crawford would enter first with the escort two or three paces behind and carrying her knitting bag on one arm and a small, white poodle under the other. Knitting was another of her obsessions. She would knit wherever she went, although Tallulah Bankhead once stopped her by taking the work in progress out of her hands, stuffing it back in the bag and saying: "At my parties nobody makes their own entertainment."

When the evening was over Crawford would drive her escort back to her house where, after a goodnight embrace of such ardour as was decreed appropriate to the occasion, he would collect his car and depart. She would then allow him exactly enough time to get home and phone him, ostensibly to make sure that he had arrived safely but in fact to satisfy herself that he had indeed gone home and not perhaps to some other woman's bed. On those occasions when there was no reply to her call, for whatever innocent reason, furious retribution would be faced by that escort at their next meeting.

Greg Bautzer, the lawyer, maintains that the only scars he carries on his face were put there by Crawford in the course of physical displays of temper brought on by the fact that he hadn't returned home swiftly enough or that he had been seen having a drink with another woman. "She could throw a cocktail glass across the room and hit you in the face, two times out of three," he said. But was that a spontaneous display of emotion by Lucille Le Sueur or the calculated reaction of an insulted Joan Crawford?

Bautzer's relationship with her lasted more than two years and ended after a party in the home of Louis B. Mayer, who was then head of MGM. During the course of the evening Bautzer was guilty of paying rather more attention to another actress than met with Crawford's approval. Nothing was said at the time but punishment for the crime was administered on the way home at about two o'clock in the morning. As usual Crawford was driving and when she had reached a deserted spot about ten miles from anywhere, except other deserted spots, she stopped the car and said: "Darling, there's something wrong with the rear tyre. Would you be a dear and have a look at it?"

The gallant Bautzer said: "Of course, darling" and got out of the car, whereupon she promptly took off, leaving him stranded. Until then, he said, it had always been his practice after a tiff to phone her and apologise, whether or not the fault had been his. But on this occasion he was given ample opportunity to reflect on their relationship and on himself — "What the hell kind of man are you?" — as he trudged ten miles home to his hotel and he never called her again.

Clark Gable once said to Bautzer: "Don't you find something kind of masculine about Joan? Not in her looks but in her approach. She thinks like a man." She also behaved like a man, grabbing the initiative in her relationships with the opposite sex in a way that clearly pre-dated Women's Lib. In her defence Vincent Sherman said: "When you consider the kind of life that she had, where she had to fight for her own independence and struggle as she did, I think she felt that men in a certain sense were her enemies and therefore she had to fight against them." Ultimately perhaps, she typified and even caricatured a new breed of women to which Hollywood had given birth—women who earned not only a living but a fortune; women who, in their professional lives, were as rich and as important as men; women who, in most respects, were totally independent of men.

In 1952 Crawford left Warner Brothers — again, so it was said, by mutual consent. By now, whatever her date of birth, she was well into her forties, her third marriage had failed and her career was slipping once more. For a while she freelanced with no great success, making among other things the musical *Torch Song* at MGM, her first musical and, coincidentally, her first picture in colour. But *Torch Song* did nothing for her and neither did its successors. She was still a star and to her devoted fan club always would be but, professionally, she was at best marking time.

But on New Year's Eve, 1954, she was studying a script in her dressing-room when, at midnight, a friend called her from New York and, after wishing her a happy new year, put Alfred Steele, the chairman of Pepsi-Cola, on the line. At that time Steele was in the process of divorcing his second wife, which was convenient because, when he and Crawford met in California a little later they swiftly decided to marry and were indeed married in May 1955.

Now a new career began for her. She was, let us say for the sake of argument, around fifty and she had already extended her career as a romantic leading lady to almost indecent lengths. The kind of role for which she was suitable in that guise was becoming increasingly hard to find and so, although she did make two films during her marriage to Steele, including *The Story of Esther Costello*, her first in England, she began to detach herself from the movies. Indeed, playing a subordinate role to her husband for the first time in her varied experience as a wife, she moved to New York and became a roving ambassadress for Pepsi-Cola, travelling the world and attracting hordes of people to the opening of new factories.

The life seemed to suit her, possibly because she had simply swapped one kind of power for another while remaining as firmly as ever in the public eye. Her friends believe that the marriage to Steele was the happiest of the four, largely because he was a dominant and successful man in his own right and because he had no connection whatever with show business. Instead of moving into her life, which her other husbands had perforce been obliged to do, he moved her into his. Unfortunately, however, the happiness was short-lived. One night in 1959, Steele collapsed and died of a heart attack. Crawford reacted as typically as ever. Whatever grief she felt she kept to herself and set about organising the funeral with brisk efficiency.

"One day," said Radie Harris, "there was Joan on the phone and she said, 'The services are gonna be at St Thomas's or wherever and the cremation is gonna be at such-and-such a place and you're gonna be in car eight and with you is gonna be blah-blah-blah . . .' like giving seats for an opening night. And I hung up the phone and I just couldn't believe it. And yet, you see, this was so typical of Joan. This was something she had to do and it had to be well organised because this is what Al would have wanted."

A week after Steele's death Crawford was offered a role in *The Best of Everything* and she accepted, probably because a return to her original career would be therapeutic at such a time of trauma, but she still retained her connections with Pepsi-Cola who, as a reward for her indefatigable efforts, gave her a lifetime appointment to the board of directors. Indeed she took this work so seriously over the next three years that she restricted her acting to guest appearances in TV shows and it was not until 1962 when she was teamed with Bette Davis in *Whatever Happened to Baby Jane?* that she made her next cinema appearance. This gothic horror story of a drunken and demented former child star (Davis) and the crippled sister (Crawford) whom she sadistically torments was to be Crawford's last film of any note at all.

Its success brought her a handful of similar roles in other, vastly inferior, horror pictures, including two, *Berserk* and *Trog*, which were made in Britain, but by 1970 her career as a movie star was finally over. For a while she continued to work for Pepsi-Cola but in the end even that was lost to her when the new management retired her, either because they wanted a younger image to promote their product or, as Vincent Sherman suggests, because she had tried to become too dominant in the company's affairs.

Losing her job with Pepsi was the ultimate indignity. Thereafter Crawford became a reclusive figure, rarely going out, rarely seeing her friends. She started to worry about money and moved to a smaller apartment, although there is no evidence to indicate that she was anything but comfortably off, to say the least.

Her friends would try to invite her out but she would make excuses, pretending that she was about to leave town and claiming always that she was extremely busy. In a sense she was, but the work was self-imposed. She would get up at six a.m. and start dictating letters to her two secretaries, one in New York, the other in California, but these letters were nearly all to members of her fan club, the strangers who had kept faith with her through all her vicissitudes and with whom she in turn kept faith to the very end.

For the most part she would stay indoors, avidly watching soap operas and chat shows on television, eating her meals off a tray on her knees. Her public appearances became increasingly rare and in the last year or so of her life they stopped altogether. By then, although her friends were mostly unaware of it, she had developed cancer of the stomach, a long and painful illness which she suffered without complaint and for much of the time without treatment because she had become a Christian Scientist and believed that the body could cure itself. It didn't. And she died on May 10th, 1977, alone.

She appears to have been a most complex person, a mixture of insecurity and arrogance, an egotist who was yet capable of great kindness and generosity. The gifts she gave to her friends were extravagant even by Hollywood standards and the help she would offer, unsolicited and frequently anonymous, to people who were ill or down on their luck was legendary. For years she maintained two rooms at the Hollywood Presbyterian Hospital, not for herself but for people she heard about who were sick and could not afford the necessary treatment.

And yet along with this went a basic distrust of people, men and women — women because she saw them as rivals and men because she was never sure that they wanted her for herself or for the very useful kudos that could accrue from being seen around with Joan Crawford, movie star. Natalie Schafer believes that she wanted to be loved but failed "because you have to love people to be loved, really loved, and I don't think she loved anybody but Joan Crawford. It's an awful thing to say but I think that's the way she was and I think that's what made her a success — a complete feeling for herself."

That she was a success is undeniable. She lasted as a star longer than any other woman in the history of the cinema and to a great extent her career was a triumph of will over adversity, of personality over sometimes appalling material. She made more than eighty films, a great many of them indifferent at best, but often the worse the picture, the better she was, though not because she was a fine actress. She wasn't. Being an actress was not what she was good at. What she was good at was being precisely what she was — Joan Crawford, movie star. Survival as a star was her aim and her greatest achievement and everything else, husbands, lovers and adopted children were sacrificed to this ambition. She was, it seems to me, an easy woman to admire but not an easy one to like.

Whether at the end she felt it had all be worthwhile, that the creation of Joan Crawford was a sufficient monument to her life, only she could tell and she never did. Charles Walters, remembering the loneliness of the later years of her life, before the onset of cancer and after the end of her film career, and the frenetic way in which she filled her days with needless activity said: "It was almost as though Joan Crawford was trying to escape sitting down with Lucille Le Sueur and saying, 'Well, honey, where are we really and what do we want?' She kept busy enough not to face it."

Far more than Myrna Loy, who was briefly accorded the title as the result of a newspaper poll, Joan Crawford was the true Queen of Hollywood, the archetypal movie star whose like had never been seen before and will probably never be seen again.

At her death she was mourned far more deeply by her fans than by many of the people who knew her. And that seems to be at once the measure of her success and of her failure.

Ronald
Colman

*The youthful Ronald Colman,
with the famous moustache
still in its infancy.*

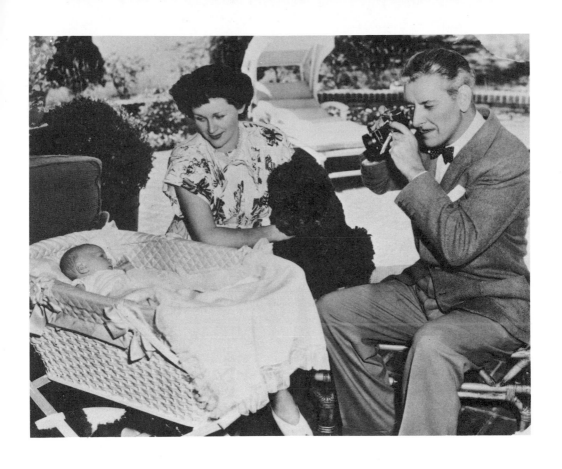

*above : The family man — left profile much in evidence — with wife
Benita Hume and daughter Juliet.*

*opposite : A classic Colman pose, though showing rather more of the
right profile than he normally liked.*

above : With Benita again in the later years.

opposite : Colman in his last film, "The Story of Mankind".

In September 1914 Private Ronald Colman was advancing across no-man's land at Messines in company with the rest of the London Scottish Regiment and several thousand others when a German shell landed beside him, fracturing his ankle and hurling him into an abandoned trench. Swiftly rejecting any idea of hopping belligerently towards the enemy lines on one good leg and a swinger, Private Colman began to drag himself back whence he had come and was making, in the circumstances, quite good progress when an appalling thought occurred to him: if he were struck now by a German bullet, and there were volleys of them flying around seeking a lodging, he would be discovered with his back to the enemy, thus leading anyone whom it might concern to the inescapable conclusion that he had been killed while running away. The prospect of such posthumous disgrace was too intolerable to contemplate, so he turned himself around and proceeded to crawl backwards to the safety of the British trenches.

This story, which he later recounted to, among others, Bessie Love, was both typical and a-typical of Ronald Colman. It was typical because his was the action of a man who cared deeply about form and style, the action of a gentleman if not, by a mere accident of rank, an officer. It was a-typical because he told it not as an illustration of his valour but as a joke against himself and on the evidence of many people who knew him well, among them Bessie Love, who was married to his agent, humour and especially self-mockery were not usually among Colman's most noticeable attributes. He was a man who took himself seriously and was anxious that others should have a good opinion of him; a man of great charm and vanity, of shyness and arrogance, an accomplished actor who might well have been more accomplished than he ever allowed himself to be, who achieved the unique feat of thriving as a romantic movie star for three decades without ever being visited by scandal.

But on that day in 1914 when, no doubt to the general astonishment of his fellows at arms, Colman reappeared from the battle backside first he was twenty-three years old and by trade a shipping clerk and accountant. He was born, in solid middle-class circumstances, on February 9th, 1891 in Richmond, Surrey, the fourth of five children. His father, Charles Colman, was a silk importer who prospered until about 1907 when his business collapsed, taking the family fortune with it and thoroughly blighting young Ronald's plans to go to Cambridge University and become an architect. Instead, he found work as a clerk with the British Steamship Company and, as a hobby, joined an amateur theatrical group, probably, in the opinion of his daughter and biographer Juliet Colman, "because he was a little introverted in character and this brought him out a bit."

After three years and by now the master of Gregg shorthand he was promoted by the shipping company to junior accountant, the post he still held when war broke out in Europe. Colman enlisted immediately, "more to get away from the office," as he said later, "than because of the fighting spirit which I did not have."

The ankle shattered at Messines was slow to heal and in May 1915 Colman was given a medical discharge from the army along with the Mons Star and bar. He had no desire to return to totting up rows of figures in a shipping office and he hadn't the money to go to medical school and become a doctor, which was the only career that had much appeal to him at this time. But while he was mooning around, wondering what he ought to do with his life, he heard that an actress called Lena Ashwell was looking for a dark young man to play a small part in her West End production of *The Maharanee of Arakan*. With nothing better to do, Colman applied and landed the job, principally because there were hardly any other young men in London.

In any case it wasn't much of a part: all he had to do was to drift onstage as an Indian herald with his face blacked-up, waving a flag and tooting a horn. He wasn't actually entrusted with any lines. Fortunately, however, Lena Ashwell rather took to him and introduced him to Gladys Cooper who gave him a somewhat larger role in *The Misleading Lady* even though she couldn't think of anything much better to say about him than that he was "very clumsy indeed". Nevertheless he seemed to flourish and very soon landed his first juvenile lead — as a young husband suffering from venereal disease in a controversial play called *Damaged Goods*. The part came his way largely because more established young actors thought that it (the part, not the pox, which many stars have triumphantly survived) might ruin them professionally. His reviews were good and by 1918 he was acting in a few modest films. In the same year he went on tour in the English provinces in the play *The Live Wire* and it was at this time that he made what appears to have been the only really grave mistake of his entire life, either professional or social. He fell in love with the leading lady, Thelma Ray, an actress of no great ability who was married to, but separated from, a wealthy Australian. In the intimate atmosphere of theatrical "digs" the affair became deeply passionate and when the tour ended and the cast returned to London, Colman and Thelma Ray set up home together.

Whether they would have stayed together if they had both been single is open to doubt. Juliet (Colman's daughter by his second marriage) believes the affair would have cooled off fairly quickly had it not been for the existence of the Australian husband who, learning of his wife's infidelity, sued for divorce, citing Colman as co-respondent. To a man of Colman's correct and honourable nature there was only one thing to be done. As soon as the divorce was through he married the lady, an action akin in gallantry to crawling backwards from a battle rather than risk being found dead with his back to the enemy. It was also, as it turned out, considerably more foolhardy.

The marriage took place on September 18th, 1920 in the registrar's office in Hanover Square. Colman was twenty-nine and Thelma Ray was thirty and almost immediately they were separated. The post-war depression was causing a general slump in Britain. There was little work in the theatre and virtually none at all in the infant film industry so Colman, equipped with hardly more than thirty-five dollars and three clean shirt collars, sailed for New York to seek his fortune, leaving Thelma behind until he could establish himself. This, however, was not easily achieved; fortune, even in New York in those days, took a great deal of finding and he existed for a while on a boring diet of soup and rice pudding while he looked for work. Eventually he got a job in the touring production of a play called *The Dauntless Three* in which he turned up as a Turkish police chief in Act One and then reappeared, heavily disguised, as a Russian spy in Act Three. He must have been reasonably impressive because after that he won supporting roles in a number of plays and by 1922 he had enough money for Thelma to join him. That this was not exactly to be unalloyed good news only emerged later, for at the time things seemed to be going very well. Soon after Thelma's arrival, Colman appeared on Broadway in *La Tendresse* with Ruth Chatterton and was promptly spotted by Henry King, the movie director, who was looking for a leading man to play opposite Lilian Gish in his film *The White Sister*.

King offered him a screen test which Colman accepted with

reservations, pointing out in his innately honest way that one of the kindest things said about him so far by British film companies was "he does not screen well". King said: "He told me I was wasting money. He said, 'I'll be no good. You'll be disappointed.'" Undeterred, King went ahead and, by way of experiment, slicked Colman's hair down and painted a moustache on his long upper lip, to see if this would change his appearance. "Well, it did," said King. "It changed him from an Englishman to an Italian, which is what I was looking for you see, because in the picture he was going to play an Italian army officer." The screen test was shown to Lilian Gish who said, cautiously, "I'll make no comment, but most Englishmen are very stiff."

In the event she was quite right. Satisfied by the test, King signed his ersatz Italian to play the role and they all sailed for Italy where Colman grew a proper moustache — which from then on he was only rarely to discard — and turned out to be very stiff indeed.

The White Sister, based on a novel by Francis Marion Crawford, told of a young girl, heartbroken by the death of her fiancé, who decides to take the veil and then finds herself torn between love of the Church and love of a glamorous Italian officer, portrayed by Colman. The crucial scene, and the one in which initially Colman revealed the English stiffness Miss Gish had predicted, was the one in which the officer had to kidnap the girl to snatch her away from the Church. "We rehearsed," said Miss Gish, "from nine in the morning until dinner and we hadn't nearly reached it and Henry King said, 'Well, I suppose we'd better come back in the morning.' I said, 'I don't think it will do any good. You're working with an Englishman and a gentleman and he'll never be able to let go and play that scene with deep passion. I think we'll have to get some whisky.' Henry said, 'All right. I'll take him to dinner and see what we can do.' They came back and Ronnie was a little . . . well, not tight but more relaxed. Well, about two o'clock in the morning he was beginning to be utterly relaxed. He didn't quite know what he was doing but Henry, with patience, got the scene and the next day Ronnie was so contrite, so worried as to what he had said in front of me. I think the worst thing he said was 'Damn', which he would never have said if he'd been himself."

Meanwhile, as Colman found difficulty in portraying passion on the screen a great deal of it was entering, ironically enough, into his private life. His marriage to Thelma had never been particularly happy, except when they were apart, but now it was becoming decidedly violent — the violence being offered by her and received by him. "One night," said Miss Gish, "she came tearing down the hall of the hotel saying that she'd killed Ronnie and we went in and he was on the floor and we picked him up and put him on the bed and, as he came to, he said, 'Oh, I fell. I must have hit my head.'" This was the third time that he had gallantly crawled backwards from the battle because, in fact, Thelma had, in mid-quarrel, hit him on the head with some blunt instrument and knocked him down. But, as ever, he was too much the gentleman to say so.

That, however, was the turning point in the marriage. They stayed together, the relationship deteriorating rapidly, for some months but when Colman was making *Romola*, his second film for Henry King, there was another and more public punch-up. While the Colmans were watching an opera from a box at the theatre in Rome, Thelma, no doubt for some reason that seemed good to her at the time, gave him a fierce backhanded slap across the face. Colman promptly got up and walked out of the theatre and also his marriage. He never lived with Thelma again, though it took him several years to get rid of her.

But, as recompense perhaps for the marital disaster, Colman's career began to thrive. *The White Sister* was enthusiastically received both by the public and the critics and, inevitably I suppose, considering the role he had played, Colman was greeted as "the new Valentino", a label that might easily have destroyed him if he had continued to play dashing Latins. But in fact while he was filming *Romola* with William Powell and, once again, Lilian Gish, he was offered a long term contract by Samuel Goldwyn, who had recently set up his own company in Hollywood, and he accepted.

Colman arrived to take up what was to be permanent residence in Hollywood in 1924 when he was already close to thirty-three and after a career that was exceptional only for *The White Sister*. But the films he made between that and *Romola* — *Twenty Dollars a Week* and *Tarnish*, in both of which he had good supporting roles — turned out well and the release of *Romola* in December of 1924 established him as a highly popular romantic lead. It was the moustache and the dark good looks that won him in the beginning the ardent female following that he was never really to lose, but he was also helped considerably by the fact that Goldwyn cast him in a couple of thoroughgoing tear-jerkers — *The Dark Angel* in which, opposite the Hungarian actress Vilma Banky, he played a soldier blinded in the war who selflessly decides not to return to his fiancée and then *Stella Dallas*, wherein by way of a change of pace, he appeared as the cad who marries beneath him and then deserts his wife.

Lubitsch's silent version of *Lady Windermere's Fan* — Oscar Wilde without Wilde, or at least without Wilde's epigrams — was another change of pace and a surprising success and then *Beau Geste* showed Colman in the kind of gentleman-adventurer roles which perhaps suited him best of all.

While all this was going on and Colman was heading towards his place as the most popular male star in Hollywood, a position to which he was first voted in 1927 and which he held several times afterwards, Thelma kept turning up in Hollywood like the bad fairy at the christening party, uninvited, unwelcome and doing her best to spread mischief. The only way to get rid of her was to pay her off and this Colman did at least twice in the mid-twenties. Nevertheless, so discreet and correct was he in his private life that no matter how hard Thelma tried to create tempestuous public scenes she was never able to damage him by causing scandal.

Indeed most people had no idea that he had a wife at all and those who did knew only of an unhappy marriage that was best not talked about. May McAvoy, who starred with him in *Tarnish*, said: "I never knew anybody to have more beautiful manners than he had and who always did the right thing at the right time. It would never have occurred to me to ask him anything personal. Although he was kind and gentle, very friendly and sweet, there was a little wall built around him and you never got beyond that."

Many years later Milton Merlin, who wrote Colman's popular radio and television series, *The Halls of Ivy*, told me: "He created a character called Ronald Colman and sustained it throughout his life, privately and publicly, and I don't know of any other actor who has done that. The greatest role he played was that of Ronald Colman and what an ordeal it must have been and how impeccable and immaculate he was in doing it." This, of course, tends to imply that beneath the Ronald Colman who appeared on the screen there was merely a succession of ever-smaller but otherwise identical Ronald Colmans, like a nest of Russian dolls, but this is to do him less than justice. If the off-screen Colman did indeed appear to differ little from the cinema idol it was because the private man, like the public figure, never allowed himself to show emotions other than those that could be expressed by the raising of an eyebrow, the twitch of a lip or a gesture of the hand. His deeper passions, for art, music, literature and, from time to time, for women, he kept to himself.

Much of this reticence was probably to be expected in an Englishman of his class and time but a good deal of it was the aftermath of his bitter experience with Thelma. From the time of his arrival in Hollywood his private life was remarkably discreet so as not to provide ammunition that could be used against him by his wife's lawyers or to provoke Thelma herself into public exhibitions of outrage and scorned fury. When he did entertain girl friends he did so at his home in the Hollywood hills and was careful never to be seen alone with a woman in public. So cannily did he conduct his amorous affairs that the identity of most of his girl friends still remains a secret. The only woman, apart from his second wife Benita Hume, to whom he is known to have had a deep attachment is Mary Astor. Bessie Love introduced him to her and for a while, this being when he was finally disentangled from Thelma, he wanted to marry her. But even this created very little stir in Hollywood, perhaps, in view of the fact that so many people had been involved with Mary Astor because nobody took it very seriously.

Colman's closest friends were William Powell and Warner Baxter and they became known as "the three Musketeers" with Richard Barthelmass as their D'Artagnan. Clive Brook and Tim McCoy, the cowboy star, were others in his small and select circle of acquaintances. Together, again usually at Colman's house, they would play tennis and a little poker, do a spot of social drinking and entertain their wives or girl friends according to taste or marital status. This kind of unspectacular social life, together with the mystery or confusion surrounding his marriage, only added to Colman's romantic allure during the late 1920s, lending him a Sphinx-like quality that gave him equal popularity with the more ebullient John Gilbert among the women in the cinema audiences.

But when talking pictures were introduced he rapidly outstripped Gilbert and indeed everybody else. Anyone could have a clean profile and a cute moustache — and in fact most actors did at that time — but nobody else had a voice quite like Ronald Colman. In 1929, when he made his first sound picture, *Bulldog Drummond*, Colman was thirty-eight, knocking on a bit for a matinée idol and decidedly late to be moving into what was, in effect, an entirely new medium. But he made the transition from silent films more easily and more triumphantly than anyone else because women who had hitherto swooned over him simply because he looked gorgeous sideways (and especially when seen from the left) were now smitten afresh by that rich, gentle and beautifully mellifluous voice.

Bulldog Drummond won him critical acclaim, an even wider audience than before and his first Academy Award nomination and established him securely as the biggest heart throb, to borrow a useful word from the fan magazines, in the cinema. The following year, playing a debonair jewel thief in *Condemned* he was nominated again and in rapid succession he then starred in *Raffles* (debonair safecracker), *The Devil to Pay* (debonair son of an English peer), and *The Unholy Garden* (debonair English crook).

By now, however, his relations with Samuel Goldwyn were distinctly cool. Fay Wray, his co-star in *The Unholy Garden* said it was common knowledge in the studio that the two men weren't even speaking to each other. In any event they were hardly compatible: Colman was the shy, dignified and introverted Englishman, while Goldwyn was the archetypal rough diamond of Hollywood, the movie mogul who had started out as a glove salesman in Minsk and became the author, or alleged author, of such classic throwaway lines as "Gentlemen, kindly include me out," "We've all passed a lot of water since then," "I had a great idea this morning but I didn't like it" and "A producer shouldn't get ulcers; he should give them." He didn't actually succeed in giving Colman ulcers but he did manage to enrage him so much that in 1932 Goldwyn found himself being sued for two million dollars for libel.

The background to this was that Colman was playing a double role in *The Masquerader* — a dissolute English MP and his doppelganger and cousin, an honest English journalist — and Goldwyn put out a publicity statement claiming that his star "looks better for pictures when moderately dissipated than when completely fit" and implying that Colman was usually a bit tipsy on the set and acted his love scenes better in that condition. Colman promptly put in the suit for two million dollars, the kind of tidy, round sum that litigants in America are very fond of, and swept out of Goldwyn's life and studios, never to return. In a letter to his friend Al Weingand, who was later to become his business partner, Colman explained: "A dirty business, as you say, but if you knew the details you would agree it had to be done."

The affair was finally settled out of court, not necessarily amicably, but before that happened Colman had taken off with Weingand on a ten-month trip round the world. At one point they took a house in Spain where, among their guests were a woman who had once been Colman's mistress and her daughter, a nubile creature in her early twenties. Not unnaturally Weingand assumed that "the chick was for me and the mother was Ronnie's". It turned out to be quite the opposite, though the philosophical Weingand took what was offered him with due gratitude. It was also on this trip that the evidence was provided to give Thelma her divorce. A friend of Colman's in Paris, acting as a benevolent and unpaid pimp, found a couple of professional co-respondents and Colman and Weingand installed themselves with these companions in a modest hotel. Colman, who loathed the whole unsavoury business, would have nothing to do with his girl, but Weingand ensured that the capital outlay was not wasted.

The divorce came through on August 1st, 1934 and so, after fourteen wretched years, Colman was finally rid of Thelma and at the same time he entered upon the richest period of his career. Henceforth he was never again to sign a long-term contract with any studio but being so firmly established — in 1934 he was voted "the handsomest man on the screen" — he was never short of work.

He shaved off his moustache to play *Clive of India* and kept it off to portray Sidney Carton in *A Tale of Two Cities*. It was while he was making the latter film that he met his future (second) wife, the young English actress, Benita Hume. By all accounts it was a thoroughly romantic business. She had seen and been overwhelmed by Colman in a London restaurant five years previously and, though they had never been introduced, had been an ardent fan ever since. Just before she left London for Hollywood in 1934 she said in an interview in a film magazine: "There are a few stars who should never marry . . . What would become of that romantic incompleteness, that hurt, frustrated romanticism of Ronald Colman if he were happily married?" As it transpired she was to discover the answer for herself at very close quarters, although not for some time.

According to Bessie Love when Colman finally met Benita Hume he "just did a nose dive. He really didn't make much sense, he was so misty-eyed. And, of course, to see Ronnie Colman absolutely fall overboard like that for somebody was great fun." The picture thus conjured up seems slightly improbable, bearing in mind Colman's traditional reserve and besides, he was not so swept away as to do anything rash, like getting married. Indeed for more than four years he kept poor Miss Hume dangling as a sort of permanent fiancée, feeling no doubt that after the traumas with Thelma he wanted to be utterly sure that a second marriage would not also lead to disaster. David Niven, his close friend, described the situation thus: "In those days the great movie stars were supposed not to drink and never to take a puff of marijuana and, above all, not to fornicate. It was supposed to upset the fans. But a lot of subterfuge went into getting that last one going and it was rather Victorian. People had a little bit of crumpet at the lodge gate. I don't mean that Benita was a bit of crumpet, but she took a little house on the other side of the wall that went all round Colman's property and he finally fell in love with her, which she intended him to do anyway, so he rather cleverly bored a hole in the wall and put a gate there and she came and went and the old dragons who ran the gossip columns never found out until they were married."

They married in fact on September 30th, 1938, at San Ysidro, the ranch-cum-holiday resort that Colman and Al Weingand had bought together near Santa Barbara in California. The bride was then thirty-two and the groom forty-seven and the marriage only came about because Benita Hume, bored with being the perennial fiancée, had declared she was going home to England and had got as far as New Mexico before Colman, deciding not to call her bluff, sent her a telegram saying: "Come home and let's get married." By this time Colman was at the very apex of his career. He had made his two best-known and most popular films, *Lost Horizon*, in which he played Robert Conway, the man who discovered Shangri-La, and *The Prisoner of Zenda*, a picture to rank with Errol Flynn's *Robin Hood* as the finest of all romantic adventure movies. He followed these with successful and creditable performances as Francois Villon in *If I Were King* and as the painter in *The Light That Failed*.

When war broke out in Europe Colman, although already forty-eight years old, was still the biggest romantic star in Hollywood. If Clark Gable was the man most women wanted to have an affair with, Colman was the one they'd have liked to marry. Nor was their admiration, in the latter case, certainly, all that misplaced. The essence of a Colman performance on screen was a noble mixture of decency, integrity, quiet strength and courage and trustworthiness, and off-screen he appears to have exhibited very much the same characteristics. When Britain went to war, for instance, he tried to join up despite his age and, out of a sense of patriotism, dropped his plans to become an American citizen and indeed never contemplated the matter again. He was, not unnaturally, turned down for armed combat and, as an alternative, worked hard for the American Red Cross and raised funds for British war relief.

During the 1940s Colman's life and career changed direction slowly but significantly. In 1944, at the late age of fifty-three, he became a father for the first and only time.

His reaction to the news that Benita was pregnant was typical. He stood for a long time staring out of the window with his hands behind his back and then he said: "What will Hollywood say?" a remark that reflected his constant preoccupation with appearance and form. Would Hollywood laugh at him for being such an elderly father? Hollywood didn't, in fact: there's a very fair chance that with the exception of Benita, who was much given to teasing him and firmly pricking the occasional bubbles of pomposity which tended to lift his feet off the ground, nobody ever laughed at Ronald Colman. His reaction to the news that his child was a girl was also typically careful. Benita wanted to call the baby Miranda, but he vetoed the idea. "Suppose she grew up ugly," he said. "She couldn't be called Miranda if she was ugly." In the end they both compromised and called her Juliet, although Miranda would have done perfectly well because she didn't grow up ugly at all.

Meanwhile, as paternity changed his private life, other developments shifted the emphasis of his professional activities. In the 1940s he continued to average roughly one film a year but he also began to appear on radio, first as a guest on the Jack Benny Show and then, with Benita, as the star of a series of his own, *The Halls of Ivy*, in which the Colmans played a university principal and his wife.

Two of those films of the forties, *Random Harvest*, in which Colman, as an amnesiac, unknowingly marries Greer Garson twice, and *A Double Life* were among the most significant of the fifty-three pictures in which he appeared — *Random Harvest* because, as a skilful and unashamed tear-jerker it won him his third Oscar nomination and appears to have acquired perennial popularity, and *A Double Life* because this, at last, won him the Academy Award. In it he played a Shakespearian actor who became so obsessed with his role of Othello that he carried it over into his private life and finished up by murdering his mistress out of jealousy.

This was an extremely un-Colmanlike part and perhaps the most ambitious he ever attempted. At first he was reluctant to do it, thinking it beyond his range but George Cukor, the director, coaxed from him a performance of great skill and depth. "He was a very careful man," said Cukor, "very logical, very intelligent — a practical man. He was a hard worker and he was conservative but he was a very accomplished actor." More accomplished, perhaps, than he ever knew; possibly it was the caution and the conservative streak which, with the exception of *A Tale of Two Cities* and *A Double Life*, made him choose his roles from within a comparatively narrow range. It seems a pity that he was not, occasionally, more adventurous but, as Cukor said: "Maybe he didn't think he had the training for it or maybe he thought, 'Well, this is what I am and I'm superbly good at it, so I'd better not go any further.'"

When he won the Oscar at last on his fourth nomination he was, Cukor said, "thrilled. I went there for dinner a few nights later and he said, 'You see how modestly I do this?' There was a series of rooms leading into each other and at the end of the last room there was a mantelpiece and the Oscar was right there. He said, 'You see how I underplay it all?'"

The year before he made *A Double Life*, in 1947, he played the title role, that of a Boston snob, in *The Late George Apley*. By then the Colman work-style was well established. Everyone would stop for tea, properly served in china cups, in the afternoon and at six o'clock sharp Colman and his fellow stars would retire to his dressing-room for a drink. Contrary to the publicity put out in the early 1930s by Samuel Goldwyn, Colman was not a heavy drinker, but he did like a whisky at six o'clock.

By this time, too, Colman's particular vanity was well known; he insisted on being photographed from the left and he was, according to Joseph L. Mankiewicz, the director of *The Late George Apley*, the "most consummate camera-hog I've ever worked with. It drove his co-star, Edna Best, mad. One day she exploded and said, 'Damn it, Ronnie, I wish you'd look at me when you talk to me.' If you had a two-shot Ronnie would never look directly at Edna, except for the most fleeting seconds as if to acknowledge that she was there and he somehow made the two-shot into a close-up of himself."

Colman indignantly denied these allegations of camera-hogging and ignoring his co-star, but one day Edna Best proved her point. As the two of them were walking down the aisle of the church in the film's wedding scene, playing the mother and father of the bride, Miss Best produced from behind her back a full black beard which she then put on. "So help me," said Mankiewicz, "Ronnie Colman walking down the aisle of that church, talking to Edna Best, never saw the beard. So when I said 'Cut,' I also said, 'Edna, you need a shave rather badly.' And Ronnie looked at her and said, 'Oh my God, where did that come from?' and she said, 'You sonofabitch, I've told you you don't look at me and that proved it.'"

As he grew older Colman's vanity appears to have become more marked. Barbara Merlin who, with her husband Milton, wrote the scripts for *The Halls of Ivy* both on radio and later when, in 1954, the show transferred to television, said: "He was a very complex man with an enormous ego which was totally under control but he was the star and that was made very plain when we moved to television. In the radio series it had been 'Mr and Mrs Ronald Colman in *The Halls of Ivy* but when it came to TV he said, 'Oh no, ducks, I don't want you to use "Mrs Ronald Colman" I want you to appear as Benita Hume.' And she asked why and he said, 'In case you don't work out.' And then he had no compunction at all about taking lines away from her. We started writing a lot of good routines for her in the TV series and he would say, 'Oh no, ducks, that's much too good for you. I'll have that,' and right in front of everybody he'd say, 'No, I like that joke. I'll take that, darling, that's not yours.' At one point, too, Benita went to Milton and said, 'Please don't praise me so much because it's not making life any easier for me.' I mean, Ronnie was the star and he was a little bit jealous of her professionally." Barbara Merlin also remembers another time when they were watching the programme and "there was a gorgeous close-up of him on the screen and I turned to him and said, 'Oh, Ronnie, my God, that's beautiful — you don't look more than thirty-nine.' And he said, 'I should hope not, my dear girl,' and at that point he was sixty-four or something."

But along with the vanity went the shyness of a man who hated to appear in public and did so as little as possible and the professionalism of an actor who had decided, rightly or wrongly, precisely what he could do and could not do.

Milton Merlin said: "I've never known anybody in my life who had such a keen awareness of his limitations as an actor and that,

I believe, was the reason he was so successful. He rejected material not because he didn't like it but because he didn't think he could fill the role. Now to me this was more important than the vanity."

By the 1950s Colman's film career was virtually over. In 1950 he played his last starring role in the cinema in *Champagne for Caesar*, an amusing but not entirely satisfactory send-up of TV quiz shows, and after that he made guest appearances in *Around the World in 80 Days* and *The Story of Mankind*. He was, in fact, in semi-retirement, living on his ranch at San Ysidro and attending to his business interests. He had shrewd financial acumen and invested his money wisely in property and in a small TV station at Santa Barbara whose board meetings he would attend enthusiastically.

Al Weingand, one of his fellow-directors, said: "The law was then that aliens could be directors and investors in television but they had no vote; they could never control the policies. Well, we'd have directors' meetings and people would introduce motions on important matters and we'd all vote and Ronnie would vote too and everybody except him knew that his vote wasn't valid. But nobody had the heart to say, 'Look, there's no point in your voting' because he loved coming to the meetings and participating and I think until the time of his death he never knew that his votes hadn't counted."

In the last two or three years of his life when he suffered a good deal from a chest complaint, Colman kept very much to himself, leading a quiet family life on the ranch and spending much of his time painting.

There was, however, one occasion when he attended, by invitation, a big golf tournament at a Californian hotel. After he'd checked in he ventured outside and, along with the other attendant celebrities, walked out and about in the crowds. But a little while later he returned to his room and stayed there for the rest of the day because the spectators had swiftly recognised the other stars, the Crosbys, the Sinatras, the Waynes or whoever, but nobody had recognised Ronald Colman and he was deeply hurt. On those occasions when he did reluctantly agree to mix with the populace he wanted people to know he was there and he wanted them to be sure who he was. That, too, perhaps was vanity, but it was the understandable vanity of a man who had made himself a star and who had sustained himself as a star for longer than almost anybody else. It was the vanity of a man who knew his own worth. When he made his brief appearance in *Around the World in 80 Days* he was offered either a fee or a Cadillac and he chose the car. Some time later a woman accosted him at a party and said, "Is that right — you got a Cadillac for half a day's work?" and Colman replied: "Not at all, madam. It was for the work of a lifetime."

Unlike that of almost every other star, Ronald Colman's career was a long, unbroken success story. Such setbacks as he had were few and unimportant and even the rarity of his screen appearances in the last few years was more a matter of his choice than of anything else. He amassed considerable wealth, remained his own man and established his own lifestyle. Before he moved away from Hollywood to his ranch he had lived, so far as such a thing is possible in Southern California, the life of a well-to-do English country gentleman in a twenty-four-roomed house in its own grounds, attended by eleven servants. Till the end of his life he remained steadfastly and unmistakably British and if he regretted anything at all it was, perhaps, that in the 1950s when Britain was handing out titles to actors on a fairly lavish scale, nobody ever offered one to him. Milton Merlin said: "Benita once told Barbara that he was disappointed that he hadn't been given a knighthood. I think Ronnie expected to be knighted and he wasn't and I think that was a deep disappointment."

Ronald Colman died on May 19th, 1958, aged sixty-seven, and was buried by the sea about ten minutes drive from his home at Santa Barbara. Benita, who later married George Sanders, lived on until 1967. Al Weingand said of Colman: "He was a much more human man than any but his closest friends ever knew. He was very warm, very generous, very gracious." Juliet Colman remembers him as "a very dear father" for whom it must have been "rather a struggle to be in his sixties and trying to keep up with this young person, me, with a piercing Californian accent which I think he must have hated. I remember David Niven's children had the most beautiful English accents and I used to say, 'Do you want me to talk like them?' and imitate their English accent and my father said, 'Yes, but that's talking normally. That's how I want you to speak.'"

Shortly before Colman's death a persistent rumour began to spread that he felt embittered because, on account of his age, he was no longer a matinée idol. To a journalist, unwise enough to bring this rumour to Mrs Colman, Benita replied coolly: "It is perfectly apparent to him, if not to you, that people are born, they live, they grow old and they die and Mr Colman has not cornered the market in this respect . . . Nor are his diverse interests in life contingent upon remaining thirty-five for all eternity. Ronald Colman is not and never will be the less magical for being mortal."

How good an actor Colman was or might have been it's now impossible to say but he was, without doubt, magical — incomparably the best, most glamorous and most popular movie star Britain ever gave to the cinema. David Niven said: "He was cautious, yes, in the selection of his roles but he was the most professional actor I've ever worked with and, although I know it's old-fashioned to say so these days, he was a great gentleman, totally to be relied upon.

"He really was at the big house and everybody else was at the lodge gates."

Jean Harlow

The platinum blonde "bombshell".

Harlean Carpentier in the years before she became Jean Harlow.

With Mama Jean.

above : *Mama Jean, Harlow and third husband Hal Rossen, the cameraman. Behind them Harlow's stepfather Marino Bello — "the Italian gangster".*

opposite : *Paul Bern, Harlow's second husband, who shot himself soon after the wedding.*

Harlow and William Powell, probably the only man she ever really loved. But note the similarity between him, Bern, Rossen and even Marino Bello.

The story of Jean Harlow is not simply the story of a girl who, exuding sex, became the prototype for all "blonde bombshells" in talking pictures. It's also a minor tragedy and, even more than that, a kind of mystery story. Harlow died in 1937 at the age of twenty-six after a brief career, spent mostly at MGM, during which she made thirty films, seven of them merely as an extra and few of them amounting to much more than the sort of run of the mill "fix" that Hollywood peddled every week at a time when the cinema was the opiate of the people. Viewed in the context of the far longer careers of such contemporaries as Crawford and Bette Davis, or Garbo and Barbara Stanwyck, Harlow was here and gone almost before she had time to attract anybody's attention. Nevertheless, such was the impact of her unique brand of bold, good-humoured sex appeal, she is still regarded as one of the greatest stars of what was undoubtedly Hollywood's greatest period.

But what makes her particularly arresting is the mystery which, forty years later, still surrounds her life and her death. What was her connection with such unsavoury characters as Bugsy Siegel, a notorious gangster, bootlegger and heroin pusher? Why did she marry a man who was twice her age and widely known to be impotent? And why, two months after the wedding, did her husband kill himself? Where was Harlow on the night he died? How do you explain the paradox of a professional sexpot who, on screen, never wore underwear, dyed her pubic hair platinum and rubbed her nipples with ice to make them stare unwinkingly at the camera, and the off-screen personality who, as everyone seems to agree, was not particularly interested in sex, lived most of her life with her mother and enjoyed childlike pursuits such as visiting funfairs and playing musical chairs? What was the truth of her love affair with William Powell? Why did she die so young? Did she, as some people have even suggested, want to die?

Questions like those, many of them unanswered and by now probably unanswerable, have led to at least one scurrilous biography of her and a host of rumours which, clinging to the poor girl's reputation like bindweed, are earnestly spread by people who will tell you, with simple candour and quite undeterred by their ignorance of the facts, that she was little better than a hooker, a sexual raver who would prowl the streets and seedy hotels picking up taxi drivers and bellhops and dragging them, protesting (feebly no doubt lest she should change her mind) into her bed.

Such is the peculiarly tacky quality of manure — whether actual or verbal — that when thrown it tends to stick and when stuck it tends to harden and becomes exceedingly difficult to scrape away. Thus when my researchers and I went to Hollywood to cast a stern investigative eye on the life and times of Jean Harlow we expected to return with a tale of wild lust, a scandal of monstrous proportions. But the facts, as we discovered them, were very different though not, I think, in their own way less interesting.

To begin, however, at the beginning. Jean Harlow was born Harlean Carpentier on March 3rd, 1911, in Kansas City, Missouri, the daughter of Montclair Carpentier, a local dentist, and his wife Jean, née Harlow.

Her mother, a pretty, plumpish blonde whose head appears to have been stuffed with a positive candyfloss of romantic dreams, concocted the bizarre name Harlean by gluing together various parts of her own two names. Not surprisingly, Harlean never really caught on and for several years the infant Carpentier was under the firm impression that she had actually been christened "Baby".

The dominant figure throughout her childhood was her maternal grandfather, one S. D. Harlow, a wealthy Kansas City property dealer, at whose insistence Harlean was sent to the right kind of school "to meet the right kind of little girl". When their daughter was nine, the Carpentiers separated, quite amicably, and were later divorced and thereafter Harlean had little further contact with her father, a fact that may have had much to do with two of her three unsuccessful marriages. After the separation mother and daughter moved in with Grandfather Harlow and lived with him for two years, at which point Mrs Carpentier — or Mama Jean as she came to be known in Hollywood — could no longer tolerate the old man's autocratic manner and ran off to Chicago where she met, fell in love with and secretly married Marino Bello, a dark, sophisticated Italian who lived by his wits and who was summed up swiftly but not, as it turned out, inaccurately by the irate S. D. Harlow as "an Italian gangster". This was, as a matter of fact, one of the kinder descriptions applied to Bello; most of the people I met who had known him being inclined to dismiss him as "a pimp".

However, with no more blessing from her father than a grunt of rage, Mama Jean left little Harlean in her parental home and took off with Bello, who installed her in various second-rate hotels and apartments while he earned a living of sorts as a food salesman or waiter or the vendor of dubious stocks and shares.

A few years later mother and daughter were briefly reunited in Los Angeles where Harlean was sent to the Hollywood School for Girls but pretty soon Grandfather Harlow, who still wielded considerable influence on account of the fact that his money had bailed the Bellos out of trouble from time to time, had the child taken away from there and sent to a finishing school in Illinois.

Here the sixteen-year-old Harlean, unhappy and homesick, met Charles McGrew at a Saturday afternoon dance. He was twenty-one and the son of wealthy Chicago business people. Harlean wrote to her family saying she liked him better than anyone she had ever met but would give him up if she were allowed to leave school and return home. The family decided to call her bluff and discovered she wasn't bluffing at all. One Sunday in March 1927, she and McGrew eloped and were married. Now both families stepped in, the couple were promptly separated and Harlean ended up in Hollywood once more with Mama Jean and Bello.

As a breadwinner for his wife and stepdaughter Bello proved, to say the least, inadequate and not particularly enthusiastic and so, inspired probably by wispy dreams of discovery and stardom, Mama Jean found work as an extra in silent films and took young Harlean with her. In the event, of course, it was Harlean who was discovered, initially by Hal Roach, the head of a comedy factory which turned out a succession of Harold Lloyd and Laurel and Hardy two-reelers.

An agent brought her to his studio and, as Roach recalls, "I took a good look at her and I knew that she was photogenic and there was no question that she had a good body and at twelve thirty when they left the office I had a seven-year contract with Jean Harlow." By this time she had already adopted her mother's maiden name for professional purposes.

The following week Jean Harlow started work at the Roach studios and, significantly, Mama Jean and Bello came with her, thus establishing a close liaison that was never to be broken. Later, after her divorce from Charles McGrew in 1931, Harlow was twice married again and set up homes of her own but not for long. In both cases she was back living with her mother within a matter of months.

Harlow's first role for Hal Roach was a bit part in the Laurel and Hardy comedy, *Double Whoopee*, in which Laurel slams the door as she steps out of a taxi and rips her skirt off. Before the scene was shot she was asked whether she was "under-dressed" — in other words, was she wearing flesh-coloured tights beneath her underwear. She wasn't, in fact, but being unfamiliar with this technical language and assuming merely that they wanted to be quite sure she had her knickers on, she said she was. The result, when the skirt was pulled off, was that she was revealed to be practically naked and the excitement was such that chaos ensued on the set. Whether news of this filtered back to Kansas City and annoyed old S. D. Harlow, or whether he merely disapproved of movies in general, she appeared in Roach's office a few days later and said that her grandfather, on whom she and her mother were still dependent for the odd handout, disliked her working in pictures and would it be all right if they tore the contract up? Roach, under the impression that she was returning to Kansas City to resume married life with McGrew, agreed.

This was in 1928 when Harlow was seventeen, and whether or not she did return temporarily to McGrew is unclear. But by 1929 she was back in Hollywood, doing the rounds as an extra again with her mother. Perhaps her grandfather's disapproval had been overcome or perhaps she simply defied him. In any event, later that year she had a small part as a salesgirl in *Saturday Night Kid* and was then signed to a contract by Howard Hughes, who had just made a silent picture called *Hell's Angels* about the Royal Flying Corps. The stars were Ben Lyon and James Hall, as a couple of Oxford undergraduates who joined up in the First World War and Greta Nissen, a Norwegian actress, as the middle-class English girl who loved them both. In a silent movie the fact that Miss Nissen had an accent that was practically incomprehensible was neither here nor there but just as the film was nearing completion talkies were introduced and Hughes decided to reshoot the whole thing with sound. Now, of course, he had problems. Lyon and Hall were not all that convincing as Oxford undergraduates but Greta Nissen, as a middle-class English girl, would be, to put it mildly, unbelievable. So, for two or three months, he sought around unsuccessfully for a replacement and it was at this stage that Ben Lyon, wandering by chance on to another set at the *Hell's Angels* studio, spotted an extra named Jean Harlow. He said: "I've never seen anything like it in my life" — this, incidentally, from a man who later on was to discover Marilyn Monroe — "she had silver hair, a fabulous figure and very tight-fitting black satin gown which showed every curve in her body. I went over to her and said, 'How would you like to play the lead in *Hell's Angels*?'"

She responded in the wary manner of every beautiful extra

believing herself threatened (or lured, according to inclination) by the casting couch. She said: "What do I have to do?" Lyon, an honourable man, explained that she merely had to meet Howard Hughes, which she did, and that night, despite Hughes' scepticism, she made a test with Ben Lyon and the next morning signed a three-year contract.

The film opened in June 1930 at Graumann's Chinese Theatre on Hollywood Boulevard and though Harlow's English accent was no closer to London than Kansas City she did at least have the advantage of sounding considerably less Norwegian than Greta Nissen. More to the point, despite the inadequacy of her acting, her obvious appeal, allied to her role as a faithless girl dallying with both leading men, brought her immediate attention as the screen's latest sex object. As one critic perceptively remarked: "She probably always will have to play these kind of roles but nobody ever starved possessing what she's got." The reviews of her actual performance were less kind but even so it was quite clear that she was already on her way.

One of the more persistent rumours about Harlow concerns this period of her life, for it is said that she had some kind of affair with Howard Hughes, who was himself still in his twenties at the time. Blanche Williams, who was Harlow's maid then and indeed until her death, thinks it's unlikely that there was anything between them at all and the evidence seems to support that view. Hughes wasn't even sufficiently interested in Harlow to find film roles for her or to help her improve her decidedly shaky knowledge of the acting craft. Instead, at a large profit to himself, he lent her out to other studios and, as Hughes cashed in on her popularity as "America's new Blonde Bombshell", she appeared with Wallace Beery in *The Secret Six* at MGM; with Lew Ayres in *The Iron Man* at Universal; with James Cagney in *The Public Enemy* at Warner Bros; with Spencer Tracy in *Goldie* at Fox; with Loretta Young and Robert Williams in *Platinum Blonde* at Columbia and, again at Columbia, with Mae Clark and Walter Byron in *Three Wise Girls*, the important difference this time being that, at last, Harlow had top billing. The roles varied from gold-digger, to faithless wife, to gangster's moll and small town girl trying to make good and her reviews were not generally a great deal better than they had been for *Hell's Angels*. But who cared what the critics thought? The public had noticed her and the male section of it most certainly approved.

During the first release of *Hell's Angels* she had made a series of personal appearances during which a public image, totally at variance with her private self, was manufactured for her by sharp publicity men. Thus she was credited with providing the punch-lines in such saucy exchanges as:

"Jean, how do you like to wake up in the morning?" — "I like to wake up feeling a new man."

"Are you wearing a brassiere, Miss Harlow?" — "That sounds like a near-sighted question."

"Would you steal a husband, Miss Harlow?" — "Wouldn't that be like shoplifting in a second-hand store?" And so on.

Well, all this together with her raunchy screen persona — those plucked eyebrows painted artificially into two startled but amused half-moons, those tight-fitting dresses which suggested, quite accurately, that underneath there was only Harlow — identified her as the blonde good-natured tart from the wrong side of the tracks, the easy, sleazy lay who would give a man a nice time and send him on his way with fond memories. Professionally, the picture thus created could do her little but good but privately the received impression of Jean Harlow was a burden under which she suffered for the rest of her life. She was not, by all accounts, in any way a promiscuous girl but she was inevitably treated as such. More than once she complained to her confidante, Adela Rogers St Johns, the writer and journalist, that even her friends' husbands, mistaking the image for the reality, would make passes at her and that she grew increasingly tired of being treated "like a bitch in heat".

She also said in an interview: "Believe me, the real Jean Harlow has nothing in common with the shadow one. Sex is something which is all very well on the screen but more than a mild nuisance off it." On the other hand, if men did follow her around like randy puppies, she could hardly claim total innocence, protesting that it was nothing to do with her. She was, after all, the first actress to appear regularly in films without a brassiere or indeed any other form of underwear, and this at a time when the untrammelled bust was a startling revelation even if, as in her case, it was only suggested and not actually revealed.

She did, after all, rub her nipples with ice and she did, after all, dye her pubic hair to match the hair on her head. Admittedly, this was not done in an attempt to delude those in the privileged position of being able to compare the colour of one with the colour of the other that she was a natural platinum blonde but, more prosaically, because she nearly always wore white in her films and a tight white dress, not backed up by underwear, would reveal a distinct five o'clock shadow unless she shaved or used dye. The fact remains, however, that as far as I know, nobody ever forced her to dress that way so the virtually naked look was presumably her own idea, suggesting that somewhere in her personality there was a strong element of the tease, a desire to titillate.

And yet none of this seems to have spilled over into her private life. Blanche Williams admits that Harlow never wore a brassiere at any time but then "she didn't need one". Apart from that unusual — for the 1930s — idiosyncrasy she dressed demurely off-screen, mostly in blouse and slacks. And, again according to Blanche Williams, she showed no personal awareness of being a particularly beautiful or desirable woman. It was almost as though Harlow herself regarded Harlow the actress as an entirely different person, or as an identity she assumed in order to earn a living but one that had little to do with her. Kay Mulvey, who handled her publicity at MGM and was a close personal friend, said she looked upon the sex image as part of the job and no more than that and that, away from the studio, she was "warm, affectionate and friendly".

"I had a little beach house and she loved to come down there and spend the night or the week or whatever. I remember one morning, very, very early, she and my young son were making mud pies and she taught him to put raw eggs in them because they stuck together better." This is not a particularly exciting anecdote perhaps, but at least it indicates a kind of knowledge you would hardly expect a dedicated sexpot to possess. Again, when she was at MGM, she would often fill in the time between takes by cutting out paper dolls, another pastime that clashes oddly with the view of Harlow as an insatiable man-eater.

Her career at MGM began in 1932 when Howard Hughes, who had presumably given up any thought of finding another film for her, sold her contract. One of his stipulations was that he would have the right to use her in two pictures over the next five years but he never bothered and that, too, seems to indicate that his interest in her was no more than slight. By the time she arrived at MGM the film *Platinum Blonde*, in which she only had third billing, had established her as *the* platinum blonde and had led to the founding of the Platinum Blonde Clubs in at least a hundred American cities. Women of all ages were beginning to imitate her dress, her make-up and her speech mannerisms. As an actress she was still finding few admirers, but as a star she had definitely arrived.

As tangible evidence of this new status she had bought a Spanish-style house in West Los Angeles where, naturally, Mama Jean and Bello installed themselves in great comfort and Bello took over the handling of his stepdaughter's money, which he proceeded to spend and invest with the foolish prodigality of one who, not having earned it, suffered no pain at its loss.

Bello was, without doubt, the most baleful influence in Jean Harlow's life and she was aware of it. She detested him and referred to him curtly in public as "Bello" but she had to tolerate him because of her mother, whom she adored. Hal Roach described the two women as being more like sisters than mother and daughter but also had the strong feeling that Mama Jean was living her own life vicariously, soaking up the limelight that she wanted but that actually fell on her daughter. Kay Mulvey said: "Mama Jean worshipped her. She was terribly, terribly proud of having such a beautiful daughter and wanted the world to see her. Her whole life was 'the Baby' and they were very, very dear friends."

But at the same time Mama Jean was besotted by Bello and remained so until their divorce shortly before Jean's death and she appears to have raised no objections when her husband tried to involve her daughter with gangsters. In the early 1930s the Mafia and other crime syndicates were thought to be trying to muscle in on Hollywood and Bello wanted a part of whatever racket was going. When Bugsy Siegel arrived in town after a no doubt lucrative career with even more obnoxious people than himself, heroin-pushing for Lucky Luciano and bootlegging for Meyer Lansky, for example, and tried to set up a protection racket, Bello was keen to get a piece of the action. But all he had to distinguish him from similar would-be racketeers clamouring for Siegel's attention was his stepdaughter.

So he used her to ingratiate himself, arranging dinner dates and the like for Siegel and his associates with Jean. There is no evidence whatsoever that she slept with any of these people, or had any kind of close association with them, but to please Bello — or more specifically her mother — she was obliged to mix with them socially and it could be that degrading experience which contributed to her embarking on the second, and quite the most disastrous, of her marriages.

By July 1932 Harlow had completed the first two films of her MGM contract, *The Beast of the City*, a gangster movie with Walter Huston, and *Red Headed Woman*, in which she played a promiscuous and ambitious gold-digger opposite Chester Morris, and was embarked on her third, *Red Dust*, the first picture in which she co-starred with Clark Gable. But also that month she married Paul Bern, the right-hand man to Irving Thalberg, MGM's head of production. Why she married Bern is a question that nobody has ever been able to answer. She was twenty-one years old and he was forty-two, a physically unprepossessing little man with receding hair and a small moustache. He was known as Hollywood's "Father Confessor", the man to whom the stars, especially the women, would confide their problems. He was also widely known to be impotent and after his death he was found to be sexually underdeveloped. That he had a liking for the company of beautiful women there is no doubt but there is equally no question that he had any sort of physical relationship with them. Hal Roach recalled that, just before he married Harlow, Bern had set up another girl in a Hollywood flat and would visit her every afternoon, the procedure being that she would take off her clothes and lie on the bed and he would read poetry to her for an hour or so. Then they would both have tea and he would leave.

Harlow first met Bern when she made *The Secret Six* while on loan to MGM in 1931 and began to go out with him regularly soon after she joined the studio the following year. Why she should have chosen him when she could have had her pick of every eligible male in a community weighed down to below the Plimsoll line with eligible males is a mystery that has never been resolved.

Several theories have been put forward, none of them wholly convincing. Kay Mulvey, for instance, believed Harlow was looking for a father substitute: "Bern was a very kind, highly intelligent man. She had immense respect for him and I think it was the father image and what he represented, his knowledge and that sort of thing, that attracted her to him." Blanche Williams thinks she married for security and to advance her career. As the wife of Irving Thalberg, Norma Shearer was given first choice of the most desirable roles at MGM. It is, therefore, possible that Harlow may have argued that as the wife of Thalberg's assistant she would at least get the pick of what Shearer left. John Lee Mayhin, the scriptwriter who wrote two of Harlow's best films, *Red Dust* and *Bombshell* goes along with the father image theory: "She always searched for older men, I think because she missed her own father terribly." Mayhin, however, took a less complimentary view of Bern than most of the other people I talked to. "He was a man who loved to hear trouble," he said. "His attitude was 'Tell me about it, tell me about it — you're having trouble, tell me about it.' That's the kind of fella Paul was. He liked misery. I think he liked misery in himself.''

What can probably be regarded as the official MGM version of the Harlow-Bern romance was advanced by Howard Strickling, the head of publicity there and the man who was privy to all the studio's secrets. According to him Bern was ''a dreamer, an intellectual, gentle and cultured. He felt sorry for Jean because of her mother and Bello. He would read to her, encourage her to read and to use her brain. He built up her confidence and wooed her. He sent her little gifts and flowers, which no other man did and he introduced her to the homes of Mayer and Thalberg. She'd never been invited there before because neither man really knew her and they thought she was the kind of girl she played on screen, just a sexpot. So Bern gave her the entrée to the homes of these powerful people.'' But beyond all the social and professional benefits that Bern could confer upon her there were two other vital elements that may have persuaded her to marry him. First, she wanted to get away from her mother and Bello and secondly, at no time did Bern try to seduce her. Strickling said that sex never meant very much to her but, because of the way she looked men treated her as a ''pushover''. At this point, he believed, she had almost certainly never had an affair with another Hollywood star and her experiences with men had mostly been confined to the rough gropings of Bello's gangster friends and the scarcely more subtle approaches of young Hollywood studs whose idea of making a gentle pass was to grab whatever part of her anatomy came most conveniently to hand. Bern, by contrast, treated her like a lady, wooed her with gentle courtesy and never attempted to lay a hand on her.

The explanation of that, of course, was quite simple: he was impotent, not just psychologically impotent but incapable of having sex. But did Harlow know that? One theory is that she must have done because it was common knowledge in Hollywood. Another is that she was unaware of the fact until after the wedding. And a third, and most astonishing of all, is what one might again call the official version, once more put forward by Howard Strickling who said that Harlow was unaware of her husband's impotence until after his death — by which time they had been married for two months. Strickling claims that the day Bern's body was discovered and before making any statements to the Press, he took Harlow to one side and asked her to tell him the truth about the marriage and according to him she said she had thought it strange that Bern had never attempted to make love to her but he had told her: "That will come later. For six months we will have a wonderful, spiritual romance together." She accepted this, she said, because at that time sex was repulsive to her. Picking up on that last statement there is yet another theory that Harlow knew all along about Bern's impotence but married him nevertheless or even because of it. The most likely explanation, however, is that she made the discovery the night after the wedding, a fairly impressive ceremony attended by Thalberg, Mayer and various other Hollywood dignitaries.

Blanche Williams, who never liked Bern because she believed he was using Harlow as a front on the principle that a man with a wife as glamorous and apparently sexy as that was unlikely to be impotent, had a brief and possibly significant exchange with him on the wedding night when he came out of Harlow's bedroom and told her: "The Baby's still a virgin." Blanche said: "I knew very well she couldn't be a virgin. She'd been married before. I'm not that dumb. What I think he meant was that he'd had no sexual relations with her."

The truth of Harlow's marriage to Bern is further confused by the sordid legend that has since grown up around it. There are stories that he was so frustrated and enraged at his inability to consummate the marriage that he would beat her up and that he inflicted upon her the kidney damage that was to lead to her death five years later. There are startling tales of Harlow, bruised, bleeding and battered fleeing to the homes of friends in the middle of the night to escape the fiend she had married. But none of this seems at all likely. As Adela Rogers St Johns says: "She was a big, strong, healthy girl and he was a puny little man. Why should she let him beat her up?" Besides, Howard Strickling says that although all Hollywood wondered about the marriage the couple seemed happy enough, until, that is, the night of September 4th, 1932, two months after the wedding.

Once more there is a considerable mystery about the events leading up to that night — the night when Paul Bern, his naked body doused in Harlow's favourite perfume, shot himself to death in front of the mirror in the dressing-room of his home. And once more it's a question of trying to sort out what seems most likely to have happened from a veritable thicket of conflicting rumours.

According to one, Harlow was in the house when the suicide occurred and she discovered the body; according to another she had been away for the night and only learned of her husband's death when MGM and more specifically Howard Strickling called to deliver the news; according to a third, which cleverly mixes up both the foregoing, she had been away but returned and then, for some unexplained but undoubtedly sinister reason, drove off again at three o'clock in the morning and at high speed.

According to a fourth — a particularly wild one this — she had murdered Bern herself and only escaped prosecution thanks to an MGM cover-up; and according to a fifth, hardly less wild, Bern had actually been killed by a Mafia hitman fulfilling a contract put out by Marino Bello, who was naturally incensed at seeing the control of Harlow's money and business affairs passing into other hands than his own.

Sifting through these different stories, it seems most plausible that Bern had indeed sent Harlow away on the afternoon before his death. Marino Bello had gone fishing with Clark Gable and, according to Harlow's own account, as reported to Howard Strickling, Bern had instructed his wife to go and stay the night with Mama Jean, who hated to be alone. He may well have had an ulterior motive in this because it now seems likely that he wanted the house to himself so that he could have some kind of showdown with a mysterious woman called Dorothy Milette who, it later transpired, had once been his common law wife — though hardly in the full physical sense — and who had turned up, unexpectedly, in Los Angeles. There is no proof that Milette did visit him on the night of September 4th but there is circumstantial evidence that somebody was there because two — or in some versions three—glasses were found bearing the remains of drinks. They couldn't have been used by the servants because the servants had been given the night off. So perhaps Dorothy Milette did call on Bern and perhaps she put some kind of pressure on him, blackmail possibly, which in conjunction with the strain he must have been undergoing in trying to keep up the pretence of a normal marriage with a young and beautiful wife, whose disenchantment with sex was presumably not going to last for ever, caused him to commit suicide.

As to that nobody will ever know because three days after Bern's death Dorothy Milette drowned herself in the Sacramento River, leaving behind very little information about herself, save that she had been living for the previous ten years at the Algonquin Hotel in New York under the name of Mrs Paul Bern. And Bern had lived in New York before he went to Hollywood.

What is known, or at least what is now widely accepted, is that Bern's body was discovered in the morning by his butler and beside the body was a note, addressed to Harlow, that read: "Dearest Dear, Unfortunately this is the only way to make good the frightful wrong I have done you and to wipe out my abject humiliation. I love you. Paul." And then there was a postscript: "You understand that last night was only a comedy." The butler phoned MGM and sometime later MGM phoned the police.

Some people, among them Kay Mulvey, believed that Howard Strickling was the first studio representative to arrive at the house, that he found Harlow already there and immediately sent her away to her mother's with orders to insist that that was where she had been all the time. Blanche Williams, on the other hand, said that she and Harlow had in fact gone to Mama Jean's the previous day and had stayed there; that Harlow had spoken to Bern on the phone from there several times and that Bern had promised to join her later. Strickling's own story is that Harlow was never at her home, either on the night of the suicide or the following morning, that she had been notified of Bern's death by Norma Shearer, who had been told to call her by Irving Thalberg, and that in any case both Thalberg and Louis Mayer were at the Bern house by the time he, Strickling, arrived.

Furthermore, he said, he met Mayer wandering away from the place, muttering that it was a terrible business and holding the suicide note in his hand, under the curious impression that it was best kept from the police. It was only after much persuasion that Strickling was able to convince him to put it back where he'd found it. Without that note it is quite possible that the police would have taken a much deeper interest in Harlow's movements the previous night than they appear to have done. As it is, Strickling says that no official suspicion ever fell on her at all.

He also says that after the police were called, by MGM and from Bern's house, he went to see Harlow and asked for an explanation of the note but she claimed then, and persisted in claiming later, that she had no idea what it meant, although the most prevalent belief now is that "the frightful wrong" and "my abject humiliation" referred to his impotence and that the postscript — "last night was only a comedy" — was a reference to some final, desperate and ultimately farcical attempt by him to make love to his wife.

Certainly the despair that caused him to kill himself was most

probably brought about by his impotence, his realisation that
he had made a fool of himself by marrying the girl and the
reasonable suspicion that she was unlikely to be happy to go
without sex for the rest of her life. A divorce on some trumped-
up grounds would now seem to have been a less drastic and
more logical solution to his predicament but a man in the mood
to kill himself doesn't necessarily seek around for a logical way
out.

MGM handled the newspaper coverage of the tragedy and
handled it extraordinarily well. Any suggestion that the sex
goddess of the screen couldn't even arouse her own husband in
bed was carefully avoided and even Harlow's rapid return to
work — barely a week after Bern's death — was explained as
medical therapy, the only way to take her mind off her grief.
She was still filming *Red Dust* and the first scene she had to do
when she went back to the studio was the famous sequence in
which she is taking a bath in a rain barrel and Gable turns up to
ask what she thinks she's doing. Her original response to that in
the script was to say: "Don't you know? I'm La Flamme, the
girl that drives men mad." "When she came to that line," said
John Lee Mayhin, "she looked over to me and said, 'I don't have
to say that, do I?' and I said, 'I'm sure you don't' and the line
was cut."

Professionally, despite Bern's suicide which, without MGM's
support could have destroyed her career, Harlow continued to
thrive. *Red Dust* in which her "effortless vulgarity, humour and
slovenliness make a noteworthy characterisation" established her
as a promising comedienne. *Hold Your Man*, another comedy
with Gable, reinforced that reputation, *Bombshell*, in which she
played, ironically, a film star surrounded by a parasitic family,
provided further evidence of her increasing ability and *Dinner at
Eight* confirmed the fact that she was now an actress of impressive,
if limited, skill.

George Cukor, who directed the latter film said that she had
the trick, later shared by Marilyn Monroe, of speaking her lines
as though she didn't quite understand them and thus creating
enormous comic effect. *Dinner at Eight* also, of course, provided
one of the classic exchanges of the cinema. At the very end of the
film, Harlow, playing once again a dumb *femme fatale*, tells
Marie Dressler: "You know, I read a book today." Dressler,
naturally incredulous, does a magnificent double-take and
Harlow continues: "It says machinery is going to replace every

profession," at which Dressler, staring thoughtfully at the voluptuous, tarty, satin-gowned Harlow, replies: "Oh, my dear, that's something *you* need never worry about."

Before work on *Dinner at Eight* was completed, however, Harlow had married again. She married Hal Rosson, the cameraman who had worked with her on *Bombshell*. Once again he was considerably older than herself — thirty-eight to her twenty-two — and, remarkably he bore a close physical resemblance to Paul Bern. Once again, though, nobody seemed quite sure why she had married him. Another father image perhaps, another attempt to escape from Mama Jean and Bello with whom, inevitably, she had been living since Bern's death, a desire to lead a quiet, normal married life. Howard Strickling said: "She wanted a bulwark against Bello and Hal Rosson seemed to provide it. He was a dull guy, who had never married and loved dogs. He was flattered by her attention."

Kay Mulvey believed the marriage was an escape, an attempt to establish her own identity away from her mother; she did not believe that Harlow was ever really in love with Rosson. John Lee Mayhin, who was a close friend of Rosson, says he was "a sweet, dear, gentle man but he wasn't the type of man who knew what to do with a girl like that. I don't think he ever helped her out with her emotional life."

Whatever the reasons, Harlow married Hal Rosson in September 1933, little more than a year after Bern's suicide. The couple moved to a tiny apartment on Sunset Boulevard and she wrote a novel, a love story called *Today is Tonight* about which she once said: "It deals with the contrasting difficulties that inevitably overtake most normal couples who are in love and happen to be sharing life together . . . Sex plays only the usual part in their story. I think they are like plenty of normal, happy people I see around me." The sort of people, perhaps, whose lives she envied. MGM bought the screen rights to the book without ever intending to film it. Kay Mulvey believed that they did so to provide some kind of allowance or annuity for Mama Jean.

This generosity, however, was misplaced. Within a very short time the Rossons had left their own apartment and moved in with Mama Jean and Bello in Harlow's house in Beverley Hills and soon after that Rosson moved out, never to return. The marriage, as such, lasted only eight months but even so was the longest of all Harlow's marriages. The probability is that Rosson was simply driven away by the hostility of Mama Jean and Bello, neither of whom liked him. And Harlow herself was not sufficiently in love with him to intervene on his behalf.

The fact that here she was, the world's number one sex symbol, but totally unable to hold a husband, both confused and distressed her. Around the time of the separation from Rosson she asked John Lee Mayhin, "What's lacking in me?" To which he replied, "The right man." She was eventually to find the right man but too late to do either of them any good.

The marriage to Rosson — the last of what she once described wryly as her "three marriages of inconvenience" — was Harlow's final attempt to get away from her mother and stepfather. In the end, ironically, Bello was the one who would leave, though not voluntarily. But before that happened Harlow made her first musical, *Reckless*, a story inspired by a contemporary Broadway scandal, in which she played a musical comedy star whose neurotic husband committed suicide. The film, a melodrama, did little enough for her career since she couldn't sing much and didn't dance a lot better, but it was important to her nevertheless because it introduced her to William Powell, her co-star. Adela Rogers St Johns says that Harlow fell in love with him the moment she met him, a remark that probably owed a great deal to hindsight and Mrs St Johns' own romantic nature, but there is no doubt that the pair of them swiftly became very close indeed.

By 1935 when the love affair, which her friends believe was the only true love affair of Harlow's life, began Powell was forty-three and she was twenty-four. Physically he had much in common with Bern and Rosson, the dark hair swept back from the temples, the small, neat moustache, and, like Bern, he was an intelligent, sophisticated man.

Harlow's great friend at MGM was Clark Gable but they were simply friends; conventionally handsome men and those who on film were the male equivalents of herself, sex objects, seemed to hold no particular appeal for her and all her life she was attracted to the type epitomised by Powell, men of real or apparent dignity and culture, men of the world who were old enough, or almost, to be her father. Oddly enough, Marino Bello fell more or less into the same category, superficially at least, and perhaps she was repelled by him because she saw him as a counterfeit version, a crude caricature of the kind of father/lover she was seeking. Well, who knows? Harlow never explained her taste in men and indeed had the grace and good sense to reveal very little of her private life.

The affair with William Powell, who had previously been married to Carole Lombard, is another of the mysteries in Harlow's life. Blanche Williams says that he "loved her with a passion" and remembers that he once sent her an enormous box which, when it was opened and masses of tissue paper removed, was found to contain a handsome cheque with which to buy a fur coat. But Blanche also says that Harlow didn't quite return that passion. Jesse Lasky Junior, the son of one of Hollywood's founders, who had a platonic relationship with Harlow after the divorce from Rosson, says that their friendship ended when she "went back to William Powell", the clear implication being that there had been some sort of estrangement between them. Lasky further believes that the affair was "constantly on and off", possibly because Harlow was a volatile and restless character "at one moment talking to you on a deep level, searching her own soul, and the next charging around, wanting to go to the beach, to ride in a roller-coaster, to drive a car very fast or play a game".

Adela Rogers St Johns disagrees with Blanche and says that Harlow was more in love with Powell than he was with her and says she was present when Harlow knelt beside him one day and asked why he wouldn't marry her. His reply, according to Mrs St Johns, was that he had already been married to one "blonde bombshell" (Lombard) and was too old to take on another.

But against that there is the testimony of Howard Strickling who believes Powell and Harlow would have married, had she lived, and "this would have been her salvation", in other words that as Mrs Powell she could finally have cut the long, tough cord that tied her to her mother. And Kay Mulvey, who probably knew her as well as anybody and who, forty years later, could still weep at the memory of her death, maintained that Powell was "the one great love of her life. There's just no doubt about that. She was very much in love with him and he was with her. They were fantastic for each other, they really were. Each had a terrific sense of humour and they were just great people together. It's very, very sad that she died before they were married." If that is so, and if, as Kay Mulvey said, they had been going together and spending weekends together on Ronald Colman's San Ysidro Ranch near Santa Barbara for two years before Harlow's death, why did they not marry sooner? The answer that she suggested, and it's a plausible one, is that "Jean wanted to be awfully sure not to make another mistake and I think Bill thought the same way. Also they were both working a lot and they were waiting for a time when their careers could let them be together for a while."

Powell himself, like Harlow, never talked publicly of the affair but, all things considered and bearing in mind the testimony of Blanche Williams that he had shown her the house he had had built for Harlow, the probability is that they would have married and that, as Howard Strickling said, the marriage would have been her salvation.

Meanwhile, as the relationship with Powell progressed, so did Harlow's career. In 1935 she vied, successfully, with Rosalind Russell for the favours of Clark Gable in *China Seas* and in 1936 she played a fisherman's daughter in love with Spencer Tracy in *Riffraff*, lost Clark Gable to Myrna Loy in *Wife vs Secretary*, won, lost and re-won Franchot Tone, the First World War pilot, in *Suzy* and lost William Powell (again to Myrna Loy) only to win Spencer Tracy as a consolation prize in *Libelled Lady*. The following year she co-starred with Robert Taylor in *Personal Property*. In all these films, whether the critics liked them generally or not, her own reviews were good and by now her position as the screen's sexiest, brassiest comedienne was pretty well unchallenged.

But early in 1937 there were rumours in the gossip columns that she and William Powell had parted and she was seen in various Hollywood night spots with Donald Friede, a New York publisher who, apart from any personal interest, was hoping to bring out her novel, *Today is Tonight*. If there had been a quarrel there is one gossip writer of the period who now says, privately, that it came about because, for the first time in her relationships with men, Harlow was not the dominant personality.

In her last two marriages anyway she had been the star, "the Baby", the centre of attention. But Powell was also a star, and one whose status was equal to her own, and he was not prepared to wander along in her shadow. He was the first man to treat her as a woman and not as a glamorous celebrity and she was unsure how to react. Whether or not there was any substance to this, whatever quarrel there may have been was apparently resolved because early in May 1937, it was reported that Harlow went to the studios with a cake bearing three candles and said that Powell had sent it to her to mark the third anniversary of their first date, along with a card saying, "To my three-year-old from her daddy."

In that month, May, Harlow was completing her fifteenth film in five years at MGM, *Saratoga*, a story of love and honour and bookmakers and lost fortunes in which once again she co-starred with Clark Gable. On Saturday, May 29th, she complained of feeling ill, and after calling at the neighbouring set where William Powell was working to break the news to him, she went home and never again returned to the studio. Just over a week later, on the morning of June 7th, 1937, she died in the Good Samaritan Hospital.

What happened in the intervening eight days is unclear. She had been in bed and extremely ill with uremic poisoning, but she seems to have received no medical treatment at all. A nurse may have been called to look after her but even that is far from certain. It has been said that early in the week after she left the studio various representatives of MGM tried to visit her but were refused admission to the house by Mama Jean on the grounds that her daughter was sleeping.

What lay behind this curious behaviour was the fact that, since her divorce from Marino Bello nearly two years earlier on the grounds of his persistent adultery, Mama Jean had become a devout Christian Scientist. She did not believe in doctors, drugs or any kind of medication; she believed only in prayer and as her daughter lay dying she sought no help except from Christian Science readers. When eventually, and after much persuasion, MGM executives and Jean's friends, among them Clark Gable, were able to gain entry to the house, Harlow's condition was appalling. John Lee Mayhin said: "Clark told me that when he leant over to kiss her he could smell the urine on her breath. He said it was so shocking it was like kissing a dead person, a rotting person. He said 'It was a terrible thing to walk into . . . I hardly knew her, I hardly knew her.'"

A doctor was then summoned by Louis Mayer, overriding Mama Jean's objections, and on the Sunday night Harlow was rushed to hospital but by that time it was too late. She was given blood transfusions and placed in an oxygen tent where she died at 11.37 am the following morning. William Powell and Mama Jean were beside her bed. A writer at MGM said later: "The day the Baby died there wasn't one sound in the commissary (the studio restaurant) for three hours — not one goddamned sound."

Whether Harlow could have been saved if a doctor had been called immediately she went home ill from the studio it's difficult to say. An acute infection, starting in the gall bladder, had spread throughout her system. Her kidneys were damaged and uremic poisoning rapidly set in. But what caused the infection was another matter for scandalous conjecture. It was said that she had suffered second degree burns while sunbathing, that she had been poisoned by the bleach she used on her hair, that her kidneys had been damaged by beatings she received from Paul Bern, that she had had an abortion that went wrong, that she had been killed by excessive drinking, even that she had died of syphilis. All of these can be discounted. Her death certificate in Los Angeles Coroner's Court declares that death was caused by uremic poisoning but how she contracted it nobody knows.

There is even a theory, suggested by, among others, Anita Loos, the author of *Gentlemen Prefer Blondes*, that Harlow may have wanted to die. In her book, *Kiss Hollywood Goodbye*, Miss Loos says that Powell had "walked out on Jean because he really wanted a 'little Miss Nobody'" and adds: "After Bill's rejection, Jean seemed to lose interest in everything and when stricken she refused to put up a fight. It was as if Jean took advantage of a minor ailment to escape from life." But as a theory this doesn't bear very close scrutiny. Whatever the origin of Harlow's ailment it could hardly be called minor. And William Powell's behaviour after her death seems conclusively to refute any suggestion that the love affair between them was over and that he had rejected her.

Harlow was buried, three days after her death, at Forest Lawn, the garish and theatrical graveyard of the stars. The funeral was arranged by Mama Jean and Powell. Two hundred people were invited and in addition more than a thousand sightseers crowded round the gates to watch the funeral cortege pass by. At nine a.m. when the service began, conducted incidentally by a Christian Science reader, a one-minute silence was observed in all the studios of Hollywood. In the chapel itself Nelson Eddy and Jeannette Macdonald sang "The Indian Love Call" and "Ah, sweet Mystery of Life", thus introducing a note of such senti-mental vulgarity (for which, presumably, Mama Jean was responsible) that Carole Lombard, who was there with Clark Gable, immediately stipulated that nothing so outlandish was to be perpetrated at her funeral. The casket was covered by 1,500 lilies of the valley and 500 gardenias, again provided by Powell and Mama Jean and it was Powell who bought the crypt, nine feet long, ten feet wide, lined with marble and costing 25,000 dollars, in which the body was interred. When the coffin was closed after the traditional lying-in-state, so beloved of Hollywood, there was a single gardenia, Harlow's favourite flower, in her hand. There are some who say it was put there by the New York publisher, Donald Friede, but Louella Parsons, the omniscient gossip columnist of the age, said that in fact it was placed there by William Powell, together with a note that said: "Goodnight, my dearest darling."

When the service was over Powell was so grief-stricken that he had to be helped by friends as he walked away and afterward he abandoned the film he had been making and went to Ronald Colman's ranch for a month to recuperate. In a column written a week after Harlow's death, Louella Parsons claimed that Harlow had loved Powell more than he loved her and revealed — safely enough since the subject of the piece was no longer around to deny it — that though Harlow had said to her, "I never knew the meaning of the word love until I met Bill," Harlow herself had never really believed they would marry because Powell was shy of matrimony. But that, too, conflicts with the opinions of the friends, like Kay Mulvey, who knew both parties. As a final postscript to the affair and as an indication perhaps of the depth of feeling that had existed between Powell and Harlow, Howard Strickling said that when, a little later, he was negotiating a new contract with MGM, Powell made it a condition that the studio should pay a certain amount of money to Mama Jean.

The impact of Harlow's death was astonishing. As the English critic C. A. Lejeune wrote: "Jean Harlow died on Monday. From the time of her death until the funeral on Thursday one national paper alone, I reckon, gave her fourteen columns. That was in England where Miss Harlow had never been seen in person . . . in England where sentiment and sensation are traditionally abhorrent. Princes could scarcely have collected more space . . . It was a bizarre fact but radically sound journalism. It reflected the wishes of a multitude of readers."

As an actress Harlow died too young to have achieved very much. She was improving all the time but her range was modest and she was far better in comedy than drama. Her great accomplishment was to make sex funny and to purvey it with an appeal that transcended all social classes. She once said: "I know I'm not a great actress and except for the early part of my life in Hollywood I never believed I was. But I happen to have something that the public likes." What she had, of course, was that lusty, healthy sexuality that made men think of her as the kind of girl who would be a glorious companion in bed but also a loyal and honest friend.

As a person she seems to have been one of nature's victims: the victim of a broken home, an ambitious mother and an unscrupulous stepfather; the victim of three unhappy marriages, one of which could have destroyed her; the victim of a love affair with William Powell which, one way or the other, ended tragically for both of them. In a sense perhaps, she was the victim of her own body because she looked what she simply was not — she was a child who happened to look like a vamp. Everyone, to the end of her life, referred to her as "the Baby", not just because she was very young but because she was childlike and simple in the best sense of that word. She was also, after her death, and indeed until this day, the victim of lies and rumours and innuendos that depict her as a tart and a harlot and she was neither of those things.

William Powell, at the time of writing, is well into his eighties, living in retirement in Palm Springs and, wisely no doubt, holding his peace. Marino Bello died, after being involved in sundry nefarious schemes with Bugsy Siegel, in 1953. Mama Jean died five years later. Jean Harlow, who herself had died so many years earlier leaving very little money and a lot of debts, thanks to the activities of her mother and her stepfather, lives on in that curious approximation to immortality achieved only by the most notable of movie stars. Her beauty, which was never classic in any case, looks dated now but her popularity lasts and the reason for that is probably quite simple; Hollywood always seems synonymous with voluptuous sexy blondes but in fact there have only been two of any real note — Harlow and Marilyn Monroe — because none of the others have shared their special qualities of naughtiness and innocence, of worldly-wisdom and human warmth, of toughness and vulnerability and, above all, of humour.

Judy Garland

The young Garland, before the hard living began to take its toll.

The three Gumm sisters. Frances — later Judy Garland — is in the middle.

The MGM starlet and "the little girl with leather lungs".

above : With Vincent Minnelli, her second husband, and Louis B.
Mayer, who called her his "little hunchback".

opposite : With her first husband, David Rose.

above : Mark Herron became her fourth husband after her
triumphant/disastrous tour of Australia.

opposite : With her mother. Their relationship was not always so
affectionate.

A month before her death with fifth husband Mickey Deans.

When you look back on the brief but eventful career of Judy Garland the overall impression is one of waste. She had talent in abundance but she never developed it to its full potential. She was certainly a great singer but perhaps she could have been a great actress, too. Admittedly, on the evidence of what, singing apart, she actually achieved on the screen, greatness is too big a word to throw at Garland the actress but her early films did at least hint at a depth of promise that was never truly fulfilled.

Well, she blamed a lot of people for that, her mother sometimes and Louis B. Mayer and MGM frequently, but in the end it was largely her own fault. Her own frailty, her own lack of discipline, her own absence of faith in herself, her own dependence on drink and drugs kept her bouncing about like a lady on a trampoline, often touching the heights and occasionally looking down on them from above, establishing new heights of her own, but never managing to stay up there. By the time she died thirty years had passed since she appeared in *The Wizard of Oz* but to most people she was still Dorothy, middle-aged and more than slightly wrecked, but nevertheless the cherished personification of the dreams and fears and vulnerability of a teenage girl. In thirty years she had accomplished nothing to surpass the performance she gave as a girl of seventeen with caps on her teeth and her breasts strapped down to make her look younger, and with her gifts she should have done a great deal better than that.

Yet, with hindsight, it's perhaps unfair to lay the entire blame for all this profligate waste on Garland herself. She was never, in any conventional sense, permitted to be completely a child or completely a teenager. How then could she ever be expected to become a complete adult, or even as complete an adult as most of us manage, somehow, to be?

Judy Garland, or Frances Gumm to give her her proper name, or Baby Gumm as she was billed throughout her infancy, is reputed to have made her stage debut on New Year's Day, 1925, at the age of two and a half and thereafter she was, above all else, a performer. Her childhood passed in a non-stop routine of singing and dancing lessons and a series of whistle-stop tours appearing down the bill at vaudeville theatres and the like as one of the Three Gumm Sisters, the others being her older sisters, Jimmy (Virginia) and Janey. And she was barely into her teens when, in 1935, she was signed to a long-term contract by MGM.

One way and another she was deprived of her childhood by the ambitions of her mother, Ethel Gumm, a frustrated singer herself, who was the inspiration, if that's the word, behind the sisters' act and she was protected from the painful, but necessary, traumas of adolescence by MGM. If anything went wrong, well, "Never mind, Judy, the studio will fix it." And the studio did. Thus she arrived at adulthood totally unprepared to deal with the ordinary problems of everyday life, never mind the extra pressure of being a superstar. If she was a psychological mess — and there's little doubt that she was — she had never had much chance of being anything else.

Judy Garland was born Frances Ethel Gumm in Grand Rapids, Michigan, on June 10th, 1922. Her father, Frank, was the manager of the local picture house and her sisters, then aged seven and five, were already veteran troupers as a singing duet, with their mother as pianist. By the time she was three Baby Gumm was a regular part of the act and, because she was so young and so tiny and already showed signs of having a remarkable voice, swiftly became the star of the outfit. In 1926 the family moved to Hollywood spending, as Garland later recalled, "three months on the road, playing one night stands in just about every city between Grand Rapids and Los Angeles" to finance the trip.

Once established in Hollywood, Ethel Gumm enrolled the girls in a dance school, arranged frequent public appearances for them and, realising that Frances was the most talented of the three, hawked her round the film studios to audition for children's roles, although never with any success. On one occasion the child was turned down for the title role in a film called *Cinderella* on account of being "too plain", exactly the sort of experience calculated to do wonders for a young girl's self-confidence. By 1934 the family trio had ceased to be the Gumm Sisters — a dispiriting business anyway because they were often wrongly announced as the Glumm, Rumm and even Dumm Sisters — and had become instead the Garland Sisters, taking the name of a well-known theatre critic of the time. And Frances, or Baby, Gumm had been further renamed Judy after the title of the song by Hoagy Carmichael.

At that time the act was well enough known to be reviewed, favourably, by the influential show business magazine *Variety* and the *Los Angeles Herald Express*, with Judy capturing most of the attention . . . "handles ballads like a veteran . . ." ". . . the divine instinct to be herself on the stage . . ." All of which was gratifying but not much more, for this was the age of Shirley Temple, a time when potential child stars had broken out in Hollywood like chicken pox and the competition between pushy mums (some of them even pushier than Ethel Gumm) to bring their offspring to the attention of the studios was deadly. The odds against young Judy Garland being picked out of the Lilliputian horde were distinctly high but in 1935 the opportunity did come along, thanks in part to Joseph L. Mankiewicz, who was then a twenty-six-year-old screenwriter at MGM.

Mankiewicz had been taken to a concert by a mutual friend of his and the Gumms to hear the child sing. He said: "Judy was about twelve or thirteen then and she worked with her sisters. Her mother told me she wanted to bill her as 'the little girl with the leather lungs', which will give you a very quick description of her mother. But Judy's voice was something incredible even then and you knew, as you sat there, that you were in the presence of something that wasn't going to come around again for a long time. She was an ungainly, awkward little thing, but I went to MGM and said, 'Take a look at this girl.' At the time Louis Mayer was busy signing anyone with talent. His approach was very simple. He would hire anyone who looked good. It's like betting on all the horses in a race and when one of them wins you hold up the winning ticket and say, 'See, I picked it.' And that was how Louis Mayer picked his stars: he hired anyone who had any talent whatsoever.

"Anyway, he sent his secretary over to hear Judy — I don't know why that professional opinion was considered important — and she thought Judy was wonderful and Judy was signed."

There were, of course, formalities like auditions to go through and there were one or two other people plugging for her but that, in essence, is how Judy Garland's career at MGM began. Just before she signed the contract her father died of spinal meningitis. As the head of the Gumm family he had been a somewhat ineffectual man, dominated by his wife, but Judy had been very close to him and had regarded him as a staunch ally in her frequent rows with her mother. When, many years later, her daughter Liza Minnelli asked her how she felt when Frank Gumm died, Judy said: "I thought, 'Now there is nobody on my side.'"

At first it seemed as if she were quite right because there was nobody much on her side at MGM either. She attended the studio school with the likes of Mickey Rooney but there was precious little work for her to do. As Joe Mankiewicz said:

"Judy went to work for MGM at the age of thirteen and became fourteen and nothing happened except that she'd sing at MGM conventions or gatherings in the executive dining room. Deanna Durbin was also at MGM at the time and she and Judy made a short called *Every Sunday* and as a result of this Deanna Durbin was fired." (In fact, Miss Durbin was not fired. Mayer was not sure he could afford two girl singers on the payroll, even two as dissimilar as Durbin and Garland, but while he was dickering about which of them he should keep, Miss Durbin's contract ran out and she was snapped up, to his great fury, by the opposition.)

To quote Mankiewicz again: "Well, Deanna Durbin ran over to Universal and became a star with her very first film (*Three Smart Girls*) and then Mayer made a star of Judy because he'd lost the other one. He loaned her to Fox — and this is how stars are made — he loaned her to Fox to do a very inferior football picture called *Pigskin Parade* which did nothing but attract people to hear this little girl sing and Judy came back to MGM a star."

But if she was already a star to the public she was still not all that highly rated by the studio and her next, and biggest break, occurred more or less by accident. She sang a special version of "You Made Me Love You" to Clark Gable at his birthday party on the studio lot and this went down so well that she and the song were rushed into the production of *Broadway Melody of 1938*, receiving such a warm response that at last Metro began to take her seriously. She made four pictures in 1938, including *Love Finds Andy Hardy* in which she played Mickey Rooney's platonic girl friend and, in the following year, she was cast in her most memorable role of all, that of Dorothy in *The Wizard of Oz*, though even then she was faced with considerable opposition from the studio executives.

Neither Louis Mayer, who had the endearing habit of patting her on the head and calling her his "little hunchback", nor his henchmen though she was a big enough star for the part and they wanted to borrow Shirley Temple from Fox. But the role and the songs had been written for Garland and besides, Fox weren't all that keen on lending their biggest asset to their biggest competitors, so Garland, aged seventeen but disguised to look about fourteen, got the job.

When the picture was finished some MGM executives thought it was running overlong and decided to cut one of the songs.

Eventually they were persuaded to let it stay but — to demonstrate the sort of acumen that was to be found in the studio that boasted "more stars than there are in heaven" — the song these perceptive fellows wished to cut out, and probably lose for ever, was "Over the Rainbow".

The Wizard of Oz was released in 1939, became at once a classic of the cinema, won for Judy Garland a special juvenile Oscar, though God knows why they couldn't have given her a proper one, and caused MGM to realise that she was now a considerable star.

But it was at this point, with her professional problems apparently resolved, that Garland's emotional problems began to dominate her life. While making *The Wizard of Oz* she had fallen deeply in love with Artie Shaw, the bandleader. Although it seems most unlikely that Shaw took the affair at all seriously, there is little doubt that Garland did. Her mother disapproved of Artie Shaw, on the not unreasonable grounds that he was too seasoned a campaigner in amorous matters to be a suitable escort for a comparatively innocent girl of seventeen. Garland, however, was not at all deterred and continued to meet him clandestinely, using her fellow child-star, Jackie Cooper, as a "beard", he being her ostensible date for the evening on those occasions when she was actually meeting Shaw.

The relationship, friendly on his part, ardent on hers, lasted into 1940 when, to Garland's utter distress, Shaw suddenly eloped with Lana Turner.

What made this particularly painful was the fact that, according to Joe Pasternak the producer, Lana Turner was precisely the kind of woman that Judy Garland would have liked to be. Pasternak knew her throughout her years at MGM and worked with her on *Summer Stock*, her last film for the studio, and in his view, "she didn't realise how much talent she had or that she had more to offer than Lana Turner or Joan Crawford or the other clever girls around the place. She never believed that she had any strength: I mean feminine strength. She felt she was a failure in her private life; she wanted to be Lana Turner and it didn't occur to her that perhaps Lana Turner might have liked to be Judy Garland."

It was possibly because of this, because of a need to prove to herself that she was as desirable as anyone else, that she had a tendency throughout her life to chase relentlessly after the men who took her fancy. Charles Walters, the director of *Easter*

Parade and *Summer Stock*, recalls that at one time she set out to seduce a very famous star for no better reason than that, being one of those rare Hollywood creatures, a happily married man, he had shown no physical interest in her. One night, at some studio celebration, she persuaded the hapless actor into her dressing-room and, encountering Walters an hour or so later, winked, gave the thumbs-up signal and said, "Got him!" It was both the beginning and the end of the affair.

However, the immediate aftermath of the Artie Shaw romance was that on the same day that she learned of the elopement, Garland also met the man who was to become her first husband. That night she appeared on the Bob Hope radio show where the orchestra leader was one David Rose, a talented musician and a kindly man who, seeing that she was unhappy, took her out after the programme. At that time he was married to Martha Raye from whom he was not divorced until May 1941. Just over a month after the divorce, on June 28th, he and Judy Garland were married. He was thirty-one and she was nineteen and Louis Mayer was furious with her because she had not sought his permission for the marriage.

As a union it was amicable but not especially successful. Apart from music they had little enough in common and temperamentally they were opposites, she being inclined to the frenetic while he was placidly easy-going. About a year after the wedding Rose was inducted into the army and in the spring of 1943 they officially separated. A year after that they were divorced.

What effect drugs — uppers and downers — had on Garland's life and personality and behaviour at this time is difficult to establish. David Rose has said that during the period that he was with her he was not aware of her taking drugs at all. But it has been suggested that, as early as the age of thirteen, she was being prescribed pills containing Benzedrine and Phenobarbital, initially to help her diet. She always had a weight problem and at thirteen, when she joined MGM, she was distinctly chubby.

"There was a constant struggle," she said later, "between MGM and me — whether or not to eat, how much to eat, what to eat." At that time little was known about the dangers of the new, and apparently harmless, amphetamines, hence the pills she was given. The effect of the Benzedrine was to make her so wide-awake that she needed sleeping pills at night; and the sleeping pills left her so groggy in the morning that she took Benzedrine to wake her up.

Her mother, realising that this pattern was potentially disastrous, took her off the pills but, with or without parental permission, she returned to them later, if only, to begin with, to help her cope with the long working days that were common in Hollywood then.

Garland herself always blamed the studio for her drug problem. "They'd give us pep pills to keep us on our feet long after we were exhausted," she said. "Then they'd take us to the studio hospital and knock us cold with sleeping pills, Mickey Rooney sprawled out on one bed and me on another." But this would appear to be a downright lie — certainly it's denied by Mickey Rooney. "Can you imagine," he said, "a company giving any kind of barbiturates to youngsters who were making a lot of money for them? Can you picture that? It just didn't happen." And Joseph Mankiewicz, who is not instinctively an apologist for Hollywood and least of all for Louis B. Mayer, said: "I think I should make perfectly clear that one of the most idiotic myths about Hollywood is that they fed Judy Benzedrine and Dexadrine. If Louis Mayer had heard that anyone so much as offered her a glass of sherry he'd have had the man beheaded. I mean, J. Arthur Rank was a libertine compared to Mayer in terms of behaviour of that type."

So if her mother discouraged the use of pills and MGM forbade them, the likelihood is that, after the original and innocent prescription of them, Garland found the drugs for herself. Certainly by 1943, when she and Joe Mankiewicz had a love affair, one that many people consider the most important of her life, she was thoroughly hooked.

At this point her marriage to David Rose was failing fast and her career, though satisfactory enough, was merely marking time. She had appeared in a couple more Andy Hardy pictures with Mickey Rooney and in musicals like *For Me and My Gal* with George Murphy and *Thousands Cheer* with Kathryn Grayson and Gene Kelly, in which she made a guest appearance. Garland was now twenty-one but still being treated very much as a teenager by the studio. It was a difficult and perhaps restless time for her and Mankiewicz, a witty and gifted man of thirty-four who had been around Hollywood since his teens and who was later to win Academy Awards as both director and writer (*A Letter for Three Wives* and *All About Eve*, for instance) was probably the first man in her life to treat her as a fully grown-up woman.

Recalling what Garland was like at that time, he said: "Here was a girl who had been told she was ugly, who had been locked away in closets by her mother as punishment when she did something that was supposed to be wrong; a girl who had built up a tremendous sense of inferiority, believing that nobody wanted any part of her except her voice. And her mother kept drilling that into her, day after day after day. But she was an extremely bright, witty girl somewhere under all that and I think I used to bring it out.

"She was very funny, very gay, and also she had a tremendous desire to know about things. It wasn't on any so-called intellectual level; it was simply a girl who didn't know a bloody thing about what went on anywhere and asked an awful lot of questions that I was able to answer. I think essentially I was probably the first man that Judy ever felt totally wanted with as a person. I've never known anyone as hungry for affection and later on, when she fell on hard times, emotionally, the empty times of the blues and the pills, out of nowhere there'd come that call in the middle of the night. It could be from London, it could be from anywhere and it was a call for help. But at the same time there was a bottomless pit, a pit of emptiness and of not being wanted and you couldn't fill it for her. Nobody could."

Still, for a while there in 1943 there were the good times, times as Mankiewicz remembers, when "we laughed an awful lot". But also there were the pills. She was taking them, he thought, as a form of misbehaviour, to attract attention, to force people to help her. Mankiewicz, whose own wife was then in a clinic suffering from mental illness, began to worry about Garland's behaviour and habit.

"I didn't think she was mentally sick," he said, "but I was afraid that she would become so because there was no way she couldn't, considering the demands that had been put upon her, the complete obliteration of her childhood, the obliteration of love and the love/hate she'd developed for her own self. She'd been made to consider herself as nothing but a voice. I mean, even if I'd said applause is love, to Judy applause was for her vocal chords. She thought nobody really wanted her."

Mankiewicz tried to persuade her to seek psychiatric help to straighten out her emotional problems and kick the drug habit but in this he encountered the implacable opposition of her mother and Louis Mayer. "Judy's mother came to the studio to complain that I had sent her daughter to see this psychiatrist. Mayer summoned me to his office and there was a screaming fight. The mother got hysterical, Mayer got hysterical, particularly at the idea that MGM stars could be crazy. He kept asking me, how could I do this? 'This girl . . . all this girl needs is a mother's love and there's the mother. How can you deny this?' And tears were rolling down his face. He must have hated his mother. And the mother was saying, 'I know exactly what to do with her. You just lock her in a closet. What the girl needs is discipline.' And I kept saying, 'Look, the girl needs help.' Anyway, the screaming reached such a pitch that I found myself making what has become a legendary remark, I found myself looking at Louis B. Mayer and saying, 'Well obviously, L.B., this studio isn't big enough for both of us. One of us has to go.' And suddenly I realised what I'd said and looked over at Eddie Mannix, the general manager, who fell right off his chair laughing. And of course I went. I went the next week. I went to work for Fox."

After that, as Mankiewicz describes it, "explosive" meeting with Mayer both he and Garland realised that their affair was coming to an end. In a way it had to end because in those days the Hollywood studios were run like independent duchies with very little fraternisation between them and when Mankiewicz moved from the duchy of MGM to that of Fox the chances to meet became limited. By then, too, Garland had started work on *Meet Me in St Louis* and had begun to fall in love with her director, Vincent Minnelli.

Mankiewicz said: "Our relationship never broke up abruptly or in a fight. She merely started seeing more of Vincent. He was a very kind and generous man and I think Judy found him more of a support than I was because I was more inclined to tell her some unpleasant truths. Liza (Minnelli) has told me that Judy loved me and I loved Judy at that time. I can't recall any incident over which we fought. We just became sort of long-dissolved, and Minnelli was there to offer marriage. I don't think I could have married Judy. I don't think I would have wanted to because of my instinctive fears of what was going to happen to her, what her stupid and ignorant mother had done to her. Put it this way — I was not at all surprised at Judy's decline."

That decline which, in effect, had already started before she met Mankiewicz was at least arrested during the early years with Vincent Minnelli. To begin with Garland didn't want to make *Meet Me in St Louis*. She was asked to play a seventeen-year-old and she thought the time had come when she should be taking more sophisticated parts. But Mayer overrode her objections and Minnelli's quiet persuasion made her believe in the role so that the finished film was her biggest success since *The Wizard of Oz*.

Minnelli said: "You could tell her twenty things and you'd never know if you were getting through to her or not because people were messing with her and making her up and so forth, but by God everything would be in place. She wouldn't forget a thing."

He believed then and believes still that Garland had it in her to be a great actress. "The surface wasn't scratched with Judy at all. She could have been a Bernhardt or a Garbo. She had great potential." By the time *Meet Me in St Louis* was finished Garland and Minnelli were firmly in love and he informed her mother, in his gentlemanly way, that his intentions were honourable and that he planned to marry her as soon as her divorce from David Rose was final.

In fact the wedding took place on July 15th, 1945, after Minnelli had directed her for the second time in *Under the Clock* in which she co-starred with Robert Walker. The start of the marriage was certainly promising.

"She was taking a lot of pills at that time," Minnelli said, "although I didn't know about it until she told me. But when we went to New York for our honeymoon she threw all the pills in the East River and said she was through with them." For a while she was true to her word but soon after they returned to Hollywood the pattern that was repeated throughout the rest of her life began to emerge. Any difficulties at the studio, any setbacks, would cause her to reach for the happy pills. Minnelli tried frequently to break her of the habit but never with lasting success, largely because she simply lacked the self-confidence to face life without some kind of prop to lean on. "At times," he said, "she knew how good she was. At times she got jubilant but mostly she was very nervous and morbid."

As she came to depend more and more heavily on barbiturates even Mayer was converted to the idea that she needed help. Minnelli said: "He would get hold of these psychiatrists and send them up and I would wait. And they'd always come out of her room and say, 'There's nothing wrong with her, you know, she's a charming girl,' and I would say, 'Wait.' And they'd be called for again at four o'clock in the morning and they'd run away screaming."

Yet this is not to suggest that life with Judy Garland was simply a kind of long-running nightmare. As Joe Mankiewicz put it, somewhat lyrically, "There was something about her that made you instinctively smile. Seeing Judy was like smelling a freshly-cut flower or a wonderful splash of rain." And Minnelli insists, too,

234

that their marriage was a lot happier than it might sound, especially around the time when their daughter, Liza, was born in March 1946. Garland didn't work for eight months after that and for much of the time she tried hard to be a good, conventional wife and mother. But then the self-doubt and the insecurity returned and by the time she went back to the studio to start work on *The Pirate*, co-starring with Gene Kelly and directed once again by Minnelli, she was already on the verge of a nervous breakdown.

She managed to complete the film but soon afterwards, in the summer of 1947, she made an ineffectual attempt to kill herself. Minnelli believes it was merely a cry for help and to some extent help was forthcoming because MGM sent her to a sanitorium for treatment. After a few weeks she returned, apparently recovered, to begin work on *Easter Parade* with Fred Astaire. At this point, however, the psychiatrists intervened in her marriage, deciding — for reasons best known to themselves — that it would be better for Garland if Vincent Minnelli did not direct the picture. MGM agreed and he was replaced by Charles Walters. Minnelli says now, rather mildly, that he thought the whole business was "peculiar" but by then the marriage was already failing and when the filming was over Garland moved out of the marital home and into a place of her own.

Over the next couple of years her relations with MGM steadily deteriorated. She made a guest appearance in *Words and Music*, was dropped because of her behaviour and fluctuating weight from *The Barklays of Broadway*, starred with Van Johnson in *In the Good Old Summertime*, and then was dropped again from *Annie Get Your Gun*. All this was punctuated by periods of ill-health and by suspensions and threats of suspension when she was too sick or too fat or too thin to do the work assigned to her. In the spring of 1949 Garland, not yet twenty-seven years old, underwent a series of electric shock treatments and in May, having been fired from *Annie Get Your Gun* because she hadn't reported to the studio on time, even though she'd already recorded the entire score for the film, she went into hospital in Boston for eleven weeks.

When she came back, once again apparently cured, she was reunited with Vincent Minnelli and Liza and agreed to appear in *Summer Stock*. But as soon as the filming began all her problems recurred. Her behaviour was as erratic as ever and she had a bitter row with her mother, the result of which was that Ethel sold her house in Hollywood and moved to Dallas to be near her eldest daughter, Jimmy. That, virtually, was the end of any closeness between the most talented of the Gumm sisters and her mother. To what extent Ethel Gumm was truly responsible for the mess that Judy Garland became is pretty well lost now in a crossfire of accusations and counter-accusations. Garland herself laid heavy blame on her mother but then she blamed practically everyone, save herself.

Joe Mankiewicz saw Ethel as stupid and ignorant; Joe Pasternak believed her to be jealous of Judy. Against that there are those who claim that Ethel was greatly maligned, a loving and caring mother who became a scapegoat for her daughter. The truth, as in most things, probably lies somewhere in between but Ethel can hardly have been blameless. Even assuming that in everything she did she genuinely believed that she was acting in Judy's best interests she must still, at least, be guilty of having driven the child too hard, of demanding too much, of being over-ambitious on her behalf. Most people are what their parents make them and Judy Garland seems to have been no exception.

However, with *Summer Stock* finished, Garland was asked to replace the pregnant June Allyson in *Royal Wedding*. She simply failed to turn up and thus came to the end of the line. Dore Schary, who by now was the head of MGM, says that some time earlier both he and Louis Mayer had tried to persuade her to undergo a full course of treatment, had indeed assured her that the studio would be prepared to take care of her for an entire year if she would go into a clinic and make a determined effort to break herself of the drug habit. Garland refused and when the irresponsible behaviour, which by now had become only too familiar, was repeated again during the preparations for *Royal Wedding*, Schary felt the time had come to get rid of her. He said: "She complained about this, she complained about that and we had finally to make a decision. I think one of the saddest things I had to do was to tell Judy that we would no longer keep her under contract."

She reacted, he said, with anger, retorting that she could do perfectly well by herself, "and, of course, for a while she did. She did beautifully but I had a hunch she was headed down a road which was going to be rather a short one. She was heavily into drugs by that time. She was going to bed soaked with drugs and then when she got up in the morning she had to bring herself up again with more drugs. Well, you can't keep punishing yourself constantly like that."

Schary insists that MGM did their best for Garland. Vincent Minnelli is not so sure; he believes that the studio could have shown more patience with her because "she made such a terribly large amount of money for them and, when she was a star, she always came through for them."

Whatever the rights and wrongs of this argument, in September 1950, Judy Garland and MGM parted company and she set off on her own road, not always as it turned out a yellow brick road. At first she did indeed do very well. In partnership with Sid Luft, a former test pilot, producer of B movies and all-round entrepreneur, who was to become her third husband in June 1952, she went to London for a triumphant season at the Palladium and then, returning to New York, enjoyed an even greater success at the Palace Theatre. In the thirties the Palace had been New York's leading vaudeville theatre but by October 1951, it had been a cinema for fifteen years and was growing steadily shabbier. The Garland season reopened it as a live theatre and created something of a sensation. She was booked for four weeks and stayed for nineteen. After the first night one reviewer described her act as "the most fantastic one-hour show in theatre history".

So, once more, Garland had hauled herself back to the top. As a concert artist and as a guest star on other people's radio and TV shows she was in great demand. She married Sid Luft and soon afterwards, having been pregnant on her wedding day, gave birth to another daughter, Lorna. In December of 1952 she signed a deal with Warner Brothers to co-star with James Mason in a remake of *A Star is Born*.

Inevitably, however, even this minor success story was not without its setbacks. She was still on the uppers and downers and in a fit of post-natal depression after Lorna's birth she made another attempt — at least her third — to kill herself, though, as before, the wound she inflicted on her throat was only superficial. But the most traumatic event of 1952 was the death of her mother.

Ethel had returned to Hollywood when Judy left MGM but her daughter had refused to see her. They had met, briefly, some time earlier when Ethel was in hospital after an attempted suicide of her own but there had been no real rapprochement between them. At the time of her death from a heart attack Ethel was living, to say the least, modestly, on her earnings as a clerk at the Douglas aircraft factory in Los Angeles. There is little doubt that because of the love-hate relationship she had long had with her mother, Garland had neglected Ethel over the last few years, both emotionally and financially, and there equally seems little doubt that she was afflicted with considerable guilt because of that. "I didn't want her to die," she said when she flew back from New York to Hollywood to help her sisters arrange the funeral.

Meanwhile the preparations for *A Star is Born* were proceeding slowly and filming didn't actually begin until the autumn of 1953. It was the first picture Garland had made for nearly four years and predictably she was stricken by nerves on the first day of shooting.

George Cukor, the director of the film, who has worked with most of the finest actresses in the cinema, found her "enormously gifted" but quite lacking in self-confidence. He said: "I asked her about that one day. I said, 'Why? You're so accomplished, you're so good — what the hell are you worried about?' And she said, 'Well, I'm always afraid that this is the time they're going to catch me out.' She was a very complicated creature."

Her performance in *A Star is Born* made her a hot favourite for the Oscar but in the event it went to Grace Kelly for *A Country Girl*. On the night of the Awards Garland was in hospital after the birth of her son Joey, surrounded by a TV crew ready to interview her should she win. But when the name of Grace Kelly was announced the TV men wrapped up and went away without even pointing a camera at her. Hollywood never had much time for losers.

A Star is Born was supposed to be the first in a three-picture deal with Warners but the other two films were never made, and it was another seven years before she was seen on film again. In the interim her career consisted of concerts and tours, TV and cabaret at Las Vegas. Often money was very short because, when she was working away from Los Angeles, she insisted on taking her children with her, travelling first class and putting up at the best hotels. Her living expenses were frequently greater than her earnings. And during those years in the late 1950s as she toured America and Europe, enjoying another success at the Palladium and an ovation at the Metropolitan Opera House in New York, the pattern of her life continued remorselessly — quarrels and reconciliations with her husband, a suicide attempt, an overdose, a serious illness when her liver became infected, a dependence on the uppers and downers.

In 1960 she returned to the screen in *Pepe* with Dan Dailey and the following year she was nominated as best supporting actress for her role in *Judgement at Nuremberg*. This was followed by another concert tour, including an appearance at Carnegie Hall, a separation from Sid Luft, followed by a reconciliation and another separation and a return to England where she made her last two films — *A Child is Waiting*, in which her co-star was Burt Lancaster, and *I Could Go On Singing*, opposite Dirk Bogarde in which she played a famous American singer touring Europe and much afflicted by emotional problems. Very nearly type-casting.

Back to America, another reconciliation with Sid Luft and then her own TV series, two sets of thirteen one-hour shows for CBS which, like practically everything else in her life, began on a high note and plummeted.

For twenty-six programmes she earned nearly four million dollars, enough — with even a modicum of thrift — to make her comfortably off for the rest of her life. But somehow, somewhere, the money was frittered away and, in the course of the series, her potential television career was frittered away with it. She had neither the temperament nor the self-control to knuckle down to the sheer hard graft that a TV series demands. Mel Torme, her musical director on twenty-three of the twenty-six shows, says she had "a short attention span"; if the material and the guest stars appealed to her she would work, if not, she wouldn't. So for much of the time she turned up days late for rehearsals and sometimes barely rehearsed at all. As CBS grew ever more disenchanted with the ragged quality of the show it had bought, writers, producers and directors came and went with bewildering rapidity and Garland's sense of insecurity increased.

Torme, who was arbitrarily dismissed himself in the end, remembers what he calls "the dawn patrol". Garland was separated again from Sid Luft at the time and an affair she had been having with Glenn Ford had recently finished. Time after time she would wake up, unhappy and desperately lonely, at four o'clock in the morning and then, Torme says, "our phones, any one of our phones, or in fact multiple phones would ring and Judy would say, 'Quick, I need you right now. Please come over instantly.' And you'd get over and find the house wasn't burning to the ground, nor were people breaking in with crow bars. It was just that Judy needed somebody there to talk to her until the sky got light."

Eventually, when he was fired from the series — largely because Garland, dismayed by the low ratings and the angry rumbles from head office, confused movement with action and decided that what she needed was a different musical director — Torme sued her for breach of contract. But on the day he was to make his final deposition to his lawyer, he changed his mind: "I said, 'I don't think the money's collectable anyway and I think that lady's had her very last chance of many last chances. Let's leave her alone.'"

As an assessment of Garland's position and future prospects this was pretty accurate. The cinema had finished with her and so, now, had television. All that was left were the personal appearances.

Parted finally from Sid Luft she took up with an unknown young actor called Mark Herron and, accompanied by him, set off on a tour of Australia where, once again, initial triumph was swiftly followed by disaster. A brilliant success in Sydney had a calamitous aftermath in Melbourne when she turned up late and, as far as the irate and impatient audience was concerned, drunk or drugged or both.

At the end of a shambling performance she was booed off the stage and, apparently, booed all the way out of Australia. According to Herron, the crowds that turned up to see her off at the airport screamed abuse, tore up her pictures, threw things at her and advised her never to come back.

In order to recover from this distressing experience she and Herron decided to stop off for a few days in Hong Kong where almost at once they were caught in a hurricane or typhoon and Garland, feeling that even the elements had turned against her, took yet another overdose of drugs. This time the attempt at self-destruction was almost successful and for a while in hospital she was given up for dead. But, like most of the people who knew her, Herron believes she went through the motions of committing suicide without truly wanting to kill herself.

"She just wanted to ease the situation," he said. Indeed it might seem that a woman who, apparently, made repeated attempts on her own life and constantly failed could have no great conviction about it. But the reasons behind the frequent throat and wrist slashings and the overdose of pills are hard to determine. Possibly she just sought periods of oblivion in the hope that whatever problems assailed her would simply go away while she was unconscious. Possibly she was sending out silent but dramatic cries for help. Or possibly, as Joe Mankiewicz suggested, the attempted acts of suicide became eventually acts of hostility against herself. Each unsuccessful try, he said, was followed by abject, grovelling apologies for all the trouble people had been put to and "at certain points I think Judy became aware that these demands she was making, these appeals for help, could not be met by one or two or three human beings and she was tired of having to grovel in apology and angry with herself and perhaps she said, 'Well, if that's the way it is, screw it, I'll go.'

"When she was young and made some very inept attempts at cutting her wrists, that might have been a ploy to grab attention. But later on, I think, the things she did became an attack upon herself. If you know that you're demanding more than life or any human being can give you, then maybe you decide that you're the one you should turn on."

Whatever the true cause of the overdose in Hong Kong, Garland's amazing resilience pulled her through yet again and she returned to America where in November 1965, Mark Herron became her fourth husband. The marriage, however, did not last long. Herron wished to pursue his own career as an actor and Garland was taking work where she could find it — guest spots on other people's TV shows, another four-week season at the Palace, even an attempt at a film comeback when she at least turned up on the set at Fox to appear in *Valley of the Dolls* which, ironically, was based in part on her own story, one of the characters being a singer whose career is ruined by a dependence on uppers and downers. To nobody's great surprise she was unable to cope and was rapidly fired.

Now with Herron gone she found another man, Mickey Deans, a musician who was managing a fashionable discotheque in New York and together they went to London where she played a five-week season at the Talk of the Town and, as was now customary, was either superb or appalling depending on her health and psychological fitness, an ovation one night being followed by abuse the next. London, next to New York, had always been her favourite city and she and Deans decided to settle there. In fact, on March 15th, 1969, they were married at the Chelsea Registry Office and moved into a mews house in Kensington.

According to Mickey Deans this was a happy time for her. Somewhere, tucked away within her, there had always been a wistful dream of settling down to a life of wife and mother, to a domestic routine. Temperamentally she was quite unsuited for it and on the two occasions when she tried it, with Minnelli and later with Luft, she had signally failed. Perhaps all she really wanted, despite the nomadic character of her life, was roots and a base of her own, a common enough ambition, after all. Mickey Deans said: "One day Judy said to me, 'You know, what I'd most like to do is just have some property so I could stand on it and say, This is mine. I own this.' But in all her life she never was able to do that. At the end of her career there was no money, no capital had been put away for her, nothing. That's the terrible thing."

During the period in London Deans did his best to provide some sort of insurance for her, trying to establish a chain of Judy Garland Cinemas in America to bring her a regular and continuing income. Something of this kind was clearly necessary for she was a most inept business woman. One night, after a concert, he collected her fee in cash, some fifteen or twenty thousand dollars in hundred dollar bills and told her: "It's yours. Put it in a bank or a safety deposit box, whatever you want." Garland decided that the safest place for it was her sewing basket. With a bizarre concept of security she took it with her whenever she went out but on the other hand she also left it for three days in the unlocked boot of a friend's car. Her appreciation of the value of money was minimal. She would wonder anxiously whether she could afford to buy a glass that cost a few pence and, on the same day, would buy a plate for £200 and use it as an ashtray.

Against this haphazard background Deans struggled to bring a little order into her financial and business affairs but before he could make very much headway Judy Garland was dead. She died in their house in Kensington on June 21st, 1969, three months after their wedding. She was forty-seven years old.

She had gone to bed early the previous night with a sore throat and when Deans, who had also felt unwell, was awakened by a phone call in mid-morning he found her in the bathroom. She was in a coma and beyond anyone's help. Inevitably, predictably, she died of an overdose of drugs but, as a final irony, it's most unlikely that on this occasion she had had any desire to kill herself. She had recently returned from an enjoyable trip to New York, she was in good spirits and the probability is that she took the pills only to overcome the discomfort of her sore throat and to help her sleep.

Garland's body was flown back to America where the funeral was preceded by the customary lying-in-state, attended by thousands of grief-stricken and devoted admirers. Nor is that at all surprising. As a star she had long been fading but this hardly mattered because by then she had already transcended mere stardom and become already a legend, a legend that has grown even more powerful in the decade since her death.

The reason, I believe, is that Judy Garland was quite simply special. As the critic Philip Oakes once said: "She is a great artist. She is Judy. She is the very best there is." Penelope Gilliatt called her "a harrowingly good actress"; Paul Dehn described her as "an alchemist who can turn corn golden". She was all of those things and more besides. Looked at from a material point of view her life was a disaster. She failed four times at marriage, she threw away not one career but many, she earned ten million dollars and died a million dollars in debt.

Whose fault? Who knows? Mickey Deans said: "She was beat out of money all through her life, sometimes intentionally, sometimes unintentionally." Frequently she was exploited by people who, as Mickey Rooney put it, would say to her, "You're broke. Get up there and sing." Yet in all this she was not entirely the helpless victim. Time after time she would reject the people who could and would help her and cling instead to those who wished only to use her. Though granted all the gifts that anyone could wish for she was, when you see her career in retrospect, on the skids almost from the start and, in a curious way, this was part of her appeal.

Audiences all over the world loved her not just for the enormous and unquestionable wealth of her talent but for her vulnerability, her unpredictability and her bravery. She once said: "What do I do when I'm down? I put on my lipstick, see my stockings are straight and go out there and sing 'Over the Rainbow'." But the difference between her and other stars who, in similar circumstances might have done the same sort of thing, was that with Garland it didn't matter how well the lipstick was applied and how straight the stocking seams were, you could always see she was down. She was like a battle casualty with his leg in plaster and his head swathed in bandages claiming stoutly that it was only a scratch. Garland's wounds and scars were always visible and there was something about her, an innate honesty perhaps, that made it impossible for her to hide them, no matter how hard she might try.

She was a superstar who, against all the odds, managed the considerable feat of converting herself into an underdog. She was a born winner who, by perverse acts of self-destruction, became a loser. As George Orwell said: "Any life when viewed from the inside is simply a series of defeats." Judy Garland's life was no different save in one respect — that when viewed even from the outside it was a series of defeats. She was open, transparent, brilliant and doomed. She was irresistible.

Charles
Laughton

*Possibly the finest screen actor
Britain has ever produced.*

above : With his wife, Elsa Lanchester, in their Hollywood garden.

*opposite : An unusually slender Charles Laughton soon after his
arrival in America.*

Laughton during one of the reading tours that helped revive his career.

Laughton showed immense talent as a director with "The Night of the Hunter". But he was never encouraged to direct again.

Charles Laughton was a large, fat, "ugly" man as, in his moments of fear and insecurity (and he had his share of those) he himself would have been the first to admit. Indeed "ugly" was his own description of himself; nobody else applied it to him because nobody else believed it. He was also a homosexual, which except to other homosexuals and a few very close friends he would never have admitted at all. But in addition to being large, fat, "ugly" and homosexual, he was quite possibly the finest screen actor there has ever been, an actor of true greatness which, in his more arrogant moments (and he had his share of those, too) he would not only have admitted but would have been swift to point out lest the fact had momentarily escaped your attention.

In the varied opinions of his friends and relatives, Laughton was lovable, hateful, kind, cruel, insecure, vain, a genius and a monster. But above all he was a great actor. Billy Wilder, the eminent director, has no doubt whatsoever where Laughton stands in the league table of greatness. "My God," says Wilder, "who was there better than Laughton?" The question is rhetorical but he answers it anyway. "Nobody," he says. "There has never been anybody that even came close."

The larger question concerning the extent to which the ugliness, the homosexuality and the greatness were connected is more difficult to answer. Would he have been as great had he not been "ugly" and a homosexual? Paul Gregory, Laughton's friend, manager, producer and the man who rescued him from a professional decline that was not only premature but was beginning to look positively humiliating, believes the "ugliness" — or more accurately, Laughton's belief in his own ugliness — was vital.

Gregory is convinced that an obviously handsome Laughton would have been a different man, possibly a happier man but undoubtedly a less successful one; that he was impelled by a determination to prove that however grotesque he believed himself to be he still had as much talent as, and possibly more than, any other actor anybody cared to name. Laughton's own view was different. He believed that the key to his ability was his homosexuality and once told Gregory so, putting forward the theory that being a homosexual gave him a talent of a finer grain than not being a homosexual. Gregory denied this, arguing not unreasonably that it wasn't actually necessary to be homosexual to be talented, but Laughton was unconvinced.

As a homosexual Laughton was at once bold and guilt-ridden and suffered under what his friend Christopher Isherwood called "the heterosexual dictatorship", as Isherwood himself had done. It was perhaps because of this that Isherwood says of him: "He was very, very insecure." He also believes that insecurity led Laughton to worry incessantly about his work "and rightly. I mean, as an artist one should keep testing the thing again and again, hammering it to see if it rings true or not." If, then, insecurity is a vital ingredient in the composition of an artist, Laughton came to his destiny extremely well-equipped.

He was born in Scarborough on July 1st, 1899, the eldest son of Robert and Eliza Laughton who owned a small hotel, the Victoria, nearly opposite the railway station. The hotel thrived and so did the Laughtons. They had two more sons, Tom and Frank, and eventually moved from the Victoria to a much grander establishment across the road.

Because hotel keeping is a demanding business the children saw little of their parents and were mostly brought up by the staff and various nannies. The dominant personality in the household appears to have been Eliza, a somewhat matriarchal figure who had the ambition and the head for business that her husband lacked. According to Tom Laughton Eliza's name was evoked by the staff or the nannies as the ultimate deterrent if the children threatened to get out of hand: "If you don't behave we'll bring your mother to you."

Nevertheless in Tom's recollection it was a happy childhood, involving visits to theatres, of which Scarborough as a fashionable seaside resort had several, and Pierrot and Punch and Judy shows on the beach. But Charles, the homely fat boy, had other memories. Years later he told Paul Gregory how other children would jeer and throw stones at him in the street.

Eliza Laughton was a staunch Roman Catholic who brought her children to heel not by beating them but by making it clear that she was going to pray for them, a much more subtle and altogether nastier and more effective punishment. By her decision the three boys were educated first at a convent of French nuns and then at Stonyhurst, the Jesuit College, where Charles was deeply unhappy. This is not, of course, surprising because in the entire history of the world no fat boy has ever been happy at an English public school and a fat boy who was hopeless at games and interested in art, literature and wild flowers was clearly doomed to years of utter misery.

The passion for wild flowers and also for art stemmed from his Aunt Mary, his father's eldest sister, who lived in a cottage just outside Scarborough. She was an ardent collector of pictures and other works of artistic merit and a devoted gardener and she shared these enthusiasms with her nephews. From an early age Charles would insist on people accompanying him for apparently endless hikes across the countryside to look at a special kind of violet or some rare wild flower.

Anyone with that kind of sensitive nature was most unlikely to find a sympathetic audience at a school like Stonyhurst and Laughton, not surprisingly, hated the place. He arrived there as an obedient Roman Catholic and left it as, at best, an agnostic with a deep suspicion and dislike of all forms of authority. Almost immediately he was exposed to another kind of authority — the army which, though probably no sterner than an English public school, would hardly have been more palatable to him.

It was 1918 and he enlisted as a private in the Royal Huntingdon-shire Regiment, resisting all his mother's attempts to make him take a commission, on the grounds that the company was better in the ranks. Apart from the fact that he was sent to France, fought at Vimy Ridge, took part in a bayonet attack and was gassed, very little is known of Laughton's wartime experiences. He had cultivated the habit of secrecy at Stonyhurst and for ever after was inclined to keep his deepest and most painful feelings to himself.

When the war was over, he was sent to Claridges in London to be trained in the hotel business for which he had no particular taste. He spent most of his spare time and nearly all his money on cheap seats at the theatre and would talk of little else when finally he returned to Scarborough to take his rightful place, as the eldest son, in the family hotel.

He stayed there for some time, although by now he was making it quite clear that what he wanted to be was an actor and, as Tom Laughton recalls, making it equally clear that he had no gift at all for the hotel business. "He looked upon the hotel as a production, which of course it should be," said Tom. "He transformed the decor and he introduced music but he didn't like the chores. He didn't like getting up in the morning and he wouldn't do the shopping. As for the guests, he found them fascinating as a study but I don't think he was very good at looking after them." Eventually he was able to persuade even his mother that Charles Laughton, hotelier, was a non-starter and was allowed to return to London to study at the Royal Academy of Dramatic Art.

By now he was twenty-four and success attended him immediately. At RADA he won the gold medal as best actor of his year and, on leaving the Academy, had no difficulty in finding continuous employment in the professional theatre. He appeared in Gogol (*The Government Inspector*), Ibsen (*The Pillars of Society*) and Chekhov (*The Three Sisters* and *The Cherry Orchard*) and by the middle of 1927 had earned such a reputation that he was offered the title role in Arnold Bennett's *Mr Prohack*. This play assumed enormous significance in his life not simply because it introduced him as a leading man, despite the handicap of his unusual and far from handsome appearance, but because it also introduced him to Elsa Lanchester, a young actress who played the part of Prohack's secretary.

Her initial response to him was not exactly favourable. "A rehearsal is a very icy thing," she said. "You know, there's a working light hanging in the middle and everybody looks grey. He looked greyer than anybody. He was plump, well, fat really, and pale. I think I said that he reminded me of a baker's boy who has just come out of the bakery and was covered in flour." But despite this unflattering first impression she found herself attracted to him, largely because they had a mutual interest in art, antiques and the countryside. By coincidence, Elsa too had an Aunt Mary who was devoted to art and wild flowers and who, like Laughton's Aunt Mary, had also passed on her enthusiasm to her niece. In the early days of their acquaintance Elsa and Laughton would often go by train into the countryside, especially to Sussex, just to look at the flowers and the gardens.

Elsa herself was small, lively, and although attractive, by no means conventionally pretty and she was not deterred by Laughton's appearance or his own opinion of his appearance. "He was really better-looking," she said, "than a lot of good-looking people who are so good-looking you could throw up." In any case, the attraction was obviously mutual for, by the time *Mr Prohack* closed they were living together and on February 9th, 1929, prompted to some extent by Laughton's mother who, in Elsa's version anyway, had a middle-class respect for the conventions, they were married at a registry office in London.

For the first two years their marriage appeared to be happy and normal enough. But then when Charles was rehearsing the role of the murderer in the stage adaptation of C. S. Forester's *Payment Deferred*, with Elsa again in the cast, there occurred what was perhaps the single most traumatic event in both their lives.

A boy, a male prostitute, arrived at the Laughtons' flat in London insisting that Laughton had picked him up in the street and had refused to pay him. He created such a disturbance that the police were called and both the boy and Laughton were notified to appear in court.

According to his biographer, Charles Higham, Laughton immediately told Elsa what had happened. His confession was both tearful and complete. He told her that he had had several affairs with boys and young men, most of them prostitutes, and that much of their activities had taken place on the sofa in the flat. Elsa, to whom this knowledge of her husband's homosexuality was a most horrifying revelation, responded first and rather touchingly by ordering him to get rid of the sofa and secondly by being stricken with a temporary deafness that was quite obviously psychosomatic. Elsa herself says now: "I hadn't thought about homosexuality, ever, in connection with him," and doesn't recall any immediate sensation of shock. "I said: 'That's quite all right, don't think any more about it. It's all right, it's perfectly all right,' but of course a thing like that, since I didn't know, since he didn't tell me, the feeling that you've been deceived I think starts to eat in . . . it boomeranged years later." The most dramatic effect of this boomerang was her determination never to have children. "I gradually felt, I think as every woman probably feels, that the father of children should be the right father for children and . . . I gradually knew I didn't want to have children." In later years when Laughton talked dreamily and unrealistically of adopting his protégée, Maureen O'Hara, or expressed his regret at never having had a son, he would accuse Elsa of having refused to have children for selfish reasons that were nothing to do with him, but she insists that in fact her resolution was formed on the night he made his original confession.

The result of the court case that ensued from the disturbance caused by the boy prostitute was extremely fortunate for Laughton. The magistrate, a man presumably of the most amazing naivety, merely warned Laughton about his "misguided generosity" towards the boy, as though all that had taken place had simply been a gesture of philanthropy on the actor's part, and the case was dismissed. Had matters gone otherwise, had Laughton been convicted, as he might well have been, of homosexuality, his entire career could well have ended there in court. He would most probably have been ruined in England and certainly he would have had no chance of an international career. As Charles Higham said: "I very much doubt if he would ever have come to Hollywood because the attitude here was then, as it is now, enormously antihomosexual. The idea of Louis B. Mayer or Cecil B. de Mille, who abhorred and despised homosexuals more than anything else, hiring such a person would have been unthinkable." And yet, ironically, both de Mille and Mayer were to be extremely important in helping to further Laughton's international career.

Elsa Lanchester says, surprisingly perhaps, that the incident with the boy prostitute made no great initial difference to her marriage. She had been brought up in a free-thinking and socialist household in which the only doctrine was the doctrine of tolerance so that when she said: "It's all right, it's perfectly all right," she genuinely thought it was. For his part Laughton started going to an analyst, Ernest Jones, whether in the hope of purging himself of homosexual desires or merely of the guilt they instilled in him neither Elsa nor probably Laughton himself was entirely clear.

In any event, he soon lost interest in analysis. "After he'd been three times," said Elsa, "the nurse called up and said: 'Well, where's Charles Laughton? He's not here.' When I asked Charles about it he said that Ernest Jones had told him that he, Charles, knew more about himself than Ernest Jones could ever tell him. This was a kind of vanity, the actor's 'I know' character — 'I know people and no one can tell me by plunging into my past what I am.' I'm sorry he didn't stick to it."

Gradually, however, and inevitably once Laughton's homosexuality was accepted, the relationship between them changed, becoming in the end a strong but platonic friendship. "It sort of separated us a little bit," she said, "but we never talked about it. I wish we had. If he'd gone on with Ernest Jones we probably would have done. I'd have liked to talk but he wouldn't. He wasn't capable of talking, he just couldn't." She believes that this inability to discuss what must, after all, be a colossal problem in any marriage where it occurs, was due to guilt of some kind but guilt about what she is not sure even now. She doesn't think he felt guilty about marrying her and not telling her about himself, but perhaps he did about not being a "normal" man and not wanting to be "normal" at a time when homosexuality was a criminal offence. His secretiveness about the matter extended even to his own family. His younger brother, Frank, was also a homosexual and had admitted the fact openly to his mother and brothers, all of whom were as supportive as a fairly close family might be expected to be. It is possible that Charles had confided to Frank about his own homosexuality but he did not confide in the others.

The middle brother, Tom, said: "I was never aware of it in any shape or form until Elsa told me and I was just astounded. I never saw the least sign that he was but maybe he was. I don't know and I don't care."

However, the run of *Payment Deferred* which, had the court case gone another way, could have ended disastrously for Laughton instead ended in triumph. It was such a success that the production was taken to Broadway where, again, it opened to good reviews, although it ran only three weeks. Laughton then directed a Broadway version of *Alibi*, adapted from an Agatha Christie story — once more to good notices — and at the end of his stay in New York he signed a three-year contract with Paramount.

Before then he had made a few modest pictures, two-reelers mostly, in London but his film career really began in Hollywood in 1931 with a series of films like *The Old Dark House*, based on J. B. Priestley's *Benighted*, *The Devil and the Deep*, with Gary Cooper, *Payment Deferred*, *The Sign of the Cross* (in which, despite the strong disapproval of the director, Cecil B. de Mille, he played Nero as an effeminate homosexual) and *If I Had a Million*, the Ernst Lubitsch comedy in which Laughton, as the clerk who has unexpectedly inherited a million dollars from a total stranger, takes a long, deliberate walk through the office building where he works to blow a farewell raspberry at the boss. By and large the films were not greatly impressive but Laughton was and he was beginning to gain recognition as a character actor when Alexander Korda brought him back to London in 1933 to play the title role in *The Private Life of Henry VIII*. This was a picture which, despite its early difficulties, turned out to have the most far-reaching consequences. It established the British film industry on an international basis, it established Korda at the head of that industry and it established Laughton as an actor of exceptional ability.

In the light of all that, it seems incredible that at first Korda had the utmost difficulty in persuading anyone to distribute it. Indeed, it sat on the shelf for six months until United Artists agreed to take it on, whereupon it was an immediate success. Laughton's huge, bravura performance won him the Academy Award for best actor, to say nothing of ecstatic reviews.

The acclaim that was thrust upon him would have been enough to satisfy most actors but Laughton, being Laughton, regarded his success with deep suspicion. In his own opinion he had missed some vital element in Henry's character and so, no matter what anyone else said, the portrayal as far as he was concerned was a failure. To make matters even worse the international celebrity that he had now acquired made him a widely recognised and widely imitated personality; every mimic and impressionist added Charles Laughton to his repertoire. Well, again most people would have taken this as something of a compliment but to a man who hated his own appearance and suspected his own gifts that kind of recognition was intensely painful.

Laughton's repugnance for his own appearance and his dissatisfaction with his acting simply increased along with his fame and success. "As an actor," said Elsa Lanchester, "he didn't have any particular method but he did try to be a real person, to get into the character and he always started off a film in desperate unhappiness because he didn't feel that he was anywhere near what he was aiming to be. In fact it's absolutely true that in every film he did he said, 'I can't go on with this unless you shoot the first three days again.' And the directors had to say 'Yes, Charles, we'll shoot it again,' but then the film went on, it would be cut and we'd see the rushes and he could never find those first three days. Even so, he was never satisfied."

Yet beneath the agonising and the self-doubt, neither of which ever left him, there was also, as there had to be, a belief in himself as an artist. Christopher Isherwood says that Laughton was not a vain man but "he liked himself", he realised fundamentally how good he was. Paul Gregory says: "He had greatness, no two ways about it. He was the only genius I've ever known. I think he thought he was great, too, and was sort of comforted by that thought and wanted people to think he was even greater." But, with it all, Gregory says, he was "one of the most frightened human beings I've ever known, frightened of himself. I think his being so unattractive as he was gave him an enormous complex and there would be times when he wouldn't want to be seen. And yet I've seen him when he was absolutely, radiantly beautiful and I told him that one time. He had done a show and he'd been hateful before, absolutely hateful, and he'd gone on stage and really I've never seen anything so beautiful as Laughton was in that performance. Afterwards we were riding in the car and I said: 'Charles, I can't help but tell you that you were absolutely beautiful on that stage tonight,' and he turned round and looked at me and said: 'You rotten son of a bitch, why do you tell me that?' and he burst into tears and it was just terrible, you know? It was like Niagara Falls because he didn't even cry lightly."

With Henry VIII serving as the foundation stone of his career as a leading man Laughton now entered on the most fruitful phase of his time in Hollywood. His portrayal of the Victorian father in *The Barrets of Wimpole Street* dominated the whole film, quite overwhelming Norma Shearer and Frederic March as the romantic lovers. MGM and Louis B. Mayer (happily ignorant of Laughton's sexual proclivities) asked him to stay on and play Mr Micawber in *David Copperfield*. It seemed a splendid piece of casting to everyone except Laughton. George Cukor, the director, recalls that "he looked marvellous, just like the illustrations, but he was not comfortable. He didn't feel that he had the geniality or the innocence and he was quite right. It was too bad but he simply didn't have the innocence to play Micawber. I believe he was generally unhappy about everything. He doubted himself all the time. He said, 'I am not good, not good.' He was a most accomplished actor — a very intelligent man — but I feel he was tormented and because of that he tormented other people I should think." After three or four days of this torment and self-doubt Laughton left the cast and was replaced, very probably at his own suggestion, by W. C. Fields.

But this was a brief and ultimately insignificant setback for he swiftly went on to appear in *Ruggles of Red Gap*, his own favourite picture, in which he played an English butler in the wild west. Then, as if deliberately showing off the kind of virtuosity which few other film actors could match, he appeared as Javert in *Les Miserables*, as Captain Bligh — his most famous and most imitated performance — in *Mutiny on the Bounty* and, returning to England to work for Korda again, took the title role in *Rembrandt*.

All this in the space of two years and accompanied, inevitably, by the usual agonising, especially when he played opposite Clark Gable in *Mutiny on the Bounty*. The two men did not get on well, each thinking the other was trying to steal the picture, an absurd delusion on Laughton's part since Gable was never in the same league, let alone the same division, as an actor. But what added to Laughton's worries, according to Charles Higham, was Gable's sheer physical presence. Here was a big, handsome man "a 100 per cent man, a masculine man", the very antithesis of Laughton and "the knowledge made him suffer horribly". Higham believes that with Laughton, more than with most other actors, the playing of great and significant characters like Henry VIII, Bligh and Rembrandt was a way in which he himself could feel significant and important. "He could become somebody greater then himself and lose himself but I don't think it led him to any deeper understanding of himself. In fact, in a way, it increased his sense of inferiority because after he cast off the robes and the costumes he had to go home and be an ugly, unappetising, unhappy man pursuing other men. I mean, what a contrast — from all the magnificence and glamour to this furtive, horrible life he was leading."

Nevertheless and whatever Laughton's own state of mind his reputation was now reaching a peak. His films were making money and in the opinion of one critic, Mark van Doren, his performance as Bligh "fixes him in my mind at any rate as by far the best of living actors". And when *Rembrandt* was revived in London in 1949, thirteen years after it was made, the *Daily Telegraph* critic said of it: "Laughton never again did anything so good."

So, in 1937, apparently secure at the top of his profession, Laughton again came to London to play in the screen adaptation of Robert Graves's *I, Claudius* for Alexander Korda. Nearly thirty years later what was made of this film became the centre of a BBC TV documentary called *The Epic that Never Was*. For Laughton the entire enterprise was a horrendous experience.

The intolerant and dictatorial attitude of the director, Josef Von Sternberg, drove him literally to tears. He was confused by the constant changes in the script and for a long time he was unable to find a key to the character of Claudius. Then, when at last he did begin to feel his way into the part, inspired thanks to God knows what actor's alchemy by the abdication speech of King Edward VIII, the filming was abruptly cancelled. Merle Oberon, who was playing Messalina, was badly injured in a car crash. Shooting was suspended while she recovered and was not resumed. The reasons for this were never explained by any of those concerned, but the generally unhappy feeling on the set, together with rapidly mounting costs, probably had a lot to do with it. In any event, Laughton greeted the cancellation of the picture with great relief and refused ever to speak to Von Sternberg again. The irony of the whole affair is that, had it been finished, it might have been Laughton's greatest accomplishment. As to what he would have been like as Micawber one can only speculate; but on the evidence of what exists of *I, Claudius* there is no doubt that a quite superb performance was in the making.

The aftermath of the Claudian fiasco was another, though different, fiasco. Laughton decided to set up his own company, Mayflower Productions, so that he could have complete control of his work. In three years (from 1937 to 1939) Mayflower made three pictures, *Vessels of Wrath*, adapted from a Maugham short story about a missionary (Elsa Lanchester) and a beachcomber (Laughton), *St Martin's Lane*, a tale of London buskers with Vivien Leigh grossly miscast as a Cockney and Daphne du Maurier's *Jamaica Inn*, one of the least satisfactory films Alfred Hitchcock ever directed. None of the pictures was particularly good and none of them made money, so the company was a failure both artistically and financially. Tom Laughton says, with hindsight, that the whole idea was doomed to disaster from the start. "It was utterly wrong. Charles was an actor. He turned out to be quite a good director on the one film he did direct but he was essentially an actor. He wasn't fit to have financial responsibility and he couldn't stand it. It took him all his time to worry about his performances and that's as much as he could do. He wasn't a businessman."

Mayflower Productions was wound up in 1939 and Laughton returned to Hollywood to play Quasimodo in *The Hunchback of Notre Dame* — his last great performance of the 1930s and indeed his last for many years. During the making of the film, while in fact he was shooting the famous bells sequence, war was declared in Europe and he thought seriously about flying back to England to offer his services, though the idea was clearly preposterous. He was already forty, grossly overweight and he still suffered from the side effects of the gassing he had received in the First World War. Eventually he decided to stay in America — for which action he was much criticised by the British Press — and did his bit for the Allied cause by selling War Bonds.

It was at this point, during the war years, that his career began to go into decline. He worked consistently through the 1940s but not to any great effect, almost as though he were living on the credit he had stored up with his handful of superb performances in the previous decade. Admittedly when viewed now, forty years later, even some of his most famous pictures — *Henry VIII* for instance, *Les Miserables* and *Hunchback* — look quaint and dated but the same could never be said of Laughton's performance in them.

In the forties, however, not only the films but even Laughton himself seemed below standard, although inevitably there were exceptions to that general condemnation: there was *This Land is Mine*, a wartime propaganda effort about the French Resistance directed by Jean Renoir, in which Laughton was highly effective as a mild schoolteacher; there was *The Canterville Ghost*, adapted from the story by Oscar Wilde, which elicited from him a clever and witty performance; there was *The Suspect*, with Laughton as a meek Edwardian driven to murder, and later there was *The Big Clock*, a thriller which once again saw him being larger and more splendid than life. But set against these were the potboilers, such as the children's picture *Captain Kidd* and the Deanna Durbin comedy *Because of Him*, which one can only assume he made simply for the money. Laughton was never above prostituting his own enormous talent in exchange for a quick fee, not out of greed or acquisitiveness but usually in order to buy a painting. As early as 1935 he had used his entire savings, at that time rather less than £10,000, to buy Renoir's *The Judgement of Paris* and ever afterwards he was inclined to invest whatever spare cash he had lying around in works of art; although invest is not the correct word. Laughton valued his collection not for its resale value but for its own beauty.

When he bought the Renoir, Elsa Lanchester said: "He called me and said, 'I've seen a painting I can barely live without. It's a great picture and the most important thing that's ever happened in my life. Do you mind if I spend our savings on it?' So we acquired the Renoir and over the years we acquired other pictures and works of art as well and every time it was something he was passionately fond of. It was a great passion. A lot of people say they have that passion, like Edward G. Robinson may or may not have had it. But everything he bought he knew he could sell for more. Charles didn't give a thought to whether he could sell a picture for more, not ever. There was a time when he was getting sort of low because the films weren't too hot for him, when we had to sell some of his collection and we sold the Renoir. But even then it wasn't because of what we could get for it. It was because he'd read somewhere that Gertrude Stein had said: 'Don't keep a picture when it's gone into the wall,' and Charles looked at the Renoir one day and said: 'It's gone into the wall,' and he sold it. But after that he started collecting all over again."

Professionally perhaps the most important event in his career during the 1940s was that he had begun to give readings and recitals in public. Originally he did this merely as part of his war effort, to entertain the troops and with no thought of making a career of it but within a few years these readings were to become a significant part of his repertoire. Also, as his films failed to make money and the Hollywood moguls, who always loved money better than any actor, began to talk of him ominously as "a commercial liability" he returned briefly to the stage, appearing in Los Angeles and New York in Bertolt Brecht's version of *Galileo*. The New York reviews were not particularly enthusiastic but the play did well during its limited run. One other development in Laughton's life that occurred around the same time was that he started holding acting classes at his home. Shelley Winters was a regular attender, Robert Mitchum, Robert Ryan, Paulette Goddard and Peter Ustinov turned up occasionally.

It's difficult now to judge precisely what these classes achieved. Shelley Winters says: "You worked six days a week from seven or eight p.m. until eleven. He demanded that your sights be very high for yourself. He made you understand you weren't just in business to make money and in those days when the studios told me I was a hunk of meat, a blonde bombshell, he made me understand I was an artist and a human being and I could demand respect and dignity."

Paul Gregory's view is altogether more jaundiced. "It was just an ego trip for Laughton. He fancied himself with people following him around adoring him."

Laughton's partnership with Gregory began in 1950, the year in which he and Elsa moved into what was to become their final Hollywood home, a large, rambling house with a tropical garden that looks like a miniature jungle, and in which they both became American citizens. Given Laughton's love of America and its comparatively classless society, together with the fact that he had never been accepted — and had never tried to be accepted — by the English community in Hollywood, this was a logical step.

But the most far-reaching event of 1950 was the meeting in New York with Paul Gregory, an agent turned impresario, who heard him recite from the Bible on the Ed Sullivan TV Show and was immediately struck with the idea of taking him on a reading tour of the country. Laughton's initial response to this suggestion was fairly cool but Gregory managed to attract his attention by talking about the potential fortune that such an enterprise could mean to them both.

"I think the persuasion was purely money," Gregory said. "When I told him that I thought we could make between eight and ten thousand dollars a week, it was pretty much the factor that convinced him." Laughton wasn't exactly hard up at the time but, as he confessed to Gregory later, his career was no longer on the peak that it had once reached and "he told me, and I like this statement, that he was down to his last 50,000 dollars." Furthermore, his film career had plunged to such depths that he had signed a contract, for a mere 25,000 dollars, to appear in a frightful movie called *Abbot and Costello Meet Captain Kidd*. The one thing to be said about that was that from there the only way was up.

The partnership lasted six years, and, financially and artistically, was a phenomenal success. The reading tours, consisting largely of passages from the Bible and Dickens were followed by more ambitious, though similar, productions in which Laughton toured with Cedric Hardwicke, Agnes Moorehead and Charles Boyer in readings of Shaw's *Don Juan in Hell*, and with Tyrone Power, Raymond Massey and Judith Anderson in Stephen Vincent Benet's *John Brown's Body*. Laughton, the reader, also made records and appeared on radio and TV and won himself a whole new audience of admirers in the United States and Canada.

The association culminated in 1955 when, again thanks largely to Gregory's help, Laughton turned film director for the only time in his life to make *The Night of the Hunter*, a strange, almost terrifying story, scripted by James Agee, about the pursuit by a psychopathic lay preacher (Robert Mitchum) of two children who could tell him the whereabouts of their dead father's money. Before starting work on it Laughton ran all D. W. Griffith's films in a private cinema to capture the mood he wanted and the result of this one essay as a director is a picture that is both lyrical and nightmarish, one that was grossly underrated in its day, being dismissed by the critics as "too arty" but that is now regarded as a classic of the American cinema.

The making of the film, however, was fraught with hazards as indeed was the entire partnership with Paul Gregory. Laughton's cavalier attitude to costs meant the picture was over budget from the first week of shooting and besides he was ruthless in his attitude to James Agee. Gregory said: "Charles Laughton could eat people up. Agee came to me one day — and he was drunk all the time — and he said, 'Laughton is driving me to drink, he's killing me.' Laughton would keep him in the house, working with him, till two or three in the morning and he didn't know, he never knew, if it was for the work or just for the company and Agee died from this treatment. He died the next spring."

No doubt the drink helped a little too, and Laughton could hardly be given all the blame for that. But nevertheless Gregory is convinced that Laughton's attitude to Agee left him a broken man, in spirit if not in health.

Gregory said: "The name Charles Laughton to me conjures up immediately about fifty or sixty different emotional reactions. He was at once wonderful, at once impossible and destructive."

Even on the reading tours, perhaps especially on the reading tours, Laughton's behaviour was often eccentric. "He did naughty things," Gregory recalled, "like going into a hospital in Salt Lake City for fourteen days when he wasn't sick — he was in there eating chocolates. He did it just to get even, with whom I don't know. With me, I guess. I don't think he enjoyed the reading tours as such. He loved it when I'd call him and say, 'Charlie, we've got 250,000 dollars worth of bookings,' but as the time neared he would think of all kinds of reasons not to have to go on this tour and postpone the first week and it would be like pulling a tooth to finally arrive at the time when that car headed out across country to meet those commitments and all the time he'd be griping about this and that . . . Have you ever tried to push an elephant? Because that's what it was like."

In addition he would wilfully, and on some mischievous impulse, ruin deals that Gregory had worked hard to pull off. Once they had a conference with a Methodist Church group as the result of which it was agreed that Laughton should record a series of Bible readings that would have brought in millions of dollars. All that remained was for the contracts to be signed when Laughton turned casually to the leader of the Methodist contingent and remarked: "Well, old boy, you know the Bible is full of shit?" The churchman, to whom this revelation came as a considerable surprise, immediately called off the entire deal.

The partnership with Gregory ended soon after the completion of *The Night of the Hunter*, partly because their joint attempt at filming Norman Mailer's *The Naked and the Dead*, with Laughton again directing, ended in disaster. "I raised five million dollars for it," Gregory said. "We had a special budget for the script and, my lord, within six months he spent the entire amount. He was sending people all over the world like he was J. Arthur Rank or somebody. So, of course, the people who were putting up the money called me in and said, 'What's the meaning of this — 500,000 dollars spent and the camera hasn't even begun to turn over?' And I'd say to Charlie, 'Look, what *is* happening?' and he'd disappear and wouldn't talk to me when I called. Well, you can't work with somebody like that. And when the deal fell apart he couldn't stand up to it and fled and left me with it." Gregory finally produced what he admits is an "inferior film" of *The Naked and the Dead* but at least the backers got a return on their money. Laughton, on the other hand, was never again asked to direct.

But, possibly by way of compensation, his acting career began to thrive once more. He returned to England to star in David Lean's screen version of *Hobson's Choice* and, in 1957, when he and Elsa Lanchester appeared in Billy Wilder's adaptation of the Agatha Christie story, *Witness for the Prosecution*, both were nominated for Oscars.

Wilder's total admiration for Laughton, the artist, stems from that picture. "He had audacity," Wilder said. "He went to the very brink of the ridiculous but he stopped there. You know, when we had finished the principal photography there was only one thing left to do and that was to shoot the reactions of the jury to all the stuff that had happened during the trial.

"Laughton came by the studio one day and asked what I was doing and I told him. He said 'How do you do that?' I said, 'Well, I'd have various shots of the jury from this side and that and they'd have to react to Tyrone Power, Marlene Dietrich, to the judge, to you and blah blah, blah.' He said, 'Well, who's reading the lines off-stage?' I said, 'I don't know. Maybe the script girl or somebody.' He said, 'Let me do it.' I said, 'Charles, this is wearisome. This is a chore.' He said, 'I must do it,' and there he was in a Hawaian shirt and unshaven — you could still see his breakfast on his shirt — and he played all the parts and it was one of the most stunning displays of a universal talent. He played Dietrich better than Dietrich ever was, he played Ty Power better than Ty Power, he was just fabulous, absolutely fabulous. I was enthralled. This was like a one-man football team. He played the goalkeeper and the striker and the referee too. It was fantastic what he did . . . Laughton was a personal friend of mine, you understand, but I found him at times petulant, at times sloppy, at times grouchy and then he wouldn't talk for three days. But my God this was an actor who brought with him a great big bag of stuff. He would discuss a scene with me and he would say, 'I could do it this way,' and I'd say, 'That's good.' Then he'd say, 'Or I could do it this way,' and I'd say, 'That's better.' And then came twenty more versions and I'd say, 'That's it, that's it,' and the next morning he would arrive and say, 'I thought of something last night. There's one other way,' and that would be absolutely stupendous too."

In 1959, and two years after *Witness for the Prosecution*, Laughton went to Stratford-upon-Avon to play King Lear and

Bottom in *A Midsummer Night's Dream*. To play Lear, a character with whom he felt a great affinity, a shared sense of having been persecuted by others of smaller stature than himself, had been a lifelong ambition, almost an obsession. He worked on his interpretation of the part for a full year at his home in Hollywood, often with Christopher Isherwood acting as adviser, critic and audience. These impromptu rehearsals took place in what Laughton called "the school room" at his house. Isherwood said: "I used to sit in that little room and watch and when I see the scene now, sort of impressionistically, it's like sitting all alone in the front row of a gigantic movie theatre where a vast face, dozens of times larger than life, is hanging right over you and saying things like, 'When we are born we cry but we come to this great stage of fools' and this kind of thing and I just wept, you know, and I was transfixed."

But, unhappily, despite all this devoted and careful work Laughton's Lear was not well received. His brother, Tom Laughton, believes Charles was already ill, with the beginnings of the cancer that was soon to kill him, when the Stratford season started and that, as a result, he was both disappointing and disappointed with the critical reception he received. Isherwood, who saw the stage performance, remembers being "tremendously impressed" but adds: "Of course, you know, nothing could be the same as those private auditions. They were something that one might have perhaps once in a lifetime."

So Laughton went back again to Hollywood, for the last time, feeling rejected by Britain or at least by the British critics, although their condemnation of his King Lear was mitigated, in part, by their enthusiastic reception of his performance in the West End production of Jane Arden's play *The Party*, in which he played a hard-drinking solicitor with incestuous feelings for his daughter. Not a cheery role but a successful one for Laughton.

At this point, towards the end of 1959, his health was deteriorating fast and he made only three more films — *Spartacus*, in which he played the Roman Senate leader opposed to the powerful Crassus, played by Laurence Olivier; a war film set in Italy, *Under Two Flags* wherein he appeared as an admiral and, finally, *Advise and Consent*, in which he gave a superb and memorable performance as a corrupt Southern Senator whose bigotry and hatred of homosexuality represented just about everything that Laughton himself detested. By making the character a soft, persuasive monster he cleverly exposed all the bigotry and intolerance. But by the time the film was made in 1962 Laughton was dying, although he would not admit it even to himself.

His friends, however, knew the truth. Billy Wilder was planning to film *Irma La Douce* and wanted Laughton to play Moustache but, knowing of the actor's grave illness, was preparing to recast when one day he received a summons to Laughton's home . . .

"He said, 'Don't listen to whatever they tell you, it's not true. I'll prove it — come and see me at my house.' I went that lunchtime . . . he had had his male nurse dress him up, comb his hair, shave him, maybe even put a little make-up on him, and he was sitting in a chair at the swimming pool. He said, 'Now look at me. Do I look like somebody that's going to die?' And he got himself out of the chair and he walked around the pool. He must have been in tremendous pain but he just wanted to say to me, 'Wait.' This was one of the finest performances I tell you. I was very touched . . . I wiped my eyes as I walked out of the house, knowing full well that I would never see him alive again."

During all this time and despite the fact that each led a separate and private existence Laughton and Lanchester had stayed together and they did so until the end. Mostly she would keep away from the house when he was entertaining a boy friend, although she got to know some of them quite well. "When he was with one in particular," she said, "I used to go to the market every day and get two peach pies for them. I didn't mind. I don't mind a bit of peach pie myself." In any event she had, understandably, friends and relationships of her own. The interests she shared with her husband were not sexual but domestic — they had their house, their paintings, their garden. Towards the end of his life, at the beginning of his final illness, Laughton said to her: "I wish this whole sex thing would finish, just disappear."

By then a gentler kind of homosexual friendship seems to have replaced the more active homosexual passions in his life. "I was very glad," Elsa said, "that in later life he got fond of people, which is a very different story, you know. That was safer and nicer." The marriage itself, she said, was not simply a front "though you could call it that if you wanted to. We were very, very attached and we wanted people to see that we were happy, so we showed the happy side. It wasn't a particularly easy life but we were both on tour quite a bit and afterwards we always came home as soon as possible and if you'd seen us at the airport you'd have thought we were Romeo and Juliet. We had, in a way, to be apart in order to become attached."

Charles Higham, the biographer, believes the marriage worked because they both decided to take second best rather than nothing at all. "In other words, if she'd said, 'No, I can't tolerate living with a man who's having affairs with men,' she would have lost Charles and he would have lost her but they meant an enormous amount to each other because they enjoyed the same things — they had gardening in common, love of flowers, love of woodlands, love of England, deep affection for the Californian countryside and a tremendously similar taste in art."

Paul Gregory said: "Elsa gave Charles a fixture in life that he needed and as much as he spat and clawed and kicked at it, he still needed it. That was the one thing of respectability he liked — he liked having a Mrs Laughton. He would like it even today. He wouldn't just come right out and say, 'This is my boy friend.' He was always very deep with all that."

Perhaps because of the reticence he learned at Stonyhurst he was always secretive about his homosexuality even with his closest friends, those he could have trusted to understand and lend encouragement. Soon after meeting and becoming friendly with Christopher Isherwood in 1959 he bought a house at Malibu, next door to Isherwood's because, he said to Elsa, he wanted to be "near his own kind". Even so Isherwood was only peripherally aware of Laughton's homosexual activities . . . "I really had, as a matter of fact, amazingly little contact with him, with his friend-ships with boys or contacts of any kind with boys. That was all rather kept a little bit aside." But from what he did know of Laughton's private life he felt that there was "a great deal of a father and son thing in those relationships, an element of instruction and being proud of the one who is instructed."

Laughton's affairs with other men need to be emphasised if only because of the historical context in which they occurred. Today it may not matter much whether an actor is homosexual or not but in Laughton's time the conditions were very different. Homo-sexuality was socially unacceptable and indeed against the law. Thus a homosexual who was in the public eye could not help but lead a furtive and even a guilt-ridden life, with the fear of being found out ever close to his thoughts. And a homosexual like Laughton who went in for casual affairs with highly inappropriate people rather than for a steady and settled relationship with one man must presumably have suffered more than most.

Because of the closeness of their professional relationship over six years Paul Gregory probably observed more of Laughton's private life than anyone except Elsa Lanchester. "Charles was aggressive as a homosexual," he said. "He wasn't a little worm in the wood. There were always people popping up whom he'd brought along, who were following on in the bus behind you. And he made it more difficult for himself, too, because he wasn't content to have just one, he'd have a menage of them. Some of them would end up in prison and you'd get calls from wardens and letters threatening him. He had set himself up as a target."

They were not then, these men and boy friends, Laughton's intellectual equals in any way? "Of course not," Gregory said. "They were the dregs, low class kind of people. He had a sort of Higgins complex about being able to make them into something. He'd say, 'I've got this young man who has star quality,' and it would be some wretch he'd met along the way and he'd have no star quality at all, except to Charles. They weren't physically similar but they were all young, very young. On a college campus or someplace Laughton would encounter someone to whom he would give a "scholarship" and he'd call me and say, 'Put 500 dollars in such and such an account,' and then I'd join him later and say, 'Well, where's the scholarship boy?' and he'd say 'Oh, I got rid of him in Palm Beach or somewhere.' They'd come and go. I didn't have too much to do with all that except to write the cheques for him and hide them from Elsa and his accountants."

With all this going on it's not at all surprising that Laughton was, by general agreement, a tormented man. To what extent that particular torment helped his development as an artist perhaps he alone could tell. But whatever the contributory factors — and homosexuality and his conviction of his own physical ugliness were undoubtedly among them — his artistry is undeniable. He was an actor of remarkable range, intelligence and sensitivity. If his performances often looked to be over the top, that was because of an unkind twist of fate: his very appearance was over the top. As Peter Ustinov said, even when he was sitting perfectly still and in repose he was already doing too much but if you look beyond that huge, remarkable face Laughton's acting was full of subtlety and wit. His film career was a thing of ups and downs, mostly consisting of splendid performances in unworthy vehicles, but at its best his work was superb by any standards.

Laughton died, of bone cancer, in the school room of his home in Hollywood on December 15th, 1962. He was sixty-three years old and he was still trying to convince himself and everybody else that one day he would be well enough to work again. Before he died, thanks to the efforts of his two brothers, he had been received once more into the Roman Catholic faith.

Thinking back, a decade and a half later, on the man he had known, Christopher Isherwood said: "It was possible to love him. I think many people quite misunderstood him, you know, or didn't see that side of him." Then, after a long pause, . . . "I rather loved him, yes. But again I was fully aware of how difficult he could be with other people."

Elsa Lanchester said: "I know that I've become a more live, complete person since he died. But if I'd died first I would say that Charles would be a more tortured man because we all think of what we might have done but didn't and I know he would suffer deeply because of what he might have done."

Tom Laughton remembers a perfectionist who was difficult to work with, a man who could be ruthless when it involved his work but also a brother who was a "kind, gentle, marvellous man".

Billy Wilder talks of "this universal, interested, fascinating man — the complete Renaissance man, one who could talk engrossingly and knowledgeably about Impressionist painting and Burgundy wine, who could phone at eleven thirty at night and say 'You must come over straightaway. I have a plant which will open at midnight and it opens only once a year and you must see it.'" Wilder says: "There was no way of saying 'Who the hell cares? I've seen plants open and close, no big deal.' Oh no, I had to be there."

I asked Paul Gregory whether, given the opportunity, he would go through his years of business partnership with Laughton again and he said: "I don't know. What I didn't know at that time was his disposition. He was cruel and I don't think we have a right to be cruel to anybody and he was cruel not only to me but to other people. There was a cruelty there that was frightening — in his rudeness, in his talk with you sometimes, the things he would say to you, the way he would attack you in areas where you weren't able to respond."

And then, summing the man up, he said: "Charles had to have turmoil all the time. Whatever the situation he'd pit somebody against somebody else. He just couldn't help it. He had to do this. But out of this garbage he'd created, he would grow a rose, a rose of extraordinary blossom would come and then it was so beautiful you would weep for the beauty and weep for the injury . . . And that was Charlie. He could embrace you out of your life. It was all enormous."

Index

Aadland, Beverley, 46, 61–2
Academy Awards, 30, 77, 82,
    107, 109, 112, 130, 135, 136,
    158, 179, 182–3, 229, 231,
    238, 256; (British Film), 88
African Queen, The, 135–6
Agee, James, 263–4
Allyson, June, 236
Anderson, Judith, 263
Arden, Joan, *see* Joan Crawford
Ashley, Sylvia, 35–6
Ashwell, Lena, 173
Astaire, Fred, 235
Astor, Mary, 28, 36, 178
Auer, Mischa, 126

Bacall, Lauren (Betty), 120,
    128, 130–32, 135, 137–8
Bad Day at Black Rock, 71,
    84–5, 90
Balfe, Veronica, *see* Veronica
    Cooper
Bankhead, Tallulah, 161
Banky, Vilma, 99, 177
Barrymore, Ethel, 73
Barrymore, John, 22, 61, 99
Barrymore, Lionel, 22, 24–5
Barthelmass, Richard, 178
Bautzer, Greg, 156–7, 161–2
Baxter, Warner, 178
Bello, Marino, 196–7, 202, 204,
    206, 209–10, 213, 216
Benchley, Nathaniel, 120–22,
    126–8, 131–3, 137
Bennett, Joan, 134–5
Benny, Jack, 113; (Show), 182
Bergman, Ingrid, 129
Bern, Paul, 203–10, 214
Best, Edna, 183–4
Bogart, Humphrey, 70, 75,
    115–39
Bow, Clara, 100, 102
Boyer, Charles, 263
Boys' Town, 72, 79
Brando, Marlon, 8, 11, 136
Brazier, Alice, *see* Alice Cooper
Burton, Richard, 138–9

Cagney, James, 124, 129, 199
Capra, Frank, 30, 105
Captain Blood, 49–51
Carpentier, Harlean, *see* Jean
    Harlow
Carpentier, Jean, (Mama Jean),
    196–7, 202, 204, 206–7,
    209–10, 213–16
Casablanca, 129–30
Cassin, Billie, *see* Joan
    Crawford
*Charge of the Light Brigade,
    The*, 50–52

Cohn, Harry, 11
Colman, Juliet, 173–4, 182, 186
Colman, Ronald, 30, 99, 104,
    167–87
Columbia, 11, 30, 88, 123, 199
Cooper, Gary (Frank James),
    70, 91–113, 256
Cooper, Gladys, 173
Cooper, Maria, 101, 105–6,
    109–12
Cooper, Veronica (Rocky),
    104–5, 108–11
Crawford, Joan, 27, 30, 79,
    141–65, 195, 229
Cuban Rebel Girls, 61
Cukor, George, 31, 72, 80–83,
    87, 89, 153, 155, 183, 208,
    238, 258
Curtiz, Michael, 49–50, 129–30

Damita, Lily, 49, 52, 58, 60
Daves, Delmar, 100–102, 105,
    111, 131–2
Davis, Bette, 52, 152, 158, 163,
    195
Deans, Mickey, 241–3
de Havilland, Olivia, 52–4, 63
de Mille, Cecil B., 11, 105, 255,
    256
Dietrich, Marlene, 101, 265
di Frasso, Countess Dorothy,
    101–5
Dillon, Josephine, 23–4, 26, 29
Dinner at Eight, 208–9
Donat, Robert, 49
Double Life, A, 182–3
Dunlop, Jennie, 22–3
Durbin, Deanna, 228, 261

Eddington, Nora, 51, 53–9, 62

Fairbanks, Jr., Douglas, 27,
    149–50, 153–4
Fairbanks, Sr., Douglas, 35,
    49, 147
Fleming, Victor, 31
Flynn, Deirdre, 51, 53–7, 60–64
Flynn, Errol, 30, 41–63, 70,
    125, 181
Ford, John, 20, 36, 75, 87, 90
Fountainhead, 96, 108
Fox, 75–6, 123, 199, 228, 233,
    241
Friede, Donald, 212, 215

Gable, Clark, 15–39, 70, 77–80,
    86, 104, 113, 153–4, 160, 162,
    181, 203, 206, 208, 212–14,
    228, 258

Garbo, Greta, 158, 195, 234
Garceau, Jean, 30–33
Garland, Judy, 217–43
Garson, Greer, 34, 158, 182
Gish, Lilian, 174–6
Goddard, Paulette, 262
Goldwyn, Sam, 113, 176, 179,
    183
Gone With the Wind, 21, 30–32,
    36–7
Graumann's Chinese Theatre,
    11, 120, 152, 199
Gray, Virginia, 20, 35–6
Gregory, Paul, 250–51, 257,
    262–5, 268–71
Griffin, Wayne, 29
Guess Who's Coming to Dinner,
    83, 86–8
Gumm, Ethel, 226–7, 229,
    231–8
Gumm, Frances Ethel, *see*
    Judy Garland

Hall, James, 198
Halls of Ivy, The, 177, 182, 184
Hardwicke, Cedric, 80, 263
Harlow, Jean, 28, 36, 77,
    189–216
Harlow, S. D., 196–8
Harris, Radie, 148, 156–7, 163
Hathaway, Henry, 100, 103,
    105, 111–13
Hawks, Howard, 26, 32–3,
    38–9, 99–100, 104, 106, 111,
    130–31
Hayes, Helen, 23, 29, 102–4,
    122
Hell's Angels, 198–9
Henreid, Paul, 129–30
Hepburn, Katharine, 10,
    79–84, 87–9, 138
Herron, Mark, 240–41
High Noon, 96, 109–10
Hopper, Hedda, 81, 109
Howard, Leslie, 124, 132
Hughes, Howard, 198–9, 201
Hume, Benita, 178, 180–82,
    184, 186–7
Huston, John, 37, 61, 129, 133,
    136
Huston, Walter, 101, 135
Hyams, Joe, 120–21, 123,
    126–7, 132–3, 137–8

Isherwood, Christopher,
    250–51, 257, 266, 268, 270
It Happened One Night, 30

Jacobs, Arthur, 113

Jaffe, Sam, 125–6, 128–9, 135–6, 139

Kanin, Garson, 71–2, 80–84, 89
Kelly, Grace, 36, 238
Kerr, Deborah, 35, 105, 112
King, Henry, 99, 174–6
Korda, Alexander, 256, 258–9
Kramer, Stanley, 78–9, 81, 83, 86–9, 120

Lanchester, Elsa, 253–7, 260–62, 265, 267–70
Langham, Ria, 24, 26–9, 31
Lasky, Jr., Jesse, 211
Lasky, Sr., Jesse, 106
Laughing Sinners, 27, 153
Laughton, Charles, 245–70
Laughton, Tom, 251–2, 256, 260, 266, 270
Leigh, Vivien, 31, 260
Leroy, Mervyn, 25
Le Sueur, Lucille, see Joan Crawford
Lombard, Carole, 30–33, 38, 211, 214
Loos, Anita, 214
Love, Bessie, 172, 178, 180
Loy, Myrna, 21, 77, 165, 212
Luft, Joey, 238
Luft, Lorna, 237
Luft, Sid, 237, 239–41
Lyon, Ben, 198–9

Mankiewicz, Joseph L., 20, 27–8, 35, 76–8, 80–81, 83, 89, 183–4, 227–8, 231–4, 236, 240–41
Massey, Raymond, 263
Mayer, Louis B., 11, 25, 28, 30–31, 161, 204–5, 207, 213, 225, 227–8, 230–34, 236, 255, 258
Mayhin, John Lee, 203–4, 208–10, 213
McAvoy, May, 177
McGrew, Charles, 197–8
Meet Me in St. Louis, 233–4
Menasco, Al, 37
Mencken, Helen, 122–3, 134
Merlin, Barbara, 184, 186
Merlin, Milton, 177, 184, 186
Methot, Mayo, 125–6, 130–31
Metro-Goldwyn-Mayer (MGM), 11, 25, 27–32, 34, 36, 38, 70, 75–80, 84, 86, 148–9, 151, 154–5, 158, 161–2, 195, 199, 201–4, 206–10, 213, 215, 225–33, 235–7, 258
Mildred Pearce, 158–9
Milete, Dorothy, 206
Miller, Arthur, 37
Minnelli, Liza, 227, 233, 235
Minnelli, Vincent, 233–5, 237, 241
Misfits, The, 37–8

Mitchum, Robert, 262–3
Mogambo, see Red Dust
Monroe, Marilyn, 37, 198, 208
Moorehead, Agnes, 263
Mulvey, Kay, 201–3, 207, 209, 211, 215
Mutiny on the Bounty, 30, 258

Neagle, Dame Anna, 53, 60
Neal, Patricia, 108–9
Night of the Hunter, The, 263–4
Night Nurse, 25–6
Nissen, Greta, 198–9
Niven, David, 58, 138, 181, 186–7

Oberon, Merle, 259
O'Brien, Bill (Pat), 72–5, 80, 89
O'Hara, Maureen, 254

Paramount, 86, 96, 99, 108, 134–5, 256
Parsons, Louella, 81, 215
Pasternak, Joe, 229, 235
Petrified Forest, The, 124–5, 132, 136
Phillips, Mary, 122–3, 125
Pickford, Mary, 149–50
Poitier, Sidney, 88
Possessed, 27, 153
Powell, William, 31, 154, 176, 178, 195, 210–16
Power, Tyrone, 263, 265
Private Life of Henry VIII, The, 256–8, 260

Raft, George, 125, 129
Ray, Thelma, 173–8, 180–81
Red Dust, 28, 36, 203, 208
Roach, Hal, 197–8, 202–3
Robinson, Edward G., 125, 129, 135, 261
Rogers St. Johns, Adela, 27–8, 32, 200, 205, 210–11
Romanoff's, 11, 90, 128
Rooney, Mickey, 227–8, 231, 243
Rose, David, 230–31, 234
Rose, Stuart, 134
Rosson, Hal, 209–11

Sandberg, Carl, 96, 112
Sanders, George, 186
Schafer, Natalie, 155–6, 165
Schary, Dory, 79, 84–6, 236–7
Selznick, David, 30–31
Sergeant York, 99, 106–9
Shaw, Artie, 229–30
Shaw, Sandra, see Veronica Cooper
Shearer, Norma, 27, 155, 158, 203, 258
Shedlo, Ronnie, 61
Sherman, Vincent, 50, 54–5, 59, 63–4, 127–8, 150–51, 157–9, 162, 164
Siegel, Bugsy, 195, 202, 216

Spreckles, Kay, 36
Stanwyck, Barbara, 25, 152, 158, 195
Star is Born, A, 237–8
Steele, Alfred, 157, 162–3
Stevenson, Adlai, 135
Stewart, James, 112–13
Strickling, Howard, 204–7, 209, 211–12, 215
Sturges, John, 71, 73, 78, 82, 85, 89–90
Sullivan, Ed, 21, 30; (Show), 262

Temple, Shirley, 227–8
Terry, Philip, 156–7
Thalberg, Irving, 27, 76, 155, 203–5, 207
To Have and Have Not, 130–32, 138
Tone, Franchot, 154–5, 212
Torme, Mel, 239–40
Tracy, John, 73–4, 80; (Clinic for the Deaf), 74
Tracy, Spencer, 24, 65–90, 138–9, 155, 199, 212
Treadwell, Louise, 73–4, 76–7, 81–2
Turner, Lana, 36, 158, 229
Twentieth Century Fox, see Fox

United Artists, 256
Universal Studios, 11, 199, 228
Ustinov, Peter, 262, 269

Velez, Lupe, 100–103
Von Sternberg, Josef, 259

Walsh, Raoul, 62
Walters, Charles, 148, 150, 159, 165, 229–30, 235
Warner Brothers, 25, 48–51, 53, 56, 59–60, 86, 124, 127, 135, 158, 162, 199, 237–8
Warner, Jack L., 25, 50–51, 61, 63, 124, 128–9, 134–5
Weingand, Al, 179–81, 185–6
White Sister, The, 23, 174–6
Wilder, Billy, 250, 265, 267, 270
Williams, Blanche, 199, 201, 203, 205, 207, 211–12
Winters, Shelley, 262
Wise, Robert, 86
Wizard of Oz, The, 31, 225, 228–9, 233
Woman of the Year, 10, 80–81
Women, The, 153–5
Wood, Sam, 107–8
Wymore, Patrice, 59, 62

Young, Loretta, 27, 76–7, 87, 199

Zanuck, Darryl F., 25
Zinneman, Freddie, 85–6